Lullabies for
Lieutenants

Lullabies for Lieutenants

Memoir of a Marine Forward Observer in Vietnam, 1965–1966

FRANKLIN COX

February 8, 2012
To My Friend —
Jerry Farber —
Your wit makes the
world a happier place.
Best Wishes and Semper Fi —
Frank Cox

McFarland & Company, Inc., Publishers
Jefferson, North Carolina, and London

Library of Congress Cataloguing-in-Publication Data

Cox, Franklin, 1941–
    Lullabies for lieutenants : memoir of a Marine forward
observer in Vietnam, 1965–1966 / Franklin Cox.
        p.   cm.
    Includes bibliographical references and index.

    ISBN 978-0-7864-4719-0
    softcover : 50# alkaline paper ∞

    1. Cox, Franklin, 1941–   2. Vietnam War, 1961–1975—
Personal narratives, American.   3. Marines—United States—
Biography.   4. United States. Marine Corps—Officers—
Biography.   I. Title.
DS559.5.C687   2010
959.704'345—dc22 [B]   2010004826

British Library cataloguing data are available

Cover images ©2010 Shutterstock and ©2010 Photos.com

Manufactured in the United States of America

McFarland & Company, Inc., Publishers
  Box 611, Jefferson, North Carolina 28640
  www.mcfarlandpub.com

To my precious children, Carolina and Frank,
who choose to ignore my many weaknesses

This book is a memoir, not a military history book. It is a personal remembrance about real events that occurred for the most part over 40 years ago. I have changed names in certain cases to respect the privacy of those people and their families.

Acknowledgments

If I mentioned all those who gave me inspiration or guidance I would run out of ink.

Most of all, I must thank my brave mother, Mary Carver Cox.

I must thank my second family, the men who served with me as young artillery Forward Observers in Vietnam in Echo Battery, Twelfth Marines. Their performance in action is well documented and their support to put this manuscript together has been exceedingly valuable. So I thank each of them: Barney Barnum, David Garner, Bob Hamel, Jim Riordan, and Jack Swallows. I also thank Dan Walsh, Harry Dellinger, and Bob Rowe, all USMC lieutenants in Vietnam and close friends.

John M. Dowd was my college roommate and is my great friend. He was an extraordinary lawyer as a Judge Advocate General Marine Corps officer just as he is today with Akin Gump Strauss Hauer & Feld, where he heads the firm's criminal litigation group. His influence at History and Museums Division, Headquarters Marine Corps, helped facilitate my work. May God bless the soul of his brother, Tom, who was killed as a Marine platoon leader in the terrible killing fields south of Danang.

I thank Milam Propst and Jerry Lee Davis for helping me get started on this endeavor.

Finally, I must thank all the individual Marines I served with who showed me what courage is all about.

Table of Contents

Preface

Marines are about the most peculiar breed of human beings I have ever witnessed. They treat their service as if it was some kind of cult, plastering their emblem on almost everything they own, making themselves up to look like insane fanatics with haircuts to ungentlemanly lengths, worshipping their Commandant almost as if he was a god, and making weird animal noises like a band of savages. They'll fight like rabid dogs at the drop of a hat just for the sake of a little action, and are the cockiest SOB's I have ever known. Most have the foulest mouths and drink well beyond man's normal limits, but their high spirits and sense of brotherhood set them apart and, generally speaking, of the United States Marines I've come in contact with, are the most professional soldiers and the finest men I have had the pleasure to meet.

—An Anonymous Canadian Citizen

It was the first movie I ever saw. My father took me to the fabulous Fox Theater on Peachtree Street. Stars twinkled in a light royal-blue sky above the 4,600-seat colossus. It was one of the wonders of the world, an original American Top Ten special effect amphitheater. We saw the stars, each constellation drawn above us by a Creator, or something. It looked real. I expected the stardust to fall, slowly swirling and glittering, in flakes upon us as if we were outside in the languid late spring evening. We gasped with wonderment when remembering, kids my age along with fathers and grandfathers, that there was a roof above the stars. Yet the pulsating stars looked so real you could look up and throw a kiss at them just like in the backyard, except there was a roof above them.

Twenty minutes into the film John Wayne walked into his squad's tent, scowling. He was wearing a cotton olive-green battle shirt and a cartridge belt crammed with clips loaded with bullets for his M-1 rifle. Emblazoned on his left breast pocket was the first acronym I'd ever seen ... four letters in a row ... USMC. It lit me up.

1

That's a really cool shirt, I thought. *I want one of those. Someday I'll wear that shirt.*

In *The Sands of Iwo Jima* John Wayne roared into my life: "My name is Stryker, Sergeant John M. Stryker. You're gonna be my squad, a rifle squad. You joined the Marines because you wanted to fight. Well you're gonna get your chance, and I'm here to see that you know how. If I can't teach you one way, I'll teach ya another. But I'm gonna get the job done. Any questions?"

There were no questions. Except for one ... mine. After our flag was raised over Mount Suribachi, after the Marines had carried the battle, a solitary Nipponese sniper fired a shot through the lungs of Sergeant Stryker. The movie was almost over, the Japs were vanquished, yet John Wayne had a mortal bullet hole in his utility shirt with USMC emblazoned on it. I was devastated. Confronted with my first glimpse of death, I wondered — how could it end like this? Decades later I saw firsthand how often those that wear that shirt, the one so hard to get, fall also, like Sergeant Stryker.

Recently while looking west from a 22-story balcony I saw in the hot summer sky soft white clouds that had been motionless like massive suspended kites stir and scuttle to the east. Streams of grey flat clouds rushed from the west to mingle with the soft cotton ones. The wind swirled and suddenly a wall of purple-violet clouds swallowed the sky. Instantly the air turned cooler as the first thump of thunder sounded. Bright flashes from lightning framed the waves of rain, which fell in a sideways spume. Rain fell on the crusted earth and the scorched pavement below for the first time in weeks. A layer of steam hovered above the asphalt below like a low fog over a swamp. The perspiration on my forehead evaporated into the sudden coolness.

When mean weather moves in with such volatility it sometimes is a reminder of similar storms decades ago in a place where the weather was usually at an extreme. Violent storms visited the Marines in Vietnam with regularity, and in the monsoon season the storms lasted for weeks.

I denied all feelings in my heart about my Vietnam experience after departing. When I was there I never thought I could escape it. When I came home I shoved its memories deep into a subconscious file, locked the cabinet drawer, and threw away the key for a long time. It was so intensely real when I was in Vietnam that once gone I renounced it, morphed its existence into a surreal cocoon, and buried it way back deep inside; the whole trip was too heavy a consideration if you wanted to get a life.

In time I allowed some of the memories to emerge and I arranged them together so that I could draw upon the past as a catalyst to create emotions: rekindled adrenalin and aggression, and sometimes hope.

Finally one day I discovered scores of letters I had written my mother

43 years ago from Vietnam. The truth and essence of my experience came to life and walked into the room with me as I read those letters. The sights and sounds and events returned with clarity into my consciousness. I decided to put words to paper. I had meant to for a long time.

Recently a friend asked me, "Why another Vietnam book, now?"

I told him it was to honor the young Marines of that strange war who were slashed across their cheeks and throats by five-foot-tall, razor-sharp elephant grass as they crossed into the thick green foliage hiding enemy ambush positions.

This book mirrors the nature of the American experience in the Vietnam War, and in it are a series of events, many of which have no connection, personal fragmented experiences in a surreal, linear, long-term episode. The only resolution is the same one reached by the Marines who fought in the war, an ending of a tour of duty with no happy ending.

PART I

Forward Observer

1

We Never Promised You a Rose Garden

The vibrant young Marine warrior that fought in the Vietnam War is getting long in the tooth now. Middle-age has already elapsed, seen through his rear-view mirror quickly disappearing in a collage of marriage, kids, heartache, and joy.

But though he may try not to, he still vividly recalls the suffering and violence he was a part of, and at unexpected moments suddenly a flood of remembrances floating on a montage of long-ago images visit him.

He remembers no hot food, but he doesn't care, because the Marines are trapped in the hottest imaginable heat in Southeast Asia. He loses his appetite while humping through the thick jungle, so he settles for a C-ration can of fruit cocktail in syrup for minimal nourishment. He can't bear the thought of anything heavy to eat. If someone brought him a cheeseburger from paradise he would retch in the elephant grass, so he lives on water and canned juices and a piece of C-ration protein every now and again. He feels the weight slide off his bones with glee because he does not want to go up into the hills with one more ounce of weight. He can't remember what ice is like, but he would give a month's combat pay for a bucket of it.

He remembers the rancid smell of buffalo dung mixed with primordial black mud floating in a malodorous cloud above the rice paddies he sloshes across, which are vividly green like the pictures of Ireland. But Saint Patrick himself won't be able to stop the terrible bullets streaming at him even before he hears the sound of the firing itself. He remembers getting the heaves the first time he smelled the putrid animal pens next to the village hooches. He remembers the first shit detail the top sergeant assigned him to for a screw-up and how the awful black smoke smells when he lights the kerosene he has poured into the waste below the wooden seats of the officers' latrine at battalion headquarters. He remembers the iron-tinged smell of the blood of his dear friend sluicing through his fingers, which are pressed against the terribly large hole in his buddy's throat, *too much blood, not enough time.* He remembers the campfire smell, finally back from another patrol, unwinding in the comparative safety of the company base camp, the only civilized home he has, which is more primitive than the ramshackle huts of the nearby peasants, smelling like the burning oak smells back home, curling up past the dancing red embers while a comrade strums some chords from Bob Dylan and everyone finally feels safe. For a few minutes.

He remembers the stench of his body. There are no showers in the boonies. He smells the ripeness of his soiled and ragged jungle utilities that are usually either drenched from his sweat or from the relentlessly assailing monsoon rains. The flooded land causes the feet of some grunts to become bloody, infected messes of flesh. The corpsmen call it immersion foot. He remembers the smell of the rotting vegetation in the jungle, a very old smell. He smells the oil and grease in the chopper swooping straight down to the hot landing zone and then the smell of his own shit in his pants. The helicopter crew chief doesn't notice that smell anymore.

He remembers the sting of salt in his eyes from the constant sweat rivulets washing down his brow. He remembers the sudden insect bite on his forearm while lying under a poncho on the ground in a night defensive position with monsoon water pellets slapping the olive-green poncho's rubber surface, and he prays it was not the bite of a scorpion. That makes him think about all the snakes everywhere, and he gets petrified, remembering the dark brown, exceedingly long, king cobra that slithered across the trail about 10 yards ahead of the patrol point man, who was a few yards ahead under a canopy of coconut trees.

He remembers checking out the interior of a Buddhist pagoda that was collaterally damaged in a firefight moments ago, and he sees a new hole as big as a basketball in the back wall, bricks blasted like eggshells, right next to a breathtaking mural in coral and lime pastel shades of the Mother Goddess, Quan Am, above an ancient altar, while loading a full magazine into his rifle.

He remembers the precious water racing down his gullet, pulled from its pool hundreds of feet below the quagmire of mud surrounding the base of the village well in a rusty, tin bucket, tasting coppery as it flows from the old, aluminum, vintage–Korean War canteens. The Air Force MPs in the rear at the Danang Airbase have new, plastic ones but not the grunts yet.

He remembers seeing the smoke. It is diesel-black or whiter than an angel's wings or the tan color of weak coffee, but it is everywhere he looks, drifting into the turquoise Asian sky from a burning helicopter, or from a thimble of C-4 plastic explosive lit under his C-ration can of ham and lima beans, or belching from the mouth of a cannon, or from flames leaping from thatched roofs of a village whose people have made the Marines very angry. Even in the pitch black night it is seen when the illumination flare bursts and smoke spirals outward like the Fourth of July fireworks display in New York City. It rises from flames dancing on burning hedgerows and gates in villages where Marines get wounded by booby traps, so they get payback. The Marine Corps is known as the "Green Machine," but in war do not expect it to be an activist in the "greening" that saves the environment.

There are some things that are so insistent they cannot be recalled. The human mind can only assimilate a certain level of pain until it finally just checks out, a merciful circuitry meltdown. He may try, but he cannot revisit the utter state of exhaustion he endures on the march in the heat, just *one step at a time, baby, try to think this is really not happening.* He will never again experience the incredible thirst after the last drop of water from his canteen is gulped scaling a steep ridge in the green jungle or feel the jolt of a high-velocity bullet or of molten grenade fragments into his flesh; *it hurts so much,* but the good news is he can't feel the white-hot pain now like when he got hit.

When it gets real hot in the summer now he tries to compare the heat to that summer he spent so long ago in Vietnam, but it's a fruitless exercise, the combination of the heat and humidity in the jungle areas between the rice paddies has no equal and thank Jesus he's endured the last of that. He can recall the arduous struggle to carry his heavy load, but today he can't feel the actual strain of patrolling on foot with suspender straps attached to a cartridge belt holding magazines of bullets, canteens of water, a machete, a first aid kit, a compass, a Ka-Bar fighting knife, a rifle-cleaning kit, a pouch of hand grenades, plus a 12-pound M-14 rifle and two nine-pound bazooka shells and a haversack with claymore mines, socks, C-ration meals, a poncho, extra radio batteries, an entrenching tool, detonating cord, and paperbacks about sex, violence, and Jesus.

But he does remember the sense of touch and yearning. He is 20 years old and suddenly from his core the hormones race unsolicited, testosterone on the run, and standing in a line to draw water from a well or to draw grenades for the ambush patrol that will start just as darkness falls and out into the countryside owned by Victor Charlie he will go, he suddenly becomes erect. A blue-veiner has decided to arrive and is about to burst the cotton of his green jungle trousers. It hurts so good; what's a young Marine to do? When he daydreams he revisits the file of each girl he ever yearned for, all the way back to grammar school. He recalls how the ones he had success with tasted when he kissed them and how they smelled and what they whispered when he touched them. Then he daydreams about the ones he wanted but never got and how he will pursue them and what he will do with them when he returns to the world.

He remembers fetching 105mm howitzer shells and quickly screwing in the proper fuse and, after jamming the round in the breech, turning away from the artillery piece and covering his ears the second before his gun team-mate pulls the lanyard and the machine recoils as the steel shell is resound-ingly fired while the smell of tart gunpowder smoke swirls in his midst. The report slams so hard into his eardrums there is only one numbing ringing sound, and even today he hears that incessant ringing because the Marine Corps didn't issue earplugs to the cannoneers like the Army did.

The veteran remembers patrolling into a village with such stealth in broad daylight that the surprised mothers, wheeling and spotting the advanc-ing Marines, fetch their infants off the hard-packed, recently swept clay floor of the village where they were slicing freshly harvested *cu cai* turnips and scurry under the shelter of a nearby thatch-roofed storage bin, looking back one last time at the Americans while clutching their babies. Their faces are contorted by such consummate fear it is matched only by the fear of deer on the hoof trying to outrace a wind-blown forest fire, and the Marines feel ashamed.

The radioman remembers suddenly halting when his lieutenant, who is issuing hand signals to his squad leaders does five paces in front of him because the man on the point thinks he has sniffed out a band of guerrillas on the other side of a copse of trees with dead vines of brown, withered leaves fas-tened to them. The radioman does not move despite the pain of the heavy radio baseboard's straps cutting into his shoulders for the last several hours while walking through a glen of exotic bushes with glistening dark-green fronds so large they are only found in the jungle. He is alert as a mother leop-ard is when her cub falls to the ground from the crook of a tree limb and the baboons approach with their big teeth shining. He is motionless, and his gaze does not waver for a second from his leader, who may reach for the radio's handset at any moment. His dog tags are neatly fastened with black tape and hang from his neck in front of his shirt, where in the left pocket he has two ball point pens in case he or his lieutenant need to write information from incoming transmissions in the pocket notebooks they carry. Suddenly there is an eruption of gunfire, and he leaps to his leader's side.

The squad leader remembers his eyes must be multitasking, glancing all about for the safety of his 12 Marines, who are wading vulnerably across the open rice paddy toward the only close haven, a dike about 30 yards ahead between the Marines and the tree line they are headed to. Once past the dike, hopefully uneventfully, and once inside that tree line, he must be wary of the many dangers that exist and search for signs of them, the metal glint of an enemy's weapon, or freshly disturbed earth under which a mine could be buried, or fighting holes below the earth with bamboo covers that a Vietcong sniper could pop out of firing an SKS carbine round into the heart of one of his Marines. He must also flawlessly maneuver his three fire teams tactically to achieve success while insuring they use fire-discipline until finally they can reach the day's final objective and shut it down and grab some food and water and fade into a restless sleep.

The captain commanding the rifle company remembers the ambivalent nature of his responsibility, to lead his 150 Marines to kill as many of the enemy as possible while at the same time safeguarding them with risk-avoidance whenever possible to keep them alive. All the Marine Corps' assets exist for one purpose, to assist him and his rifle company, the Corps' center of the universe, to accomplish its mission. The air wing, artillery, and armor units exist to provide his company close fire support. The logistical, maintenance, transportation, educational, and training units exist to teach, clothe, feed, motivate, and arm his riflemen. The U.S. Navy provides the doctors, the clergy, and the corpsmen. In the heat of the moment as contact with the enemy begins the company commander must assess the enemy's size, location, strength of numbers, and types of weapons, then describe to his three platoon leaders the tactics they must utilize to destroy the enemy. At the same time he is describing over the radio to his battalion commander the rapidly changing environment and simultaneously calling in artillery air bursts and close air support, making sure the incoming medevac helicopters are not harmed by friendly fire. He has requested them to bring water and 7.62mm ammo for his riflemen, who are running low on bullets. Even though surrounded by chaos and besieged with scores of details that he must immediately address, he marvels at how effectively his brave Marines fight and sacrifice for each other, not for the U.S. Constitution, not for the cause of democracy, not for God or the good old Red, White, and Blue, but for pride. Pride for each other and for the exquisite pride in being a Marine.

The grunt remembers incessantly cleaning and oiling his rifle, which he pampers more than his own body, for it is his lifesaver. Each time after ramming an oiled cotton white patch down the bore to remove the carbon deposits inside the barrel — because a malfunction could be the death of him in a firefight — he releases the magazine and removes the live metal-jacketed cartridges and wipes each one clean before loading them back into the magazine he has cleaned the grit out of, which he inserts back into the receiver. Then he moves the safety to the "on" position before opening his dinner in a tin can, beans and franks.

The grunt remembers the special times he would remove his muddy, sodden jungle boots and tug his filthy socks off and lay them in the sun next to his poncho, where his rotting haversack and web gear and rifle are placed. His feet are wrinkled and blue-white and the sunlight warms them. He pulls his utility shirt off and sees white vertical streaks of salt on it that dried from his sweat, and he strips off his trousers and lays on his back naked on the poncho. His body tingles from the warm sun, and soon he falls into a slumber.

The grunt remembers going back with his company after long stints in Indian country looking for Victor Charlie on search-and-destroy operations to the relatively safe area of the battalion base camp. There are good things there like a chow hall with hot food, showers, tents with wooden floors, mail from home, chaplain services —*Bless me father for I have sinned*—vehicle runs to the ammo dump in the rear and on the way back a quick stop at a skivvie house —*Maline I make you so happy!*— but the flip side, too, when the motherfucking first sergeant makes him fill sandbags for hours at a time on work parties.

The grunt also remembers his backpack is not balanced, so one of the straps is cutting into his left shoulder and it is one more nuisance he must forget about because he cannot stop until his squad does. His soggy jungle boots have created angry blisters on both heels and the sores on his thighs are leaking pus. Everyone has some sort of infection if they are out in the boonies long enough. So he returns to a favorite daydream, the one where he is back home sitting in the living room with the air conditioner on 60 degrees, making the windows stream traces of condensation, watching the Red Sox pound the Yankees while eating the chilled chunks of watermelon his gal Vivian just served him wearing only her pink panties and a snug little shirt she has just put back on after they came together at the very same second.

An explosion at the front of the column wakes him from his reverie and he is back on the march humping a narrow trail. He is comforted knowing that each of the many more thousands of steps that will have to be endured will lead to that final step of freedom as he climbs the top stair of the ramp and enters the airplane bound for America.

2

Landing at Red Beach

A ship without Marines is like a coat without buttons. — Admiral David
G. Farragut, USN

July 7, 1965 — Danang, Republic of Vietnam

The grey ship chugged through the Pacific waters at a sluggish rate of 12
knots. It headed southwest across a smooth dark blue sea at an angle of about
210 degrees once it cleared the southern chalky cliffs of Okinawa and entered
the South China Sea. In early July 1965 it was part of a group of amphibious ships sailing to the shores of Vietnam, hauling the Second Battalion,
Ninth Marines, Battalion Landing Team.

The USS *Pickaway* had ridden the seas for decades and, despite the best
efforts of the U.S. Navy, whose mission was to ferry Marines to combat, she
was like a sloppy old drunk as she wallowed slowly through the troughs of
the tropical sea. Marine troops were stacked four high in the rotting webbing
of their bunks breathing malodorous fumes of diesel and sweat. They rejoiced
when each morning the gunny sergeants led them up ladders to the top deck
to participate in physical training under the climbing red sun that by noon
turned almost white. The platoon sergeants worked the shirtless young enlisted
Marines without mercy until the deck was slippery with sweat. Marine riflemen fired their weapons off the fantail into targets in the roiling waters of the
ship's wake and then went down the ladders to their cramped compartments
inside the sweating belly of the ship to clean their weapons and discuss ways
to fuck over the sailors.

The USS *Pickaway* was commissioned November 4, 1944. The amphibious assault ship carried Marines to the battle of Iwo Jima in February 1945
and participated in the Inchon landing during the Korean War.

The first night at sea I visited the stern and looked back at the moonlit
black and lustrous shapes dancing in the sea behind, then glanced up at the
heavens and its countless celestial objects. The black vastness forced me to

13

consider eternity, always a hard bargain for me to put my arms around; the concept was too vast for me to comprehend. There were a lot of places to be in this world and somehow I had acquired a one-way ticket to Vietnam. I futilely tried to find the horizon. Heat lightning lit up the western cloudless sky, yet nothing was to be seen but silvery crests of dark ocean waves.

I was a new artillery officer attached to the infantry. Certainly I would be somehow involved in whatever contact with the enemy awaited. Would it be like the consensus the young Marine officer contemporaries of mine forecast, a walk in the park against a weak, ill-equipped bunch of weakly led 135-pound gooks? A two-month rout and we would all get medals, become instant heroes, and come home to skies filled with shredded white ticker tape? Or would it be like facing the tenacious enemy our predecessor Marines had faced in Asia in the most recent two wars, at Iwo Jima and Tarawa, and at the Chosin Reservoir? You could get killed quickly in that kind of format. I flicked my glowing cigarette into the sea. We would become only the fourth Marine Battalion Landing Team to wade ashore in a country in conflict we knew little about. Whatever will happen will happen, I thought. Nothing good, nothing bad, just do your job and it will work out, I told myself. I headed to my berth to finish reading Ken Kesey's *One Flew Over the Cuckoo's Nest*.

We sailed at first heading southwest between Taiwan and the northern tip of the Philippines, taking dead aim at the palm-dotted coastline of I-Corps in northern South Vietnam.

Then we steamed west, plying the sapphire-blue waters of the South China Sea, accompanied by scores of flying fish by day and bright moonlight that made the sea look almost electric at night. The ship was host to rumors of all kinds: we were headed to the Mekong Delta to fight Vietcong amidst mud and mosquitoes; we would land in the harbor of Qui Nhon to be trucked out Highway 13 to Pleiku in the Central Highlands, where the enemy had become brazen with multiple murderous attacks against Americans; we were to be a roving BLT afloat at all times, on call for amphibious assaults (this rumor we feared the most).

One morning we awoke in Danang harbor.

H-hour commenced at 1000 on July 7, 1965, when the order to land the landing force was issued. That morning a friend and I snapped pictures of each other with single lens reflex cameras with the breathtaking coastline of the harbor framed by mountains behind us. The landing had been progressing for several hours with no enemy fire when the time came for my group to disembark. We climbed down the green-brown rigid rope rigging slung over the ship's side into our landing craft that joined up in a circle with six others knifing through the blue water, and then in a straight line dashed toward the sandy beach called Danang Red Beach One. The sea in the harbor bowl was stirred up by activity, and frothy, salty spray doused us, but no bullets glanced off the metal sides of our little boats during our race to the shoreline.

The front ramp fell open and the scene in front of me was one of energy and turmoil with no apparent method. Marines followed their leaders up the slant of the beach to a string of olive-drab trucks in a convoy. Artillery cannons were winched up and connected to the trucks. Vietnamese peasants tried to sell Coca-Colas and freshly caught fish. U.S. Navy shore parties with red and green markers provided directions to the beach from the sea and from the beach to the waiting transportation spread out for hundreds of meters on a road that went into the city of Danang.

Scores of vehicles formed the convoy, and we departed the beach and the landing area, working our way to Highway One, the *Street Without Joy*, and headed straight for the center of the second largest city in South Vietnam. I rode shotgun in the jeep assigned to me and we tailed a truck carrying Marine riflemen with loaded M-14 rifles. Our destination was south of the big city, the assembly area where the 2/9 headquarters and battalion Command Post were to be established that day. The convoy was moving at a quick speed and churned up clouds of amber dust in the soggy July heat, an enervating warmth so intense one's sweat never dried. Quickly the gritty dust coated our exposed skin.

The streets were teeming with Vietnamese peasants setting up shop on the side of the road, having brought rice and vegetables in from the countryside to sell to the mobs in the city. Fishmongers placed their products on wide frond baskets in market cubicles. Crabs scuttled in large glass jars, bluefish and catfish slowly flopped, and basa, tra, and sole, all just landed from the nearby shimmering South China Sea, lay in lines of fillets. The smell of *nuóc mǎm*, the Vietnamese ubiquitous fish sauce hung in the air like foul incense and hit me like a sledgehammer, triggering my gag reflex. The treads of several tanks in our convoy pulverized chunks of asphalt that had torn loose from the roadbed. The steel monsters whined terrible mechanical noises and spewed diesel exhaust that hung in the air like black-grey filmy clouds.

The convoy raced along the river and through the city. Young children poked heads out of their makeshift homes crafted from cardboard and smiled and whistled. Older children brazenly and desperately raced up to our vehicles when we slowed, begging for cigarettes and candy. The adults didn't smile. They dispassionately observed us with cold, stoic faces.

We passed blue and orange pock-marked pagodas and smashed bridges and mothers washing clothes on the rocks on the bank of a river while nearby small children splashed and laughed in the water. After we dashed through the city our pace quickened even more. It appeared someone had a damned good idea where we were headed.

Scenes of a country in turmoil raced by like clips from a science-fiction movie, an ancient green bus on its side just off the edge of an intersection with chickens crawling from windows facing the ground, slum hovels with children and pigs staring back at us through open doors, white uniformed policemen thrashing bystanders with batons, young women refugees in near-panic guiding their children away from the roar of the convoy, pastel-color juke joints with mini-skirted bar girls flirting with sailors with bell-bottom white trousers while familiar high-decibel rock and roll music blasted from amplified speakers. The Animals, a wildly popular rock band from England, were screaming about young men raising hell in a whorehouse in New Orleans.

And then we were through the city and the road released a layer of vermillion dirt clouds that hung in the air, stirred up by the tires and treads of the convoy's vehicles bearing a battalion of Marines on the move. The countryside changed and water buffalos with small boys riding on them trod on the side of the road toward vast marshy rice fields that stretched around tree-lined village islands into the horizon and certainly beyond. Guessing where those lush green paddies ended would be like guessing how many stars lay in the eastern sky.

Silver U.S. Air Force F-5 Freedom Fighters and grey U.S. Marine F-4B Phantoms roared just overhead on final flight paths before landing at the massive U.S. airbase in Danang. Columns of South Vietnamese soldiers (ARVN) sloughed across the dusty soil on patrol headed toward some objective with no spring in their step. We passed our first rural villages and old roadside checkpoints inside blown-away sandbagged bunkers. There were no South Vietnamese army soldiers to be seen when we headed south past the airbase.

We took a right off the main road and climbed up a hill, and there on a high, wide ridgeline was the 2/9 battalion headquarters, blossoming before our eyes. Marine working parties were placing concertina barbed wire around the compound's perimeter, filling the first of thousands of sandbags for security against enemy incoming mortar and rocket shells, erecting huge GP tents for the mess hall and the Operations Center and smaller CP tents for the HQ Company's headquarters and officers' quarters. Late in the afternoon work had begun on the construction of two major ammo bunkers, a four-hole latrine for officers, and the shower area.

By twilight smaller two-man tents for Marine grunts dotted the area. After dusk I checked in for situation reports from the four Forward Observers from my 105mm artillery battery that were beyond the wire out in the countryside with their respective rifle companies.

We were to operate in a hotbed of entrenched Vietcong activity. ARVN operations for the past year south of Danang had been perfunctory with little emphasis on closing with the enemy.

The 2/9 battalion command post was on a high-ground bluff three miles south of the U.S. Airbase at Danang. At the southern end of the perimeter the terrain angled down several hundred feet in elevation and leveled off at the S-curved Song Cau Do River a mile south of our position. It was a very wide and deep green-brown waterway that carried its essence, volumes of fast-moving water, to irrigate the fertile rice bowl valley that stretched endlessly to the west and south. The river's origin was at the base of the dark blue-green mountains 30 miles to the west, part of the Annamese Cordillera chain that cut through the length of the country for 600 miles. The river and the valley beyond the river were exquisitely beautiful; the whole vista was a giant wide-screen tapestry of colors that would have made Paul Gauguin envious, an endless stretch of glimmering rice paddies that separated hundreds of villages with heavy populations of agrarian residents. It looked so peaceful and timeless. It was impossible to conjure the peaceful, bucolic landscape would become an unspeakably horrific stage for thousands of U.S. Marine casualties over the next six years.

There were over 1,300 men and officers in the 2/9 Battalion Landing Team. Just a handful of senior officers and salty first sergeants had seen previous combat and that was in Korea. The rest of us were new to warfare. And all of us were new to the surrounding terrain and environment. We were the first American unit to operate south of Danang. Marine intelligence was minimal and tactical lessons were nonexistent. It was the on-the-job training of the first order, filled with trial and error, and at first it was mostly error.

Our first night in Vietnam the sky was a raven background for thousands of glittering stars. Just before midnight I was relieved from my watch in the operations center and walked 75 yards to my tent. I took my boots off and slumped onto my cot and closed my eyes. And listened. For hours. I listened to my first sounds of combat and the clouds blocked the bright moonlight.

A quick 10-second firefight erupted a mile to the west with single bursts from carbines and then one four-second burst from an automatic weapon, then nothing.

What happened? I wondered.

I heard the thump of a single artillery piece firing a shell and then heard the shell explode downrange 15 seconds later.

What was the target? I asked.

But what really got to me was the powerful low *whump* noise made by exploding hand grenades less than a mile away where an ambush had been sprung. The enemy had to be really close to you to attempt to throw a grenade. A nearby *whoosh* sound brought me off my cot. A young Marine on our perimeter got nervous and fired an illumination flare and lit up the entire southwest quadrant of the perimeter. His gunny sergeant raced to his position through black and white and grey swirling light shadows and threatened to break his neck if he did it again. The adventure had begun. I finally fell asleep.

3

Forward Observer

January 30, 1966 — Ha Dong Bridge, Song Bau Xau River

For the first half of my tour I was the artillery liaison officer attached to the Fire Support Coordination Center of the infantry battalion headquarters that my artillery battery supported. My job was to help coordinate all supporting fire for the battalion's four rifle companies and advise the infantry commanding officer and operations officer when my input was needed. Four other lieutenants from the battery had more dangerous jobs, artillery forward observers imbedded with rifle companies on combat operations out in the boonies.

One afternoon I was ordered to report and meet the new commanding officer (CO) of Echo Battery, Second Battalion, Twelfth Marines. After our introduction the captain told me he had decreed immediate personnel changes. I heard imaginary warning alarms shriek and claxons wail. A feeling of dread made my temples pound like drums. I was told to be ready in an hour to be driven to my new job, artillery forward observer (FO) for Foxtrot Company, Second Battalion, Ninth Marines. My new CO told me I would have to wait a few days before meeting Foxtrot's company commander. I was to hook up with the company's second platoon position and man an observation post above a built-up railroad trestle on the south bank of the Song Bau Xau River, several miles south of our base camp.

Forty minutes later a "Mighty Mite" jeep skidded to a stop in front of the battery's tent for lieutenants. I had just finished packing my haversack with my precious inflatable "rubber lady" air mattress, poncho, extra socks, extra maps, grease pencils, a flashlight, and insect repellant. I had drawn an additional 20-round magazine filled with 7.62mm cartridges for my M-14 rifle and filled my canteen with fresh water and attached it and a new compass to my web cartridge belt.

"You ready, Mister Cox? Your limo has arrived," the driver called outside.

"You bet, Corporal Raines, I need to go where the living is easy. Thank

Artillery forward observer team for Foxtrot Company 2/9 mans observation post at Ha Dong Bridge, January 1966.

God the new skipper is cutting me some slack after the ordeal of dealing with this tough battery life back here with hot chow and real wooden floors. Besides, the grunts are more fun than a barrel of monkeys."

A little humor goes a long way with the troops.

Raines laughed. "Gee, Lieutenant. Maybe I should beg the CO to let me go along with you."

I smiled back. "Okay, Corporal, I can arrange that most riki-tik."

Raines raised his hand in mock resignation. "Sir, you know I'm just screwin' around."

A battery clerk was in the rear of the vehicle with his M-14 slung across his legs for security. We stowed my equipment in the back of the jeep including my flak jacket and a pair of binoculars in a dark green leather case and headed south.

We left the moonscape setting of the battery that was entrenched in a white salt flat with small pools of water settling in low areas from a recent deluge. We passed peasant women bouncing along the side of the road in knee-flexed jogs that helped them balance their load distributed at both ends of a bamboo pole atop their shoulders. The humid smell of rottenness and new growth filled the air. Brown-eyed eight-year-old boys smiled and waved at us straddling their fathers' water buffalos in the rice fields. The fathers in the nearby villages were absent, doing whatever mischief the Vietcong were into at the time. An occasional field with elephant grass swaying in the slight breeze bordered rows of vegetable crops.

After a two-mile trip south we came upon the infantry position. It was next to the old main north-south coastal railroad elevated bed. It had been years since trains ran north to Danang and south to Quang Ngai. There were no tracks anymore. The Vietcong had removed the valuable steel a long time before. The old railroad steel bridge had been blown in the middle and formed a perfect "V" as it dipped into the center of the river from each bank. The giant stream flowed toward the sea in sweeping turns. Villages dotted the vast landscape filled with many shades of green, from lime green to jade to emerald to sea green. Everything Marine was colored in olive-drab green.

The infantry platoon was bivouacked on the south bank of the river on flat hardscrabble ground. There were no permanent bunkers and little natural cover. There were a few foxholes and a string of barbed wire strewn across the front of the position. The 28 Marine troopers were doubled up in small tents and there were C-ration cases open next to each shelter. Most Marines were shirtless in the late afternoon heat and any movement at all stirred up red dust. Grey smoke swirled from a small campfire and hung low. The scene matched one I had seen a long time before, a picture in a history book of a bunch of hobos camped out on an Oklahoman plain during the Great Depression. The platoon leader shook my hand and welcomed me aboard. Staff Sergeant Jimmy Crowley was now in temporary command after his lieutenant had been wounded and evacuated a few days before.

"Welcome aboard, Mr. Cox, we're delighted to have a real FO with us. Your timing's outstanding. We're scheduled to conduct a full day search-and-destroy patrol beginning at first light."

I pulled out my map. "Just my luck. Where are we headed? Please trace our route on this."

"We're headed first to this village where we got shot at last week. There is another place further along our route where I think it might be necessary for you to call in arty."

"Do me a favor and put an 'X' on the probable hot spots and I'll set up some pre-planned fire missions. We'll get the fire a lot quicker if we can guess correctly."

He pointed, "Okay, here, and here. And, Lieutenant, I'd like it if you would follow directly behind me. I'm damn sure we'll be bustin' caps at those bastards tomorrow."

The map is the alter ego of the FO. He must read it with perfection; there is no room for any error. A misplaced 95-pound cast-steel artillery shell packed with high explosives is to be avoided at all costs. The FO is so caught up in keeping exact track of his map position that he is often asked the unit's precise whereabouts by his nearby infantry commander.

The platoon's present position gave it a deeper stance into the enemy's territory than any other Marine line unit in the Ninth Marine Regiment.

I introduced myself to the other three members of my FO team. I exchanged greetings with my scout/observer Corporal Tommy Weaver from the piney woods of Mississippi, who would become the finest enlisted Marine I would serve with. Next I shook hands with the team's two radio operators, Lance Corporal Jeremy Cowart from Lawrence, Kansas, and Lance Corporal Randolph Cassidy from Brockton, Massachusetts. Only Weaver had reached his 20th birthday. Their lives depended on my ability to make proper decisions, and they quickly tried to read me.

Cowart began my initial examination, "Welcome aboard, sir. Are you a Chevy or a Ford man?"

Cowart's eyes matched the color of his native state's brilliant blue flower, the salvia. Cassidy edged forward. Obviously the two communicators had a failure to communicate on at least one subject. Cars were right up there with getting laid in importance with 19-year-old Marines. Weaver just leaned back and winked.

"I'm trying to decide. You guys tell me. I kind of like them both."

Cowart was among the minority of the young enlisted men who had graduated from high school. As he began, Cassidy started changing the battery pack in his PRC-25 radio.

"Sir, when I get back to the world I'm gettin' me a '56 Chevy. I know a parts shop in Emporia where I can get a discount and get me a power-pack two-carb setup. I'll raise it and rake it and paint it solid black and get me more chicks than you can shake a stick at in east Kansas. Bitchin', sir, bitchin'!"

Cassidy responded, "Never happen! Sir, I know just the '55 Ford I'm going after in Lowell. It's cherry and as red as the dick on a dog. I'll drop a three-quarter Isky cam in her and suck every Chevy I meet up through the carb and blow it out the exhaust. Fords are just flat out fuckin' groovy, sir. Fuck a bunch of Chevys."

I looked at the two auto enthusiasts, "You guys both have a good point. So maybe I gotta get me one of each, unless one of you can convince me otherwise. No sweat, we've got a long time to figure this problem out. Meanwhile I'm getting chow before I hit the rack. We have a busy day tomorrow starting at oh-dark-thirty."

Cassidy looked hard at Cowart. "Lieutenant, do they even got gasoline in shit-kickin' Hicksville, Kansas?"

Cowart responded, "Shove it, pogue. You ain't not only never been laid, you can't even speed shift gears, dip-shit!"

"Oh yeah, shitbird, you ain't no fuckin' scivvie honcho yourself."

It was just their way of showing love for one another. Weaver smiled at me as the sun started to ebb below the distant high western mountains.

My quarters were the right half of a pup tent I would share with Cassidy. It was suppertime in the bush and I had a choice of C-ration entrees, spiced beef or ham and eggs. As I was reaching for the beef I flinched when I heard a sudden, unexpected explosion-implosion 20 yards behind me. Marine riflemen were catching their dinner by throwing M-79 hand grenades into the slowly drifting waters of the river just behind my tent. Soon several fish popped to the surface, floating aimlessly, killed by the concussions. The young Marines plucked them from the water and quickly roasted and ate them. Fresh protein was a rare commodity on the battleground. They enjoyed their isolation from the rest of the company; there was no first sergeant to screw with them.

Soon the sun slid down the backside of the hills and darkness enveloped our remote outpost. I inflated my air mattress and climbed as a co-tenant into my new home, a seven-by-six-foot floor on the ground inside a makeshift tent redolent with the smell of rotting canvas and old rubber. I tried drifting to sleep, slowly letting go not only of my fear of my new vulnerability but also of the new sounds found at a truly forward combat position. Frogs, cicadas, and birds created an animal stew of noises mixed with the sounds of remote quick rifle bursts, distant, hearty explosions of solitary harassing artillery rounds, and the barely heard *c-r-r-u-m-p-s* of slung grenades. Once I thought I heard a monkey scream.

We were the forward unit, at the very tip of the spear. And there were less than 30 of us. In the open. I stopped thinking about it.

"How's your first day been with us, Lieutenant?" my radio operator asked.

"Fine. Thanks for asking."

"Well, I'm glad you're with us. To tell the truth, Lieutenant, I've been scared shitless out in this grunt position."

"Oh, hell, Cassidy, this is skate-city compared to all the crap they hand you in the rear. What could be finer than a nice, peaceful night in beautiful downtown Southeast Asia? Hell, we could be somewhere worse, like Las Vegas or Hollywood. Good night, my man. Don't let the bedbugs bite."

The troops really sought solace from their officers; they were just kids, growing old quickly, and constantly on the lookout for the bogeyman. They needed their leaders to provide reassurance through strength and maturity. Compassion and friendliness went a long way, too.

I turned over on my side and the right side of my face sunk into the folds of the rubber mattress. A stream of bright moonlight shone through a hole in the shelter, lighting up my cartridge belt next to my feet. I always slept with my boots on, even in the rear. My rubber poncho was also next to my feet, having been discarded. I started the night off with it as a makeshift blanket, but all it did was make me sweat.

An alien brittle, scratchy sound startled me out of my sleep, and I felt pressure deep in my left ear. The sound and pressure in my eardrum soon became more insistent. An insect had invaded my ear canal and couldn't escape. I imagined maddened spiky caterpillars, misplaced swollen Asian ants, and deranged tsetse flies. I slapped my head and reached down my ear canal as far as possible with any safe object I could find. Every movement the critter made in its confusion was amplified fractions of inches from my eardrum. I decided it would be a terrible example to freak out. So I just let it go. After a long time the thing finally died. For several days little brown crisp particles fell from my ear.

I heard more alien noises, including one unmistakably linked with childhood, the *whoosh* of a roman candle. But now the noise just meant another illumination flare was about to pop. The resultant incandescence made the world go *black-brightwhite-grey-brightwhite-grey-brightwhite* after it was released from the container. The light was jagged and made you dizzy as shadows did somersaults. A half-mile south a solitary grenade serenaded the cicadas with a mournful pop. Then sleep came.

The next morning I took a stick of black cosmetic camouflage paint and drew black lines up the length of my fingers and then halfway up my forearms until the streaks reached my rolled-up cuffs. I then drew olive-green streaks next to each black streak. Then I used the green paint stick to make my face the color of the nearby grasses and bushes. I tore sprigs of pointed leaves off a tall shrub hovering on the riverbank and placed them in the slits cut into my leaf-pattern camo helmet cover, twisting them so they stood upright. Then I stuck eight-inch-long blades of elephant grass I cut off with my KA-Bar knife and placed and secured them in other slits. Then I painted the faces of my three team members and told them to spruce up their helmets, too.

Cover and concealment; if you can't see me you can't shoot me. I was ready for my first combat patrol.

4

Ambush

In the midway of this our mortal life,
I found me in a gloomy wood, astray
Gone from the path direct: and e'en to tell,
It were no easy task, how savage wild
That forest, how robust and rough its growth,
Which to remember only, my dismay
Renews, in bitterness not far from death...
— Dante Alighieri, *The Divine Comedy*

February 7, 1966 — Bich Nam Village

Fifteen men in black peasant dress with Chicom hand grenades lay abreast motionless and undetectable facing the tree line across the short field in front of them with forefingers firmly placed on their triggers, waiting for the unsuspecting U.S. Marines to emerge openly through the tree line and close toward them. The Vietcong fighters each carried two days' worth of rice in bags tied to their backs, a small amount of water, and 20 to 30 rounds of ammunition for their carbines and AK-47 rifles. They had carefully slashed the thick yellow-green bamboo stalks and the undulating five-foot tall, razor-sharp elephant grass just in front of them to allow fields of fire for their weapons. They could not be seen from across the field.

The afternoon sunshine came from behind them and illuminated the brilliant green field of vegetables, spicy peppers and fat, pulpy peas, between them and the jungle cluster of darker green trees across the far edge of the field. Clouds flew between the sun and the field and made the landscape dance.

The Vietcong soldiers had rehearsed the ambush operation during the morning, correctly estimating the very hour the Marine patrol would arrive at the site. The hardcore guerrillas had quickly learned that the Marines repeated patterns while patrolling. They knew the Marines were very dangerous but took comfort knowing that despite the Americans' vastly superior weaponry, their predictability coupled with the guerrillas' nimbleness and knowledge of their homeland envi-

25

ronment made it at the least a level playing field. The small yellow men were patient, feeling assured the moth would fly into the flame. Sweat trickled from the soldiers' foreheads and temples covered by green pith helmets onto their forearms supporting their rifles, then fell drop by drop from their wrists into the soil supporting their elbows. They paid no attention to the sweat or other discomforts, nor did they speak or move for several hours. They would not fire until the first echelon of Marines had crossed most of the field toward them.

A photograph appeared of me in the July 1966 issue of *Leatherneck* magazine, snapped by a combat correspondent. It was sent to me after I rotated back to America, discovered through happenstance by a previous comrade-in-arms. I never knew the photo was snapped. The photographer, Sergeant Bob Bowen, was attached to our unit to capture Marine combat images during what was expected to be a likely encounter operation in an area 10 miles south of Danang in Quang Nam province.

The Marine Corps has always been the ultimate media hound. If the national press is not available for combat operations, the Marine Corps will often embed its own correspondents with combat units to encapsulate and memorialize the next great photo opportunity. The stirring photograph of the flag-raising on Iwo Jima prompted James Forrestal, secretary of the Navy, to proclaim, "The raising of that flag on Suribachi means a Marine Corps for the next five-hundred years." The Corps has forever fought for its existence against political enemies, hence its insatiable thirst for public relations.

We were briefed the evening before the photograph was taken in the bunker headquarters of Captain Carl Reckewell, the commanding officer of Foxtrot Company, Second Battalion, Ninth Marines. The bunker was positioned in the middle of the company's latest forward base camp. The large bunker's wooden walls and roof were stacked with hundreds of olive-green dusty sandbags.

Our mission was to search and sweep several villages in the Bich Nam complex south of our base camp, which was 1,000 meters east of the Main Supply Route (MSR), a road that provided vehicle movement in the Ninth Marine Regiment's Tactical Area of Responsibility (TAOR). The MSR replaced the old railroad that before had carried generations of Vietnamese from Danang to Saigon on a raised, sturdy bed elevated above the sea of rice paddies. It ran north to south, parallel with Highway One, which was almost three miles to the east. The area bristled with mined rice paddies and vegetable fields and booby-trapped tree lines, which in past operations had inflicted many Marine casualties. We had recently begun flinging three-pronged grappling hooks tied to ropes as we approached tree lines. We would then yank the rope to detonate any booby traps hidden in the thick brush.

WAITING...

by Sgt Robert Burgoyne

Photos by Sgt Bob Bowen

First Lieutenant Franklin Cox takes a breather on patrol. *Leatherneck* magazine, July 1966.

Captain Reckewell was sending a smoke generator so that when we discovered air holes leading to underground Vietcong tunnels we could smoke them out. His last instructions were, "When we get shot at we've got to get moving against them fast and charge the position. The VC will not stand and fight against a concentrated Marine effort."

It was an area in which the Second Battalion, Ninth Marine Regiment, had been assigned to conduct operations to find and kill the enemy. When the last Marine units finally left Quang Nam province six years later the objective was never fully accomplished. Despite all the resolve and will the Marine Corps could summon by fully applying its assets and firepower against the enemy, the North Vietnamese Army (NVA) and Mainforce Vietcong, he was never vanquished. It was his home and he knew every foot of each rice paddy, every spider-hole position he could climb into and cover with natural camouflage and shoot from after Marines walked past, every tree in each thick thicket, and every entrance into the elaborate tunnel honeycomb beneath his hamlets. He used the same hidden fighting holes he had used for centuries, including recent decades when he stopped the Japanese Imperial Army and later the French Foreign Legion troops.

Victor Charlie was a history major, summa cum laude. We were too busy calling in medevac choppers for our grievously wounded to reflect on the past. Of the 14,838 U.S. Marines killed in Vietnam, 6,480 died in Quang Nam province alone. For six years Marine units suffered casualties in the same villages their predecessors had in the same way. It's hard to learn from mistakes when history is thrown out of the mix.

It was another very hot day, one of the first at my new job as artillery forward observer for Foxtrot Company. I had been out in the boonies on a few uneventful search-and-destroy patrols and had not yet called in artillery fire to support my rifle company.

We were to head southeast to the first village, then generally westerly to the second village, and then go north back to the base camp. We were conducting a search-and-destroy sweep like scores of similar exploits across the breadth of inhospitable I-Corps. Between each village were mucky rice paddies, as green and beautiful as the marshes back home dotting the Savannah coastline. They provided no cover and had to be crossed. You had to be careful and you had to dismiss the soul-sapping heat of those expanses. If you thought about the 105-degree cocoon you were trapped in for very long it would suck you down into a near unconscious spiral of thermal claustrophobia, near to the point of imagining an easy way out, maybe a well-aimed AK-47 round could enter and leave you painlessly and you'd never know the difference, thank God.... *It's too hot here anyway.*

We traversed several rice paddies and crossed a rickety, partially destroyed footbridge across a turgid stream. We set up a base of fire as our forward troops approached the first village objective. While searching through the village we found several tunnels. Combat engineers used C-4 plastic explosives to wreck them. We had swept through the width and length of the village when the platoon leader called for a quick water break.

"Take ten," he ordered. The troopers collapsed onto the chalky brown earth of the village's floor.

"If you got 'em smoke 'em," suggested the platoon sergeant.

Soon we headed for the second village. The operation had been typical so far, edgy nerves, tunnels explored, the thatched roof of a hovel where ammunition was discovered torched, gooks questioned, VC bunkers blown. Two Marines were maimed from a booby-trapped grenade hidden in the brush below a banana tree that yielded misery, not fruit. No fire had been exchanged, no enemy neither seen nor heard, just another typically murderously frustrating gig, *please show your face motherfucker*. But he wouldn't, not until it suited him.

I pulled hard and up came the bucket from the well's depths, filled with water, the difference-maker, as precious as a queen's platinum in the humid envelope of the village surrounded by burgeoning vegetation snatching the available oxygen. I poured water into the outstretched canteens held by my radio operator and the platoon corpsman as he dropped an empty morphine syringe that he had just sedated one of the wounded Marines with. The Marine's moans dropped in volume, then stopped. I filled my canteen and poured the remnants down the neck of a young trooper next to me; his face had gone from florid to pale in minutes.

No other issues of any sort had arisen. Passing through the village we heard a few sounds, the yelp of a dog, the wail of a baby, the clucking of hens, women scrubbing clothes. It was the same familiar background noise of domesticity we had heard on the plains of Kansas or in the hollows between the hills of West Virginia or even on the asphalt streets of Detroit, neighborhood all–American sounds, the very sounds that made you want to take a nap back home. We ploddingly and carefully worked our way past each possible danger. We kicked open some grain bins looking for weapons but found none. We asked a few questions of the old women residents with blackened betel nut gums and unforgiving eyes. They solemnly answered the only reply to the interpreters they ever provided, "*Khong biet!*" In any language the answer was inevitable and the same and you knew they would sooner die than reveal anything about our enemy and their sons, which were one and the same, Victor Charlie to us, precious flesh and blood to them. We had been on a mind-numbing stroll for four hours under the laser beams of the midday Asian sun, now directly above us, turning the blue sky white with sunshine. We were on a trail just inside the westernmost tree line, which served as a border for the village complex.

As I examine the photograph from *Leatherneck* magazine, I see me sitting and leaning back against a hedgerow in some shade, resting. I am sure I had just holstered my canteen into its web pouch. My M-14 rifle's butt is on the ground between my bent legs. Its muzzle is above my left shoulder. My fingers are loosely wrapped around the two magazines I had taped together. I am sure it was my first week out in the bush because I see something amiss. There is a fragmentation grenade attached to my jungle utility shirt. I removed the grenade sometime during the patrol, perhaps just after the picture was taken. Only bad things could result if something, anything, happened to the exposed grenade. So I removed it from its vulnerable position and gave it to a nearby trooper.

There is a rifleman a few feet off the trail to my right. He is on one knee peering through the brush behind us. I am staring slightly to my right across the trail. It looks as if I am lost in reverie. It is at that instant the photograph is taken. The caption for the picture and story in the magazine spells "Waiting..."

A few minutes later the platoon leader yelled, "Saddle up!" The next leg required us to cross an open 70-yard field to reach the tree line on the far side. I was just behind the platoon leader with the third squad as we passed the last hedgerow and entered into the open field. The first squad was halfway across the field on line followed by the second squad some 20 yards behind.

Suddenly the VC sprang their surprise. Several automatic weapons joined by small arms erupted from the far tree line and broke the monotony of the hot afternoon. Bullets whizzed by us slapping into the tree line just behind us. The sudden noise from their weapons was deafening, a surge of adrenalin instantly took away the Technicolor, everything was now starkly black and white and scary, scores of bullets were hosed at us, the singing sound they made sawing through the air was like that of swarms of angry, vengeful hornets on a high-speed mission. Everyone instantly hit the ground, trying to crawl under the incoming fire. Tree limbs snapped above and behind us and for several seconds time was suspended. I had never been shot at like that before, so unexpectedly, the fire delivered so closely, the total surprise shocking my soul. On the ground for a few seconds I wondered, almost in denial, what that violent noise was. Then almost instantly I was on my elbows, checking my map once more to pinpoint the coordinates of the enemy shooters to call in artillery. Instinctively the first squad sprinted into the tree line, charging the fire. Seconds later the second squad also frontally assaulted the enemy position. I jumped up and ran to catch up with the command group and the third squad crossing the field. I didn't want to be the last one left back there, all alone. Who knew what might be back there now.

It's all happening too fast I can't quite get my shit together how can I read my map when I'm running at bullets passing me and why is it my radio operator and I are among the last to get across this field with a damn draw straight across the center of it makes it hard to run fast going up the slope I can hear noises of rifles firing quick bursts and soft sounds of boots pounding the wet green ground and metallic sounds of magazines with live rounds rattling and slapping noises of packs and equipment bouncing on Marines on the move — slap-slap-slap, jostle-jostle, run-run-run Hail Mary Full of Grace the Lord is with Thee.

Finally across the open area and just inside the tree line I linked up with the platoon leader. The whole event took less than a minute. Miraculously no Marines were hit. The first two squads gave chase for several hundred meters. I studied the terrain and my map trying to decide the most likely avenue of escape the Vietcong would take. The platoon leader agreed with me and I sent in a request for artillery fire. After an eight or nine minute wait I aborted the first mission; too much time had elapsed. The first two squads rejoined us. There had been no further sign of the enemy. The VC had vanished, hunkering down and disappearing like will o' the wisps, like ghosts into a different dimension, slipping into the friendly concealment of the green, lush, wet Asian environment, as elusive to hold as mercury in the fingers of a five-year-old child. Gone ... where?

It was almost incomprehensible that not one Marine had been hit by the torrent of fire, delivered at us almost point blank. It was as if nothing had transpired, a surreal feeling. But the sudden sounds of the weapons and their bullets had been unmistakably real. It is a sound you never forget. Frustrated again by the enemy we headed to the base camp, no scalps in our saddlebags.

Similar patrols resulted in different consequences. Sometimes we found a few enemy bodies. Sometimes we found only blood trails. Victor Charlie also collected his wounded and rescued them from the battlefield. Sometimes we received no weapons fire; there were no enemies in the area, but a sudden explosion by a hidden mine thunderously announced more Marine casualties. We became frustrated and insisted our enemy square up and face us. He knew better; he was into attrition and mind games. Time was on his side.

5

Hearts and Minds

February 18, 1966 — Quang Dong Village, Republic of Vietnam

"Shit! Split!" screamed the U.S. Marine as his right ankle separated the hidden trip wire, no thicker than a filament of common fishing line, from the delayed-action fuse which set off the M-18 Claymore mine, a Bouncing Betty, recently captured when ARVN soldiers fled their nearby compound, attacked just before dawn by a pack of Vietcong sappers. His warning was too late for himself and two others as 700 dime-sized balls of steel were unleashed at warp-speed when the mine sprang waist-high from its hidden nest several inches below the wet black earth and exploded. The force took apart some nearby coconut trees. Young American flesh and bone was even less of a match against the torrent of hot metal. The booby-trapped trail snaked across tropical brush then cut through a thick green-forested tree line that formed a line of defense for the village behind it.

I lay prone in the flattened brush just off the trail. I waited for the VC to follow up with more violence and traced my finger to a point on my map at a likely enemy escape avenue upon which I had created a pre-planned artillery fire, just in case. The platoon leader was 10 yards to my right intently assessing the situation, screaming and hand-signaling tactical maneuver orders to his small unit leaders. An old rusty water bucket between us teetered and spilled it contents through four new holes in the metal. To my left my radio operator held the handset next to me, just in case I needed to send a fire request. I listened and heard nothing except the ringing from the concussion. Soon the sawing sound of cricket wings and then the trilling of red-winged laughing thrushes ended the silence. I smiled at my radioman.

"No fire mission, Randy, Charlie's long gone."

The squad leader, a 21-year-old corporal and graduate of the Choate School who had joined the Corps after his freshman year at Brown University to "collect his thoughts" lay writhing on the trail after tripping the wire. The femoral sheath in his right thigh was dissected and it was spewing blood in foot-long crimson spurts. A corpsman tried to lace a tourniquet around the corporal's slick thigh to stem the torrent of blood, but the Marine quickly died while looking behind him, still trying to warn his comrades.

Two 19-year-old riflemen had also been wounded by the explosion. Private First Class (PFC) Clem McCrae was from the highlands of Elkins, West Virginia. Jerry West's blue and gold posters covered his bedroom walls back in Appalachia. He only had a few weeks left on his tour; he was so short he told people he had to jump up to look down. As he lay on the ground he saw his left thumb and forefinger were missing. He glanced at the royal blue sky and looked back at his mangled hand and just shook his head and cried as the medevac chopper was summoned.

The other wounded trooper was from "the Valley." PFC Wynn Metcalf had been in junior high when he attended the funeral held in San Fernando for Ritchie Valens, the first Mexican-American rock star, who perished in the same plane crash that claimed Buddy Holly and the Big Bopper on February 3, 1959, the day the music died. He had a sweetheart back home and was going to marry her and get a part-time job in the local refinery. He intended to become the first in his extended family to go to college and become somebody and race dirt bikes in the desert. He had lost a portion of his jawbone just under his left ear, and he was a mess. He quickly went into shock. Months of surgery awaited him.

The platoon leader, a second lieutenant, who just a year before had taken his final examinations as a history major at the University of Denver, had recently warned the village chief to report all enemy activity in the future. After the casualties were airborne the lieutenant sent his Vietnamese interpreter to locate the village chief.

We advanced in three columns and entered the built-up area of the sprawling village complex where among the structures was the district elementary school. The platoon leader dismissed the classes. Young children headed home, passing by us with wide-eyed curiosity and dimpled smiles.

Other mines were discovered and disarmed. Scores of needle-pointed punji stakes were found in hollowed traps just below the earth's surface throughout the hamlet. Armed grenades were affixed to hinges in gates leading to the animal pens. Fighting trenches crisscrossed the village complex, some dug with bare hands and tools by villagers three and four generations earlier. Through the centuries invading armies tried to seize the countryside and subjugate the populace, but the Vietnamese people would never yield. Several hooches away a grenade exploded inside a tunnel containing food provisions for the enemy. Troopers whooped cheers. Mothers' eyes shifted nervously in otherwise stoic faces.

Marines patrolling the area near Hill 55, seven miles southwest of Danang, were constantly on edge. In a matter of months Marine rifle companies suffered 30 to 40 percent casualty rates, mostly from mines and other booby-trapped explosives. Two battalions of the French army had been wiped out in the Indochina War 15 years earlier on the same hill. It belonged to the VC. It was bad country. The Marines knew about the ghosts of the past and fought nightmares that visited them continually suggesting new disasters. It only took a few times at night to hear the old Asian refrain, shouted from outside the perimeter in the darkness, "Malines, you die!" to give you the shivers.

With such an environment testing them it was no wonder a cultural change transpired in the dialectics of the confused young Marines. Their interactions with the locals morphed down a moral ladder — from protector, to antagonist, to murderer.

The village chief arrived. "Goddamnit, why didn't you warn us the VC had placed mines here?" the lieutenant asked, his fury making his voice brittle and hard.

"Me no see VC. We your friends! No VC here now. VC bad, no welcome here! I told VC to *di-di* two weeks ago and not come back."

"Oh, yeah? Then how the fuck did that mine that just wasted my Marines get buried there and explode?"

The platoon sergeant said, "Lieutenant, this slimy gook is one lying motherfucker, he's gotta be a VC sympathizer. Let's send him to the rear as a VC suspect for interrogation."

I added, "All this evidence shows us there have been *beaucoup* VC here not just two weeks ago but also today. This place is lousy with VC."

The chief got the gist and screeched, "No! Me no VC! This village no VC! We help you kill VC."

He became panicked when considering the treatment his ARVN interrogators would provide him. He especially didn't want a helicopter ride to the rear. Sometimes "accidents" happened to suspects high in the air.

The interpreter slapped the village chief's aide hard across his cheek.

"Where are the VC?" he demanded.

The aide didn't know, the chief didn't know, no Vietnamese ever admitted knowing the whereabouts of the VC. In this part of Vietnam most sons and brothers and cousins were VC. The population knew which side their bread was buttered on; they'd take their chances with the VC. Opposition to the National Liberation Front often meant death.

Thirty yards down the wide trail a young Marine screamed at another, "Don't waste that fuckin' water buffalo, man." The other Marine sheepishly lowered his rifle. The penned animal stared dumbly, then bleated.

The lieutenant stared at the chief who had assumed the traditional Asian hunker stance, deep-squatting, rocking slightly, faking insouciance, muttering, "No VC here." The lieutenant's eyes hardened. "Okay, asshole, I warned you."

The lieutenant grabbed the handset to his PRC-25 radio and contacted battalion headquarters. Continual intermittent explosions provided the background sound effect as Marines destroyed enemy fighting positions — trenches and spider holes just below the earth's surface — by blowing them up with C-4 plastic explosive.

Soon an M-50 Ontos, a tracked vehicle with six mounted 106mm recoilless rifles, wheeled noisily up to our position. A wake-cloud of brown dust settled over it as it stopped. The platoon leader pointed at the schoolhouse 30 yards away and said, "Blow the shit out of it!"

Seconds later shells from the direct-fire weapon resoundingly hit the walls and roof of the schoolhouse. Masonry and thatch and wood disintegrated amidst ear-splitting heavy concussions as warheads filled with high explosives found their mark. A brass Buddha statue settled in two pieces by the place where the front door once was hinged. Light-blue support columns bearing scenes of long-ago village life painted upon them, timeless scenes of children at play and warriors beheading invaders, lay at weird angles on the portico. Orange roof rubble was scattered on the ground outside the walls of the school, already pockmarked by bullets from earlier fights. Through gaping holes in the walls the destruction inside could be seen. Charred books smoldered and tiny chairs had been flipped and broken. A Bunsen burner lay mangled. I wondered how early the children were taught chemistry.

Marines looked at each other, then looked away, then looked down, savage warriors saddened. Women's shrill lamentations rose like the wail of sirens. Children blinked and cried. The village chickens fluttered off the ground and squawked. The lieutenant stared back at the village chief, who showed no emotion whatsoever. It was maddening.

He asked the chief, "Have you learned your lesson now, you son-of-a-bitch?"

A few months later something happened to another Marine platoon when it entered the same village. Only someone pathetically dumb would have to wonder what happened.

6

Night Vertical Assault

March 3, 1966 — Phu Bai Marine Airbase

Striking swiftly at night in late February 1966 the 810th Mainforce VC Battalion supported by unknown elements of the North Vietnamese Army savagely attacked and routed an elite Black Panther ARVN unit near the U.S. Marine airbase at Phu Bai. The possibility of an enormous enemy surge by the emboldened NVA leadership caused Marine intelligence to crank up a major operation to smash the increasing threat. Operation NEW YORK was created and handed to Marine Task Force Hotel to execute.

Reinforcements would be needed for the only battalion of Marines in the sector and Foxtrot Company, Second Battalion, Ninth Marines, was among the units selected. The troops had not had a break for almost three months, constantly in motion conducting ambushes and sweeps; they were sleep-deprived to near exhaustion. Scuttlebutt raced through the ranks of the young troopers suggesting we would get the easy duty of providing security for the airbase. But senior non-coms feared the mission would be much more dangerous. I was the company's artillery FO.

A string of olive-green six-by trucks with their canvas tops missing pulled up adjacent to our base camp south of Danang forming a long line on the dusty road that before the war had been the north-south railroad in Vietnam. With all the tracks missing the roadbed was now the MSR for the Ninth Marine Regiment. Mine-detecting teams regularly swept it. Foxtrot Company headed north up the road, our muzzles pointing outboard, alert.

We had been told to move out just an hour before for a mission that could last several weeks. We were to board the three-axle trucks and travel to Danang Air Base and climb aboard C-130 Hercules transport aircraft. Our destination was the Phu Bai Marine airbase just outside the old imperial city of Hue, up north, just below the Demilitarized Zone (DMZ). Intelligence estimated several divisions of NVA were in the area. We would be attached to the Second Battalion, First Marines, and would be given our mission and maps upon arrival.

For the first three days all we did was provide security at one end of the large perimeter, resting, eating, and sleeping after nightly movies with a few security watches thrown in. Meanwhile in the nearby brilliant green countryside trouble was mounting and contact with the NVA was increasing.

Late in the fourth afternoon our company commander, Captain Carl Reckewell, returned from battalion headquarters, his face in absorbed concentration; you could feel his excitement. Foxtrot Company had been given a special mission. He gathered the officers and non-coms together in the large hard-backed GP tent that was our temporary home.

"Gentlemen, in an hour and a half our company will board choppers, head west for about fifteen clicks and vertically assault the headquarters element of the 324-B NVA division," he began.

Nobody spoke; it was almost dark now.

Holy shit! The 324-B was elite, highly-motivated, and formidable, an historic unit fearlessly led by the smartest of generals, imbued with pride from victories won for decades over different enemies, and bristling with the best of weapons including light machine guns, powerful mortars, and long-range rockets.

This at night? We would be big bait this time, the pick-of-the-litter red wrigglers.

"We are to destroy the enemy headquarters element and its weapons and attempt to gather prisoners," he informed us.

"Our Landing Zone (LZ) is here on this map," he pointed.

"It will not be prepped. We're going to surprise the dinks. A rifle company from 2/1 is standing by as a reaction force if needed. Air support is on call," he added.

The sun slid under the top of a tree line of hardwoods to our west and a lively breeze stirred leaves that cast dancing shadows across the faces of the Marines standing in a semicircle around the captain.

"This is history, gang. This is the first nighttime combat company-sized helicopter vertical assault in the history of the United States Marine Corps."

He turned to me and said, "Frank, set up some pre-planned arty fire missions." I responded, "Will do, skipper." The captain was consumed with saving his men.

Weeks earlier we had just moved across a steamy verdant rice paddy, passing the young adolescents who ignored us and our weapons as they drove the water buffalos under their legs across the deep muddy earth, plowing rows for soon-to-be planted seedlings. Except for our presence and the whacking of gunship blades against the thick Asian air you could swear you were just on a nature field trip with your fellow classmates in your science class watching the same beautiful bucolic scene that had been played upon this field for eons, birds swooping for insects dancing on the paddy water, coconut tree fronds lifting their skirts at the field's edge, the same breeze giving us delicious relief. The gunship broke the spell as it fired a burst of mini-gun fire into a nearby tree line; hundreds of bullets ripped the fruit trees and carefully designed hedgerows in seconds. The rice paddy birds sprang from the water's edge, meal interrupted, their hearts in their throats.

We came to a halt on a gentle slope covered with hardwood trees. On the other side of the slope was a sugar cane field. You could have concealed the population of a mid-sized town in the lush thickness of that field. In fact, just three weeks before we had taken sudden fire from the cane field. The enemy broke contact before I could get the artillery fire approved. Three more of Foxtrot Company's Marines were wounded. The rules of engagement made it mandatory for each fire mission request to be approved at battalion level, then regimental level, and also with the South Vietnamese army. The bureaucracy created delays. All the junior officers, the ones actually in the firefights, were beyond exasperation. Over 20 minutes had elapsed without my fire request receiving approval. I aborted the mission; the bad guys were in the next village by then.

Captain Reckewell's light gray eyes shifted from the top of the slope seeking me. "Frank, you all set?" he asked.

I responded, "Ready to go, Skipper."

He ordered, "Then do it."

Before our initial departure that morning, I had created a pre-planned fire mission on the cane field that now lay before us. The fire mission had a name, "Concentration 101." I grabbed the handset from my radio operator and yelled into the receiver, "Wagon Master, Wagon Master, this is Echo Two, I have FIRE MISSION, over." Wagon Master told me to send my mission.

"FIRE CONCENTRATION 101 ... VC WITH AUTOMATIC WEAPONS ... SHELL MIXED, FUSE MIXED ... FIRE FOR EFFECT! OVER." With that I fired my Colt .45 pistol twice into the sky. The discharges rang loudly into the handset I held next to my weapon. The radio transmission carried the sounds of gunfire to the rear ... the sounds of contact with the enemy. Without delay approval was granted. Within two minutes I heard the intoxicating words from the artillery Fire Direction Center, "ON THE WAY! OVER."

I repeated the words as loudly as I could to notify the infantry troops to burrow lower. And then I grinned at my radio operator like I always did when I knew the shells were shot and driving through the air to paydirt. I grinned because it always scared the bejesus out of the grunts. There was an old squad sergeant who had seen a lot of action years before in Korea.

He said, *"Goddamnit, Lieutenant, they never called it in that close in Korea!"*
I told him Korea was for pussies, and he laughed.

But it was true. *Never before had Marines directed artillery so close to them-selves so often within 100 yards, sometimes even closer and the old maps didn't allow for that much error. The artillery was called in so tightly in Vietnam because that's where the trouble was, nearby, ready and preparing to waste us.*

In minutes salvos rushed over us, smashing into the sugar cane field a hun-dred or so meters ahead. Pieces of lumber fell in our midst as shrapnel from the huge shells sliced above into our hardwood cover. The sugar cane field was splin-tered and ablaze as white phosphorus was flung against the impacting high explo-sive shells, a hellhole if you ever saw one.

(Twenty years later I saw a similar incredibly white cloud after an explo-sion on TV; white fatal thick whorls of smoke spun into cobalt-blue space. The smoke filled the screen and the nation moaned. All astronauts aboard the Chal-lenger died. I turned away that morning, never wanting to watch the replay, ever.)

We swept through the scorched stalks, found a charred corpse, several weapons and some fresh blood trails, evidence the Vietcong had split quickly with their wounded. Captain Reckewell and I greeted each other with smiles. He was com-mitted into protecting the lives of his Marines and said, "Now we know how to deal with the rules of engagement."

For once we had beaten the system.

Dusk was closing rapidly as Foxtrot Company humped to the runway where a line of Marine helicopters sat, motionless, our mounts' blades unmov-ing, like giant green metal wasps half asleep.

My God, I wondered, *whatever lay before us?*

Fifteen minutes later we were ordered to stand down. We ambled back to our company area, elated. Maybe the brass at Marine Amphibious Head-quarters had decided the risk-reward ratio of our mission was poor and had overridden Task Force Hotel. First Lieutenant Everette Roane, Foxtrot's exec-utive officer (XO) and I began a card game after refilling our canteens. The troops sprawled to the floor of the hard-backed tent and wriggled out of their haversacks and started cleaning rifles, laughing at each other, and writing let-ters to friends back home.

In less than 20 minutes the gunnery sergeant appeared, "Gentlemen, mount up. We have been requested to return to the choppers."

In five minutes we were at the strip again. The evening sky was turning to slate with no moonlight.

Good, I thought, *they won't see us.*

We boarded the H-34 Choctaw choppers, 10 of us in each one with weapons loaded, safeties on, jaws clinched, sweat glands already working overtime. The engines whined to life, driving the blades around slowly at first, then faster and faster with increasing torque until we were up and off.

Boy have I done it now if the gooks don't zap us in the hot LZ they'll surely first rain enough lead into this steel trap vibrating like jack hammers had been turned on it are those rounds I hear ripping through the floor? boy that would hurt I think I heard the rear blade get smashed in back are those sparks? this bird is shaking like the scariest ride ever even worse than the time the ferris wheel stopped we at the top and Wingfield next to me swinging our cradle back and forth but not as terrifying as when this shuddering out of control beast we're in just stops and drops straight down gravity has its clutches on us and it drops like an elephant falls after instant death straight down and we're trapped in the bowels of the elephant as it plows into the earth, into the heart and teeth of the dreaded 324-B and Blessed is the Fruit of thy Womb Jesus.

Your imagination can work overtime in the sky at night.

We headed for our objective to the west, swiftly climbing high at first as the air became chilled, racing turbulently through the open door manned by a machine gun man. After a few minutes we shifted lower and cut between the tops of ridgelines like we were threading a needle in the hills.

In the daytime you are entranced by images flickering by in quick frames of the landscape below out past the door gunner checking his M-60 machine gun, maybe a glimpse of a jungled ridge just below and way below that a valley with an orange-brown river making huge "S" turns like a giant snake, or perhaps a beautiful quick shot of the blue sky and green mountains and dark blue sea coinciding on the horizon. You steal glances at the others sitting on the steel floor or stuffed in canvas webbing to see the emotions on their faces; if you see none maybe there's nothing to be terrified of after all. Each time a chopper hurtled toward the LZ there was really only one question by all aboard, would the LZ be bristling with murderously destructive weapons of fire and steel ready to take the chopper out, or not?

But on this night there was nothing to see out those doors, anywhere. Fifteen minutes later the birds dipped and swung very low as we grazed tree-tops for our final dash to the LZ.

My jungle boots hit the firm soil of the dry, grassy, open area that was our LZ. Marines scampered to preordained positions and deployed in a large perimeter circle as dusty wind bursts from the choppers almost knocked them down. The captain and I were in the center of the circle, instantly orienting our maps. Most importantly so far we had heard no incoming hostile fire.

Let's see, I thought, *the map says... What the fuck?*

I looked at the skipper, seeing his consternation also. It couldn't be, but it was true. Marine air had dropped us off in the wrong grid zone at night in the suspected midst of one of the most dangerous enemy divisions seen by Marines since World War II. Fortunately there was no enemy contact yet.

"Skipper, we gotta know where we are or we're toast," I said.

"Okay, let's solve this quickly," the captain calmly replied.

I jabbed at my map, showing him a river running mainly west to east a little north of us. All around us the landscape was flat and dark with no distinguishing features.

I suggested, "Let's split to this river. At least we'll know where we are when we get there."

He gave the word to the three platoon leaders. We were at the river's south bank, where it took a sharp turn in a matter of a few minutes. Happiness is knowing your own location.

We still had not engaged nor seen the enemy. We reconciled our location on our maps and moved due east toward a village on the way to Highway Route One which had become our makeshift objective. The only inhabitants in the nearly deserted village were several old crones who made a tasty bouillabaisse for us, mixing our C-rations with their rice in boiling vats.

Everyone was in a festive mood. Captain Reckewell had the troops in laughter telling stories about colorful episodes of different young troopers in his command group. It was as if the whole company was out for a summer camp comedy night around the campfire. There was not one hint of an enemy the whole night and it became the most enjoyable of nights, for we knew the purest of truths: we had escaped a double-edged sword — the suicidal half-baked plans of Marine brass and the mind-numbing negligence of Marine air.

We humped east again early the next morning until we reached the Truoi River Bridge for Route One that we occupied as a blocking force. The best-selling book by Bernard Fall about the French defeat a decade earlier in Vietnam gave a special name to the road, "Street Without Joy."

Two other Marine rifle companies had been inserted by helicopter 3,000 meters south of us and advanced toward the bridge. Marine intelligence hoped to trap major elements of the 810th Mainforce VC Battalion thought to be retreating somewhere in the middle of the trap. On March 3, 1966, Operation NEW YORK was cancelled. Somehow the 810th had slithered out of the trap and made good their escape.

A few hours later C-130s deposited the company back at Danang airfield. We were going home to our mother battalion.

Foxtrot Company had not fired a single shot in a week that had once promised too much enemy contact to consider. Our mission had been enigmatic, but the moral of the story was not. In Vietnam if you think it will happen, it won't. If it happens, you never considered it.

7

Her Majesty

March 10, 1966 — Ha Dong Village

Ha Dong, a nasty hornet's nest of a hamlet and a staging area and way station for main force VC units, rested just north of a large bend in the Song Bau Xau River some 12 miles south of the vast Danang airbase. Just south of the hamlet a large, old steel bridge had been destroyed years before and it lay in a "V" shape across the river where it had been buckled by explosives. Now a footbridge a few yards to the west of the ruined bridge buoyed by flatboats allowed north-south traffic to cross the river. Marines bathed in its emerald waters and threw hand grenades near its banks to collect fish for evening dinner, supplementing their fat-laden C-rations.

The village recently had been the venue for a myriad of U.S. Marine casualties. The hidden mines and booby-trapped grenades on gates, hedgerows, and trails inflicted more casualties than the bullets fired from the Vietcong SKS carbines and the shrapnel from their Rocket-Propelled Grenades (RPG). So in response Lieutenant Colonel W.F. Donahue, CO of Second Battalion, Ninth Marines, issued Operation Order 3–66 on March 9, 1966.

The mission for Foxtrot Company was to enter the village the next morning from the west and north before dawn after Golf and Hotel Companies had sealed off the south and east approaches. Foxtrot was to conduct an extensive search of each house, adjacent land, tree lines, hedgerows, and likely hiding places, and destroy enemy personnel, fortifications, equipment, and supplies. I was the artillery FO for the rifle company.

The rifle company of Marines had entered the village complex before dawn and at 0630 loudspeakers ordered all villagers to report to a detention center on the east flank of the hamlet. Then the company started clearing the area and the engineers immediately went to work to eliminate the village's fortified positions with prejudice. Every bunker, hedgerow, trench line, and spider-hole was to be destroyed by C-4, the powerful plastic explosive of choice. They all were birthplaces for booby-traps that lay dormant, waiting for a misplaced tug to waken them so they could dispense terrible agony.

Only the roar of arriving choppers interrupted the sounds of the explosions. They swooped onto the temporary landing zone, racing in with whirling blades that stirred the earth into dust devils, blinding and terrifying the young village children who waited in a long queue tightly grasping the steadying hands of their mothers. Fifteen villagers at a time were shoehorned into the belly of each chopper and their eyes looked like those of horses trapped in a burning barn. Mothers howled as they and their children were shepherded into helicopters and deposited at a "safe" camp nearby. The few local males present were old men. Still, they were roughly handled by the Marine riflemen whose collective frustration had reached the boiling point. The whole village was evacuated, except for one.

Suddenly out of the corner of my eye I saw her come into view. I don't know why she came rushing with her plea to me but suddenly she was there, frantically jabbering, pulling at my utility shirt, in my face, demanding to be heard. Even though I didn't understand her words, her emotions were revealed by her sepia eyes with a speech of their own, hooded by the crinkled russet skin of the lids and folds around them. She looked as old as the dirt we were standing on.

An off-white bandana tied in a knot above her forehead held her wispy bun of grey hair in place. She wore a dark brown thin blouse with maroon brocade buttoned to her throat and black pajama pants. Her feet were bare and she was kicking up the dirt next to me. Her eyes told the whole story; their expression spoke to me as if we had conversed for years, transcending the language barrier. After a while I didn't need the South Vietnamese Army interpreter to explain all her words. I could sense her wisdom and sincerity, but it was her courageous spirit that swept me away. I listened.

Her body language helped me understand her. With her arms crossed over her torso she said she was outraged by our intrusion, but that was secondary, she shrugged, widening her eyes and lifting her shoulders like a Frenchwoman. After all, she had seen Japanese Imperial Army soldiers in World War II and French Foreign Legionnaires during the Second Indochina War also parade along this very trail. Their efforts had been futile. Invaders had tried to conquer the Vietnamese before Rome ruled Europe, but the small, resolute people were indefatigable. The resident village mama-san and ancient village elder had seen it all.

No, she explained, her ancient eyebrows arching, she wasn't getting on any damned helicopter, and she was not leaving her village. Why now, she implored? After all, she had never left the district of the village complex before.

Not for 90 years, she said, flashing all but one of the digits on her hands. She was it and it was she. She was born here and birthed her own children here and fed them her milk to make them strong enough to work next to her in the adjacent fields of green grain.

She tugged at my hand and led me to a clearing 30 yards off the trail, just behind the first set of hedgerows on the east side of the village. The cemetery had been there for eons, a sacred place that faced the first rays of the life-giving sun each morning. Immaculate white gravestones were reverentially marked with Buddhist prayers and shaded by small trees. A few were adorned with yellow and violet flowers. Urns to burn incense sticks were near each grave.

She had buried her loved ones herself in the cemetery, over there she nodded, a brother tortured and beheaded by the Japanese, and behind him her maternal beloved grandmother who taught her the history of the Trung sisters, who in A.D. 39 commanded a 30,000-man Vietnamese army that drove the invading Chinese out of Vietnam.

Her husband had been buried with the rituals extended to a chief and a hero. She knelt and placed her hands on each side of his gravestone and slid them to the earth and leaned forward and pressed her lips to the cool stone and kissed his name etched into the stone. She turned and faced me with no pretense as tears trickled down her weathered face and dropped from her chin. Her precious grandson was extended the same burial courtesies, she explained. He had taken many French lives before they extinguished his own. She stopped her spiel and slowly raised her chin. Her sharp cheekbones were glistening. She took a deep breath and her trembling brown-spotted hand involuntarily dabbed at her wet cheek and then she just smiled. I took her request to Captain Carl Reckewell, the company commander. He listened and allowed her to stay behind and added she was my responsibility.

She reached for my hand, like a grandmother does, slowly and gently, and led me to her home in the center of the village. I took my haversack and cartridge belt off and placed them with my rifle and helmet at the base of a banyan tree and looked at her for her approval. She smiled and nodded. I sent my radio operator to tell Captain Reckewell I had found the best place for the company command post, in the old mama-san's front yard.

Bricks were missing from the arch that attached the grain bin to the right side of her house, which was shaded by coconut trees. A shelling a long time before had damaged the bricks. The aroma of boiling fish in a stew with vegetables and strange spices wafted from inside her home. It reminded me of a bouillabaisse I had tasted in New Orleans a few years before. She gestured for me to sit with her on her portico. I told the interpreter to go away. I knew a

Top: First Lieutenant Franklin Cox visits with Linh, heroine of Ha Dong Village, March 1966. *Bottom:* Linh, matriarch of Ha Dong village, eats a rice lunch in March 1966.

little French, and like most Vietnamese, so did she. I wasn't good with the Vietnamese language. So I tried what I knew best.

"I am Frank." I pointed at my heart.

Then I gently pointed at her, "*Votre Nom?*"

She understood, smiled, and answered, "Linh." The meaning is "gentle spirit" in Vietnamese.

"Phwang?" she asked. Her face lit up with the effort to communicate and she knew she had almost nailed it from the start.

Close enough, I thought. "*Bonne!*"

She giggled and said "Phwang ... Linh!"

"Oui," I said. "You can be my *grand-mère.*"

She was touched by that and took me again by the hand into her home and showed me a Buddhist altar dedicated to her husband and son and grandsons, all gone forever into the nearby earth, murdered by enemies from Japan and France, sleeping the long sleep a hundred yards away.

She gave me a bowl of fish stew and asked, "*Jeune fille?*" It was spicy and the fish meat was delicious.

"*Non.*" Through sign language and theatrics I explained I would find a lovely woman when I returned to America.

Then we heard a series of M-14 bursts followed by one of our M-60 machine guns delivering fire at the south end of the village. Voices rang out and then there was silence.

Her smile slowly disappeared, replaced by a frown of worry. Her face turned pale and she motioned for me to follow her into a side room. She pulled up the fold of a tapestry that covered the handle to a trap door. She pulled the handle up and led me down into the crawl space of a bunker. I could see daylight from it, streaming in from vents where rifles could shoot through at approaching enemy soldiers. There were unobtrusive small bamboo stakes 10 yards out in the yard to help guide the bullets into the killing zone where the foreigners would likely approach. The bunker had been there for over 60 years, she said, and those attacking have never seen the slits. I knelt in a prone firing position and through the slits I saw my radio operator next to my friend, First Lieutenant Gary Loudermilk, the forward air controller. He and I had a standing argument as to who could call in the most destruction, he and his warplanes with bombs, or me with my artillery howitzers. They were 30 yards away and I could have yelled at them and still they would never have been able to detect the small openings of the bunker. If I had a motive to I could have shot and killed them like fat ducks 20 feet over a blind and no one could have guessed where the shooter had been.

We went back up to the main room in the house and I thanked her for showing me the bunker. She shook her head and said Marines are kind, not like the French. Then she grabbed my chin and twisted my face to hers. No words were necessary. Be very careful, her wise old eyes warned me.

Late in the afternoon she sat smiling next to me on the solitary step that led to the entrance to her home. She fussed with a pouch she held and fetched out a small piece of paper on which she poured some tobacco and rolled her own cigarette. When she finished she offered it to me and took a long drag after I politely declined. Her smile was peaceful despite the warning cries of "Fire in the hole!" as detonation cord ignited nonstop explosions. I pulled out a red pack of Marlboros, lit one and smiled back at her, my new dear friend. Thankfully my radio operator took a picture of that scene. It is my daughter Carolina's favorite of me.

The next afternoon the choppers came for us. At 1610 Foxtrot Company reported, "we have destroyed the following: 700 meters of treeline, 450 meters of fence row, 15 one-man fighting holes, 250 meters of trench lines, 300 tunnels blown, a large amount of railroad ties destroyed, 15 gates blown, 10 caves destroyed, a 60mm booby trap destroyed." The company had also killed three Vietcong and captured six VC suspects while suffering no casualties. The mission had been successful.

As the command group started to move out to the landing zone Linh glided up to me. She smiled and handed me two tangerines and she squeezed my hand hard one last time.

"*Merci beaucoup. Vivre en paix.*"

"*Adieu,*" I said.

The helicopters soared in, grabbing a bunch of Marines at a time. Captain Reckewell, Loudermilk, and I and our three radio operators were among the last to leave.

It is a lonely feeling when you are one of the final few still on the ground, waiting and feeling very vulnerable, but there's nothing finer than when you jump in and watch the village get smaller as the chopper spins upward into cooler air and safety. I tried to spot Linh's home but all I could see were the tops of the banyan trees.

8

Surrounded

> I will tell you ... as officers, that you will neither eat, nor drink nor smoke, nor sit down, nor lean against a tree until you have personally seen that your men have first had a chance to do these things. If you will do this for them, they will follow you to the ends of the earth. And if you do not, I will bust you in front of your regiments.
> — Field Marshal William Joseph Slim, British Army

March 18, 1966 — La Tho Nam

We busily used grease pencils to mark objectives and checkpoints on the clear plastic covering our ancient maps created by French intelligence decades before, maps that noted terrain features that had vanished in the wind, like the souls that howled to the heavens as death resulted from war after war that plagued this green hell of Southeast Asia. Well, screw that, we were U.S. Marines. We had read *Street Without Joy* by Bernard Fall and dismissed it. We would write a new history — hadn't we always?

Captain Carl Reckewell, CO of Foxtrot Company, Second Battalion, Ninth Marines, was holding court, giving his officers marching orders for the operation to begin within the hour. He was consumed with his task. We would be the point of the spear of Operation KINGS to find and destroy the VC units south of us, ensconced in their friendly clime 15 miles below the Danang airfield, an enemy we prayed would engage with us finally in full-tilt combat. The daily nicks the VC had inflicted on Marine patrols via booby-traps and heavy-trauma two-minute ambushes had enraged us. Adrenaline filled the swampy humid air at the base camp. Sounds of combat preparation abounded — metal rounds being fed into magazines, canteens clanking with the rush of water, sweet short prayers mumbled at low audio, the seasoned gunnery sergeant cursing while touching young Marines gently on their cheeks, imploring, "Do what I do."

Corporal Tommy Weaver made his rank at 20 years of age. He was an incredibly gifted youth who approached his daily regimen with optimism and

Marines with Foxtrot Company, Second Battalion, Ninth Marines, on a search-and-destroy operation in the village of La Tho Bac on March 18, 1966.

intelligence. He was a Marine's Marine, rare at his age. He grew up in the rural fields of the south trapping and hunting and never missed a beat in the bush. He was at home in the jungle as the enemy. He was my scout-observer. My artillery forward observer team consisted of Weaver, two radio operators, and myself. Often we would split up on company-sized operations to offer maximum coverage. He and his radio operator would embed with one platoon. I would normally join the CO's group in a different platoon with my radio operator, Lance Corporal Randolph Cassidy.

On this day, March 18, 1966, Weaver's team would join the First Platoon led by First Lieutenant Joel D. Ward from Wilma, Alabama. My team joined Captain Reckewell's command group positioned with the second platoon. We would be followed in column by the third platoon. We packed C-rations for three days. The operation order called for us to conduct mobile operations for five to seven days. Our mission the first day was to sweep through several villages and reach the northern bank of the Song La Tho River late in the afternoon, several miles south of our jump-off point, deep into Indian country with no friendlies anywhere nearby.

"Saddle up!" shouted First Lieutenant Everette Roane, Foxtrot Company's executive officer, at 1330.

Everette was an Ole Miss graduate and each time the company moved out into the fight I circled behind him and yelled into his ears his school's cheer.

"Hey, Everette, baby!"
Hotty Toddy, Gosh Almighty
Who the Hell Are We, Hey!
Flim Flam, Bim Bam
OLD MISS BY DAMN!

It always caught him by surprise. He was a locked-in, squared-away Marine officer who soon would command his own rifle company. I considered the jingle to be a good stress suppressant for him. He pinched his lips together and glared at me and finally cracked up with laughter.

"Just follow me, cannon cocker," he said.

In previous operations we always vied with each other to be nearer the CO during movement to an objective — when the combat begins the closer you are the better the chance nothing gets lost in translation.

"Makes sense, Everette. That way I can read your map for you when you get lost."

The white sun jammed heat under our helmet liners and the air was so thick our sweat would not dry. The reinforced rifle company departed the assembly area and began sweeping out of the base camp, its three platoons heading due south in a continuous column.

Shortly we came upon a rice paddy network and crossed the shortest route to a far tree line, silhouetted by tall palm trees, to get out of the open expanse of the vast emerald fields. The palm tree fronds and the chest-high sharply-edged jungle grass beneath them were still; the day was windless and no birds were to be seen.

First Lieutenant Franklin Cox at Foxtrot Company's Line of Departure for Operation KINGS on March 18, 1966.

We were over 130 strong including attached combat engineers and a Forward Air Control team. Heavy weapons included M-60 machine guns, 3.5-inch bazookas, and 81mm mortars. Captain Reckewell providently placed ample flank security to either side. We were ready for bear. We closed toward an unseen enemy, bait to induce a fight.

At 1410 P.M. the first platoon halted. The entire company then stopped. Ward backtracked to us and whispered to the captain. Thirty minutes later an H-34 helicopter powered from our position, carrying two fresh replacements close to death, their body thermostats balking, out of control from the unfamiliar heavy heat—*can't breathe, can't live*—their skin florid, their lips white. They were 19 years old and in shape but they didn't last an hour. Everette and I locked eyes: every slope in I-Corps now knew our whereabouts. Stealth? Surprise? Gone. The deaf and dumb could have been aware of our approach; the elephant was in the room and it was Foxtrot Company.

We trudged forward, performing radio check transmissions with battalion headquarters in the rear. At 1450 enemy carbine fire cranked off a few rounds at us harmlessly, fired from a tree line several hundred meters across a large brown field to our left. It was inconsequential.

We kept our same azimuth when suddenly near the southern edge of the large field we received automatic weapons fire. It came in high, singing over us, tearing the air with a sound like weasels in heat. Once again Everette's eyes met mine as we fell next to each other at the base of a red, rusted fence strung along a hedgerow. *My God!* We giggled like first-graders, mainline adrenaline rush pumping into each of us. His pupils shrank to needle points.

Roane called, "Rockets up!" and Marines pumped 3.5-inch bazooka white phosphorus rounds at the VC position across the field. Through a gap in the fence I saw an A-1E Skyraider dump high explosive 250-pound bombs, stomach-tossing ordinance, on top of the snow-white smoke we had marked the enemy position with. The VC weapons became silent.

The first platoon answered a few bursts of small arms fire that suddenly came in from their front with a few machine-gun bursts. It was a quick firefight.

We continued our advance, finding blood trails. Random solitary sniper shots continued from our left flank as we advanced, only a nuisance. We cleared a nearly deserted village, La Tho Bac. A few peasants in conical hats squinted at us through the brilliant sunlight with mistrustful glances. Pigs squealed at us from filthy pens. We found a body and more blood trails. We destroyed a small bunker system with some C-4 plastic explosive; just a pinch of it would set a can of C-ration ham and limas aboil in milliseconds. After clearing the village we continued due south through some wide, dried rice fields.

Marines with Foxtrot Company, Second Battalion, Ninth Marines, on Operation KINGS on March 18, 1966, just before the company is ambushed by the R-20 Doc Lap Vietcong Battalion.

At 1600 we had two more heat casualties, creating more helicopter activity and noise that displayed our latest position.

At 1725 mortar rounds exploded a hundred yards in front of our command group into the heart of the first platoon as it neared the river, high-explosive impacts heralding the massive ambush Foxtrot Company had entered. The rifle company had made its way into a terrible trap in the open against a concealed, numerically superior enemy with more firepower. The elite Mainforce Vietcong R-20 Doc Lap Battalion (reinforced) had us in a noose and began to tighten the knot.

The late afternoon stillness instantly transformed into a world I can only equate to that of a dwarf star exploding on a PBS science documentary special about far-away galaxies.

Cacophonous noise and steel and flame engulfed us, generated by interlocked automatic weapons fire, impacting mortar rounds, and incoming B-40 rocket-propelled grenades. In seconds American bones splintered and U.S. Marine blood trickled onto the powdery surfaces of the potato field and the dry rice paddy we were trapped on.

Automatic weapons fire erupted out of the trees across the field to our left, pouring rounds into the second platoon and our command group. Three or four Marines fell. Behind us 57mm recoilless-rifle shells slammed violently into our third platoon from the right.

Cassidy, his radio handset dangling, grabbed me, screaming, "Mister Cox, Weaver just got hit!"

There was an eerie stillness for several seconds. Then the company and its platoons sprang to life and reacted, everyone doing his job; the unit was Marine-trained. In seconds the second platoon frontally assaulted into the left tree line. The third platoon did likewise, sprinting and firing into the enemy position to the right, no hesitation, just innate Marine reaction to a sudden crisis, as natural as childbirth. Marines fell in those dashes, some killed, some wounded.

Cassidy and I sprinted at full speed toward the first platoon in front of us. There were burrows in the soft brown dirt of the tilled field. *Wow*, I thought while running, *a fucking potato field?* Puffs of dirt from incoming rounds accompanied our path, the dirt chewed up by VC bullets. Adrenaline powered our feet faster.

"He's over there!" yelled some grunts. Four Marines lay side by side, dark patches of blood oozing through their green jungle utilities. A corpsman was applying a compress to the abdomen of one of the wounded. Weaver was on his left side; smoke poured from his back where a 60mm mortar shell sent most of its mayhem. He saw me and gave an apologetic, laconic smile.

I had found it rewarding and mutually beneficial to treat the troops with respect. I chatted with them about their families and experiences in their earlier youth back in the world. They all had issues of some kind or other, either in Vietnam or back at home. I listened and tried to help them think through their problems. Few of the officers I served with took their troops for granted. If you were supportive of your men, they loved you and would do anything for you.

Weaver knew my favorite C-ration meal was chicken and noodles. So in addition to the skinny Marine's regular load he jammed every can he could scrounge into the haversack slung across his back at the base camp. The troops were always doing something like that, taking care of their officers, providing unsolicited help. The mortar shell had detonated on the ground directly behind him. Ninety percent of the blast impacted into the pack, into the C-ration cans. The pack was blown open, the cans shredded with white-hot shrapnel. Blackened shreds of chicken and noodles covered him. He was wounded across his back by scores of tiny metal shards, but not mortally.

Ward called for a medevac. First Lieutenant Gary Loudermilk, the for-

First Lieutenant Joel Ward calls for medevac helicopter during Operation KINGS on March 18, 1966, 15 miles south of Danang.

ward air controller, had just called for air support to suppress the enemy mortar gunners. Gary had been an F-4 Phantom flyboy hotshot, but his orders to Nam placed him with the infantry to direct close air support. He repeated a daily mantra, "For this shit I went to fucking flight school?" Loudermilk ordered the scrambling air support to give the medevac the right-of-way. The mortar rounds had been fired from the south, across the river, from the village of La Tho Nam. That would be the first target for our air strikes.

I requested artillery fire on the tree line to our left from where huge volumes of automatic fire had been delivered into our whole left flank. The second platoon had collected its wounded and moved into a hasty perimeter in a wooded area with convenient trench lines just behind us. The third platoon had stopped the initial VC fire from the right after its assault but suffered six casualties. Within seconds after the initial attack its platoon leader was severely wounded. Two of its three squad leaders fell in the cone of incoming fire. The three platoons finally linked up with the command group in deep existing trench lines in the wooded area less than 100 yards north of the river, laboriously dug in the loamy soil by Vietnamese fighters for decades past. The three platoons formed a large 360-degree circle. Captain Reckewell and the command group were in the middle of the circle. So were many casualties, the dead just there, the wounded being attended to.

"On the way!" Cassidy repeated. The spotting rounds shrieked overhead and impacted into the very coordinates I had requested.

"Fire for effect!" I ordered.

We could hear the howitzers from Echo Battery respond. Instantly the salvos exploded into the tree line.

Loudermilk cursed. His high-tech radio had just gone on the blink. I switched the frequency on my radio to communicate with the UH-1E gunship pilots on their way to support us from Danang airfield. I had to relay through another radio operator who had access to the air support net. I warned them a medevac was airborne and to expend their ordinance on an east-west axis just across the river.

The medevac chopper landed and we placed the casualties aboard. Weaver rolled his eyes at me, the morphine making him mellow, smiled, and slowly pointed to his pack. It was to be the last medevac chopper to reach us until first light the next morning. It was to become one of the longest of nights.

The green Hueys strafed and fired rockets in passes just across the river, their Lycoming engines howling and moaning, the high explosives being felt in our bones even on our side of the river. The troops cheered. An hour and a half had passed since the battle began.

After our artillery shells pounded the target, my radio operator and I left our open space and made a beeline to the woods where the company had established itself in the defensive perimeter. The terrain was covered with generous clumps of bamboo and thick foliage that provided advantageous cover. We hopped into the command center's trench-line in the middle of the company circle. A gunpowder smell of the battlefield explosions was encased in a vast begrimed cloud of bomb smoke that hung low over the surrounded Marines.

I slumped next to Captain Reckewell.

"Sir, our artillery can help bail us out."

"I know, Frank. I want you to call in every round they'll approve in the rear. How can we ruin those mortar tubes on the other wide of the river?"

"Sir, I can request area fire missions; large chunks of real estate a lot of our cannons together can totally waste."

"Go get 'em, Frank. Call it in as close to our position as you see fit."

"Roger, Skipper. Will do."

The night was pitch black when the rotor-thud wash noise of an approaching medevac chopper filled our ears. The CO's radio operator left the perimeter and stood alone in the open field, bravely signaling with a strobe light in the darkness so the chopper could find the tiny LZ. Tracers inside our perimeter sought out the approaching chopper as VC bullets snapped the bamboo nearby. The chopper made a dive and a final swirl when it was hit just 20 meters above the LZ. It made one more awkward circle and crashed just outside our perimeter. Minutes later the crew was huddled in our trench line, shaking and laughing, thankful to be alive.

Captain Reckewell gave a situation report to the 2/9 commanding officer, Lieutenant Colonel W.F. Donahue, at 2100.

"Because of machine gun and mortar fire we are unable to have choppers come in. Mortars have the LZ zeroed in. At first light I request close air support, other than Hueys, and emergency med evacuations. Also 40 five-gallon cans of water. We have additional casualties. The medevac crew is safe in my perimeter. We have incoming mortars at the present moment. We have killed four VC by body count, but many more than that in reality. Cannot physically assess enemy body count now."

At 2340 incoming 62 enemy mortar shells cracked loudly as they burst on impact with the hard ground of our defensive position, providing brief flickers of bright daylight from explosion flashes. Then the darkness returned, as black as the devil's soul. Just after midnight, the VC launched another 30 mortar rounds upon us. At 0210 the VC struck us with another cascade of 42 mortar shells. They shrieked in, creating more Marine casualties. We now had over 30 Marine casualties, and four were dead.

I continued to call artillery fire onto the unrelenting fire coming from across the field and from the south side of the river. We were beyond radio range of my artillery fire direction center so I had to relay my transmissions for fire requests through other units. Several times my requests got garbled into wrong information and I had to scream into the handset to abort the fire mission. Captain Reckewell wearily nodded; we both wanted no artillery blunders. There were already enough dead Marines.

For hours I called in fire mission after fire mission, trying to stop the VC murderous fire. At 0050 an aerial observer reported seeing large secondary explosions across the river. The captain and I grinned and shook hands.

We became so beleaguered I radioed in fire missions I had never before considered. My home battery, Echo Battery, Twelfth Marines, fired the following fire mission in response to my urgent request:

"Sunrise, Sunrise, this is Echo 2 ... Fire Mission! Coordinates, from 001607 to 007607, all available!" This meant I wanted every Marine howitzer that could reach the 600-meter wide target to do so, not just the normal one battery with six guns. "Continuous Fire!" This means every howitzer shooting the mission should continue firing until told to stop; normally in a fire mission each of the six guns in a battery would fire two rounds. "Fire for Effect!" This means do it now, no adjusting, I know where they are, where we are, and I need it now.

Within several minutes 60 high explosive rounds and 57 white phosphorous 105mm shells lit up the massive target.

Our trench line was almost four feet deep and nearly three feet wide. I placed my M-14 rifle, my Caliber .45 Colt M1911A1 pistol, and my KA-Bar utility knife with its honed seven-inch blade on the ground above the trench, within easy reach. I had plenty of room in the trench to read my map and use the radio handset to request fire missions. My position was next to Captain Reckewell.

Three rounds of mortar fire hit directly on our command post at 0425. Somehow there were no casualties. At one point, after another intense enemy probe was repulsed, Reckewell directed me to call in a pre-planned fire mission to be used as the final answer if the unthinkable should happen.

"Frank, better plot a big one on top of us if all fails."

"Yes, sir," I responded. That's when I knew in my heart the battle wasn't all just a muddled dream.

Holy Mary, Mother of God, Pray for Us Sinners, Now, and at the Hour of Our Death, Amen.

Other helicopters tried to provide assistance (medevac and resupply) during the dark hours. All were waved off due to intense enemy fire. It went on all night. Wounded Marines administered to each other's wounds. We all prayed for first light. The night is no good when you hear the nearby bamboo cracking from incoming enemy bullets. The night is terribly wrong when you see tracers from inside your own perimeter racing in green streams toward your hovering resupply chopper.

It worked. That evening, that night, and early the next morning the batteries of the Twelfth Marine Artillery Regiment fired 1,740 heavy-metal artillery shells around our perimeter, pummeling the enemy and placing a protective ring of fire and steel around our vulnerable circle of Marines. Echo Battery fired a record-setting 829 rounds in one nonstop engagement by a single battery. Hundreds and hundreds of our artillery shells were accurately placed all night just outside our perimeter. It protected us through the night.

It was too dark and the enemy was too close to request close air support. The deep trench lines, our home for the night, and the accurate artillery saved us from disaster. Our company lost four KIAs and 36 WIAs that long afternoon and night. That's an unacceptable number for a day's work but I thanked God it had not been worse.

Villagers reported the next day the VC Main Force battalion had fled south. Many of the black-clad guerrillas were wounded, they told us, and they carried more than 40 of their dead comrades with them.

"Sorry 'bout that!" yelled the young Marine riflemen when told about the disposition of the enemy.

The next day the rifle company with engineers used over 1,000 pounds of C-4 plastic explosive to destroy more than three miles of trench lines, over 1,000 spider holes with bamboo covers (concealed underground positions VC soldiers could hide in, pop out of, and shoot Marines), 35 small caves, 40 fighting positions, and other underground tunnels and bunkers in the La Tho Nam village complex. Our artillery had significantly damaged the honey-combed tunnels and the fighting positions that were just days old.

For the next four days we conducted search-and-destroy operations on the south side of the river. It had been our first full-scale engagement with the Vietcong R-20 Doc Lap Battalion which showed great willingness to accept appalling losses in night attacks against Marine rifle companies. The 400-man enemy elite battalion had withdrawn from the battlefield to lick its wounds. Although outnumbered 3–1, we won round one — but we knew we would face them again, sooner rather than later.

A Swedish newspaper correspondent had requested to join us the morning we were assembling for the operation, saying, "I need to be where the shit is." He was on the first medevac chopper out at daybreak, pale as a ghost and so weakened from the experience he had to be helped aboard. The Marines, exulting in their own survival, laughed at the comic-relief sight of the terrified journalist stumbling into the chopper.

9

A Captain of Marines

April 6, 1966 — Foxtrot Company Base Camp — Phong Luc

The bird colonel hopped from his olive-green Huey which had just arrived from III Marine Amphibious Force (MAF) headquarters in Danang. The turbo engine's exhaust scattered dust across the LZ at Foxtrot 2/9's latest forward base camp and sprayed blasts of grit into the faces of the Marines welcoming the dignitary. It was show time. The colonel's minions led his way inside the perimeter wire where Captain Carl A. Reckewell of Smithtown, New York, the infantry company commander, greeted him. The colonel was on a dog-and-pony show; he could no more have learned anything about the local tactical situation during such a short visit than if he had landed on the University of California, Berkeley, campus. He strutted past the perimeter bunkers, pompously bobbing his head, pigeon like, demonstrating his approval of the lay-of-the-land of the compound. He did not look like an infantry colonel.

Just inside the perimeter he stopped as abruptly as if his boots had been suddenly nailed to the rich brown earth just outside the entrance to the company command post. He stared at the prominently displayed wooden sign that stretched seven feet above the ground with a scarlet background with gold graphics.

WELCOME TO FOXTROT COMPANY 2/9

SINCE 29 DECEMBER, 1965

Company Operations	17
Patrols	274
Ambushes	423
VC KIA	129

The removable block numbers constantly updated the ongoing missions of Foxtrot Company and visually portrayed how active the unit had been

81mm mortar position at Foxtrot 2/9 base camp, Phong Luc, April 1966.

against the VC. That's a lot of work for one quarter; 1966 did not start out idly.

When he saw the sign his face turned apoplectic.

"You two men there!"

He pointed to a pair of nearby lance-corporals.

"Yank that monstrous sign down!" he screamed. "No company in this whole division has that many kills. This is a damned disgraceful lie."

With that he hustled his brood back to the LZ. The Huey whined as it rose and cut for the rear. Every trooper within earshot stared at the disappearing chopper, outraged by the colonel's contempt.

John Wayne himself visited our position just days before the colonel. A photograph was snapped capturing him admiring the sign. Then he stepped away and smiled and addressed the men. The "Duke" said, "Great work, Marines." He had walked off the screen of *The Sands of Iwo Jima* and into my life. I had to pinch myself.

The rifle company of Marines took great pride in the way it had conducted operations against the Vietcong in the enemy-infested coastal plains and rice paddies south of Danang. The ARVN had not aggressively sought the enemy for several years.... "No way," they said. "Too much VC." The company conducted large-scale search-and-destroy operations with its mother battalion, sent reinforced platoons out on multiday patrols into the deep perilous bush, ran quick raids on suspected enemy concentrations, set up furtive squad-sized night ambushes deep in Victor Charlie's backyard, quietly manned listening posts in the darkness outside the wire, and stood dead-tired watches in the bunkers. The rest of the time they filled sandbags, improved defensive positions, humped heavy boxes of ammo, cleaned weapons, and avoided the first sergeant who always had additional chores to be attended to. The troops were in a constant state of near-exhaustion and went weeks at a time without hot meals.

But they worked unswervingly for their skipper, Captain Reckewell. Even though they were in constant danger, they knew that he was at the same time taking measures and precautions to save their lives. Whenever possible he would recon by fire before sending his Marines into a known hotbed. Third MAF headquarters demanded a rigid SOP; each company was to run a minimum number of daily patrols, no matter the local situation. Captain Reckewell complied but improvised and did it his way, protecting his troops, never sending them out under strength and never unprepared, protecting the lives of his Marines in every way he could under the circumstances. They knew how hard he fought for their safety and they loved their captain, a warrior with a soul.

He was a Hamilton College graduate. I asked him why he had chosen to become a Marine officer. He was sitting on a five-gallon water can, his face smudged from black-green camo paint mixed with sweat. He and his company had just returned to the base camp after a two-day foray into the countryside to the southeast. A series of quick, uneventful firefights with Vietcong elements firing from brilliant green tree lines had been fought. His sweat-drenched jungle utilities were tinted rusty from dust. A later afternoon sun framed his face, and his eyes lit with pride as he answered me, scanning his company's base camp.

"Frank, there was only one thing I ever wanted to become ... not a doctor, not a lawyer, not a banker. I dreamed of becoming a rifle company commander in the U.S. Marine Corps."

His outstretched arm swung slowly across the expanse of his base camp. Riflemen were cleaning their M-14 rifles with the same detail as given to a Stradivarius by a violin maestro. Platoon leaders checked the blistered and swollen feet of troops. The gunny sergeant berated a fire team for its inadequately constructed bunker.

"Maybe you dumb fucks don't mind dying but I sure as shit do! Do it again!"

Nineteen-year-old boys growing old prematurely read letters from home under shelter-halves; any shade was Number One. A spotted puppy bounded from a bunker, his presence in the community no longer a secret. A young Marine crossed out one more day from the calendar drawn on his helmet, one step closer to home. Each "X" was an event worth celebrating.

"It doesn't get any better than this," said the captain.

The next dawn broke as an ambush patrol led by Sergeant Fred Remington returned to the company position. A frenzied nearby firefight had awakened me a few hours earlier, violent and quick. Remington's team conducted a near-perfect ambush on an enemy squad walking down a trail near a wide creek in the moonlight.

He radioed back the good news, "Foxtrot 6 this is Sharpshooter 3. Six VC KIA, no friendly casualties. Out."

Remington reported directly to Captain Reckewell's CP with several team members to give his briefing. Upon the conclusion of his after-action report, he slammed a clear glassine bag on top of the captain's makeshift desk and said, "Captain, maybe that fucking asshole colonel will believe our body count from now on."

In the envelope were six human ears, each from a different donor, and all with freshly dried blood.

Reckewell shook his head and said, "Great ambush job, Sergeant. Now get this abomination out of my sight. You know better than this."

"Sir, yes sir."

"Sergeant, you had best quickly dispose of that bag without showing it to any of my troopers or I will have you busted."

After the Marine patrol left he turned to me and whispered, "I don't blame him, I understand his frustration. But we have higher standards than our enemies."

The young Marines dug him, even exalted in him. I remember late one afternoon Foxtrot Company was patrolling into the setting sun through thick brush that lay just east of the hamlet the captain had chosen as the day's final objective. We were to set up there in a night defensive position. We had taken a long walk on a steamy day and seen nothing of Victor Charlie. We were ready to call it a day and warm up some C-rations.

Abruptly, sniper shots fired from VC rifles rang out about 50 yards in front of us. Captain Reckewell was a few yards away from me with his head cocked, listening. He told the platoon leader nearby there were only a couple of snipers. Immediately he was besieged with volunteers who were vying with each other for their leader's attention.

"Cap'n! Send third squad!"

"Send first squad, skipper. Send first squad!"

"Sir, second squad! Sir, second squad, please!"

It was as if I were back in the seventh grade when all the smart girls knew the answer to the nun's question and raised their arms, begging to be acknowledged.

The Captain decided the competition by saying, "Okay, third squad, hi-diddle-diddle! Go get 'em!"

In seconds the third squad leader had his three fire teams on the move through the thick growth, quickly coming in from the snipers' flanks. In a jiffy the Marine squad returned with a dead Vietcong and his sniper rifle with a scope. The squad leader beamed at his captain.

In early April 1966, the Buddhist-led 1st ARVN Division joined a brewing countrywide rebellion that threatened to overthrow the Saigon government. Demonstrators took over radio stations in Danang and Hue.

ARVN Colonel Dam Quang Yeu, a devout Buddhist who sided with the rebel movement, spearheaded a convoy of infantry, armor, and artillery from Hoi An toward Danang to assist in a coup d'état against the government aligned with Premier Ky's regime. Marine aircraft spotted the large convoy of ARVN towing heavy artillery moving north up Highway 1 toward Danang and so informed intelligence at Third Marine Division headquarters. So Major General Wood Kyle ordered the Ninth Marine Regiment to block Route 1 in order to stop the convoy.

Captain Reckewell's rifle company's base camp was a mile west of the Thanh Quit Bridge, about 12 miles south of Danang. The 2/9 battalion commander instructed Reckewell to take some Marines, defend the bridge, and block the ARVN force from crossing it. The skipper took the only platoon from Foxtrot 2/9 that was not out patrolling, supported by two Ontos anti-tank vehicles, and hightailed it at a blistering pace. He ordered a two-and-a-half-ton truck to be stalled on the bridge and placed his Marines in a blocking position across the bridge on the north side of the river.

In minutes the motorized ARVN convoy came into view, racing at a swift clip straight for the bridge. Then Colonel Yeu, the ARVN commander, spotted the Marines and stopped the convoy short of the south side of the river. He placed two of his howitzers on the river's south bank and ordered his troops to dismount from their trucks and lock and load their weapons. Several hundred ARVN soldiers, backed by heavy weapons and two cannons, stared across the river at the 35 Marines from Foxtrot Company. Suddenly South Vietnamese Air Force A1-Skyraiders showed and buzzed the Marines.

Captain Reckewell met Colonel Yeu in the middle of the bridge over the Thanh Quit River and drew a line in the sand as Marine F-8E Crusader attack aircraft, loaded with rockets and bombs, circled overhead.

"Sir, if you fire your guns I will destroy you," the outmanned Marine officer declared.

Thirty suspenseful seconds passed. Suddenly Colonel Yeu wheeled around, retraced his steps, and ordered his unit to mount up. In no time they were headed south back down Highway 1 to renew the fight against the Vietcong.

The following was extracted from *U.S. Marines in Vietnam—An Expanding War—1966* by Jack Shulimson, History Museums Division, Headquarters Marine Corps (1982):

> On 7 June Operation LIBERTY began with heavy preparatory artillery fires. Marine artillery neutralized 35 objective areas in front of the advancing infantry. Initially, the enemy countered the Marine offensive with only small arms fire and mines. The mines were the more deadly of the two. The most significant mine incident occurred on 11 June in the 9th Marines central sector. Captain Carl A. Reckewell's Company F, 2d Battalion, 9th Marines walked into a large minefield in a grassy plot just south of the La Tho River. Two detonations killed three Marines and wounded 21. While the wounded were being evacuated, four to five additional explosions occurred and the grass caught fire, but fortunately there were no further Marine casualties. The following day, the artillery fired a destruction mission that caused seven secondary explosions in that same field.

The delivery of such an austere description in clipped military lexicon doesn't sound so horrible. Military history's jargon is usually accurate but almost always emotionless.

Shit happens. Sorry about that.

But the recitation fails to describe the monstrous noises in the minefield that day when two powerful H-16-A1 Anti-Personnel mines, buried below the earth's surface, under green, waving grass, within sight of the dancing lime waters of the La Tho River, exploded with no warning, spewing chunks of white-hot metal into American flesh. Just the concussive waves could induce brain injury.

One of Captain Reckewell's legs was blown away, but somehow he clung to life.

The following summer I saw a newspaper picture of him on the front page of the *San Francisco Chronicle* outside the Oakknoll Naval Hospital Chapel. He was in a wheelchair dressed in his Marine officer dress white uniform with battle ribbons, and garlands of scarlet and gold flowers, the Marine Corps colors, were woven through the spokes. His bride stood next to him in a flawless alabaster wedding dress, smiling at him. Joyce was beautiful.

10

Anger

April 6, 1966 — Phong Luc

I followed the footsteps in front of me, stepping upon each one carefully, as I had for hours that day. They were easily discernable on the trail we were following, left by the rubber-soled jungle boots of the Marine five yards in front of me, bootprints etched into the spongy soil of a jungle trail by a 19-year-old American 9,200 miles from home. A watercock gulped a creepy, mournful cry from a nearby marsh.

The brush had gotten thicker. A sharp branch bowed and sprang back across my cheekbone. I hadn't seen the rifleman in front of me glide past it with his arm extended. I chided myself to be more alert but I was lulled by the tedium of hours on the move. The men on the point blazing the trail were new to the game and exceedingly slow. The thick bramble we traversed was darkened by the shadows cast from full-bloomed tree canopy that blocked most of the brilliant light strewn by a midday Asian sun. An occasional steady beam of sunlight streamed through and illuminated spider-webs and dust particles swirling in the light. The air was heavy and hard to pull in. Tiny spiders scuttled across vines that wove through the outlandishly lush growth.

Horseflies struck and withdrew when slapped, then struck again. Sudden streams of sweat broke free and dumped salt into my eyes, stinging differently than the insects. The trooper's shirt in front of me was now alabaster from his past dried sweat-salt, no longer olive-drab green. I extinguished a black ant as it bit a chunk of flesh from my forearm. I was dizzy from the march through the enervating heat. Each of these things was soon forgotten. Everything in the bush is irrelevant, except for your unit and the enemy.

Pay attention! Don't let your mind wander. Someday soon you'll be on the sofa in an air-conditioned den, watching The Mick crack another line drive into the short right field porch in Yankee Stadium, while drinking a frosty green bottle of Rolling Rock beer. But for right now watch what you are fucking doing!

Young Marine FO team radio operator in jungle on patrol 12 miles south of Danang, April 1966.

I said this for the benefit not only of my radio operator just in front of me but also for myself.

The second platoon of Foxtrot Company, 2/9, was conducting an extended find-and-kill patrol south of the Song Bai Xau River, 12 miles south of Danang and a few miles west of Highway One. I was the rifle company's artillery FO. The good news was we had encountered no VC; the bad news was we had tripped a number of booby traps and mines and there had been several Marine casualties, no firefights but wounded Marines still the same. Frustration and fatigue consumed us.

The column halted for a short rest. I took my pack off and placed it beside me, kneeling down and wiping the sweat from my face and throat. I could breathe again. I reached for my canteen and remembered what thirst did to me several weeks before.

Foxtrot Company was in a string of green Marine helicopters heading for our landing zone. Several thousand feet below I could see the white beach line meet the sunlight-speckled deep blue South China Sea. Soft powder puffs of clouds floated above us, seen past the door-gunner checking the linked belt of ammo in his M-60 machine gun. A fishing village below had sent its watercraft out for spoils on a balmy morning. We veered away from the sea and headed west and up, up to the steep green hills of jungle that peered over the Bong Son plain. It was one large redoubt for battalions of VC strengthened with newly arrived North Vietnamese Army units. Marine intelligence estimated the enemy strength to be 6,000 regulars, reinforced by approximately 600 guerrillas. We were going there to try to correct that. We were a small part of a huge operation called Operation DOUBLE EAGLE. *The goal was to find as many VC as possible and turn them into dust for their families' altars. The chopper slowed and descended. I could see Marine gunships prepping and spraying our landing zone as we made our final approach. We encountered no contact at the LZ or on our way to set up camp for the night on a nearby wide ridge with miles of visibility in all directions.*

The next morning I was sent to work with a company of the 1st Calvary Division, one of the most decorated and elite units in the U.S. Army. Only Marine artillery was available and the army wanted a Marine forward observer involved in case it became necessary to utilize our howitzers. I was chosen. I spent a full day with them running a sweep operation through the jungle.

Late one morning three days later we were into our fourth hour of nonstop humping up and down the steep hills, at times slowly slashing our way through jungle so thick it was impossible to see more than five yards ahead, looking for NVA soldiers. The smothering heat sucked out our sweat until we were on the south side of dehydration and challenged our body thermostats. Then we were out of water. As we descended a hill we saw our first sign of any civilization in two days. A lone peasant and his water buffalo were hard at work in a rice paddy. There was a place where the mucky brown paddy water slid off a ledge to a lower level. That's where we filled our canteens. The platoon sergeant gave halazone tablets to those without them. It sterilized the water and killed bacteria that could eat holes in your guts. But it took 20 or more minutes to work after you dropped the tablets into the canteen. I weighed my risks. I was dizzy and had stopped sweating, not a good sign when you know you are overheated.

I unscrewed the cap and said, "Fuck it, sergeant. I'm not waiting."

I chugged huge gulps of the paddy water and felt mud particles in my teeth afterwards. I tried not to think about the buffalo waste that was pervasive in the paddy.

"Fuck it, if the lieutenant's drinking it I am, too," said the platoon sergeant. Now that's thirst for you.

After the short rest we got the order to move out again. I decided to move forward and take over the point as we resumed our patrol. The new Marines were too slow, I thought. I turned to my radio operator and pointed to the head of our column. He smiled like he was getting an early Christmas present, anything to break the desultory mood that held us captive.

"Randy, stay four yards behind me and keep your eyes peeled," I told him.

He nodded, squelching the static from his radio as we leapfrogged to the front. The previous point man was surprised when we took over the lead. Officers don't usually walk point unless they are bored or pissed. In this case I was both.

I moved up the trail scanning for anything unusual, enemy footprints, slivers of fishing wire strung low between trees, freshly cut vegetation. I glanced back at Randy. He was alertly checking our flanks; our new role really had his attention. I stopped after about 10 minutes to listen for ... whatever. The column of Marines behind me stopped, ordinary movements became robotic from the monotonous march and the blistering heat. Their bodies lurched and pitched. Young faces telegraphed signs of disassociation. I looked at the green canopy above us and pulled from my canteen and heard nothing. I moved forward once again.

We came upon an open crop field that stretched in front of us for over 200 yards. At its other end was a village complex behind a thick jungle tree line. I spotted a man in black bending over near the far end of the field next to a path we would likely take. He hadn't seen us yet. I halted and motioned at the four or five Marines just behind me.

"What's that gook doing?" I asked.

I was met with blank stares. They were all new replacements with no answer.

"Is he a farmer, or is he planting a booby-trap?" I asked.

Once again, none offered any assessment.

"Hey, you," I screamed. "Stay still!"

He looked up and froze. Two hundred yards away American Marines were sizing him up. Six, maybe eight seconds passed slowly. He made his decision, and like a jackrabbit made for the safety of the tree line behind him.

"What the fuck are you waiting for?" I screamed at the Marines near me. "Waste that fucker, he's a VC!"

I brought my M-14 quickly to a firing position, aligned my sights below his bobbing head at the widest part of his torso, breathed out slowly, and fired. And missed. The others next to me then opened up. The man in black was angling toward the nearest point of the tree line, running for his life. He made it. We fired over 15 rounds and missed him. If it had been a rifle range the scorer would have raised "Maggie's Drawers," a red disk signifying the target was missed.

Why had I fired? It was unclear whether he was a farmer, an enemy guerrilla, or both. Therefore my action was against the rules of engagement.

It was also very easy to rationalize. It was an ethical dilemma. He could have been an enemy warrior planting a booby-trapped grenade or a farmer planting yams for his family's next Buddhist feast. The combination of frustration, heat, fear, and exhaustion hijacked my heart and produced cold malice. Anger became the catalyst for unacceptable behavior. But I'll tell you what it really was. It wasn't just another example of our ongoing failure to win the hearts and minds of the South Vietnamese citizens. It was attempted murder.

11

The Lieutenants

Come on, you sons-of-bitches, do you want to live forever?— Gunnery
Sergeant Dan Daly, USMC, Battle of Belleau Wood, France, June, 1918

Part One—1965, 1966—Republic of Vietnam

I'll skip the suspense and tell you we all lived, all six of us who were new
artillery officers and Forward Observers with Echo Battery, Second Battalion,
Twelfth Marines. No way, Jose, the odds were heavily against that proposition. If you check out America's roll call of battle casualties you find that
Marine junior officers fall frequently, slain like fresh fawn on opening day —
see Iwo Jima, the frozen Chosin Reservoir, Belleau Wood, and Tarawa, names
just part of a much longer list. When you are exposed with radio antennas
whipping around you the enemy will spot you and try to dispatch you.

Our war was as bad as any before, maybe worse in I-Corps, the northern part of South Vietnam where the Marines fought an intransigent enemy,
the Vietcong and the North Vietnamese Army soldiers. Each day held the
potential for a ferocious battle to suddenly erupt. In previous wars time in
combat lasted a few weeks for Marines, almost never longer than a few months,
and our troops exited the scene. But not in Vietnam. A Marine's tour was 13
endless months; that was the one thing he could count on and the only way
to leave early was a dreadful, unacceptable option.

The role of the Forward Observer is fraught with personal risk and packed
with moments of astonishing action. The responsibilities for the young officer
are filled with grave consequences.

He must anticipate trouble and prepare pre-planned fire missions. He
must be aware of restricted areas of fire to avoid striking populated villages
or friendly air traffic. When his unit makes contact with the enemy he must
quickly and accurately assess the size of the force and the types of weapons he
is facing. He must move to a position where he can gather all the information necessary to fire artillery at the enemy to not only destroy it but to save

his Marines. Often he must quickly move from one position to another under incoming fire. Sometimes the situation requires him to be exposed and vulnerable out in the open in order to make his observations accurately.

He must determine precisely the enemy's location on his map. He must decide which type of artillery shell to request. There are choices. White phosphorous (WP) shells ignite and incandescently shower targets with particles that stick, then burn, then set on fire. Its effects are good against equipment and excellent against enemy troops. High-explosive (HE) shells blow targets up by disseminating hot, sharp fragments of steel at high velocity.

Next, the FO must decide which type of fuse is best. An HE airburst just above enemy troops can be most demoralizing and effective. Obviously a direct hit by a high-explosive shell against a dug-in enemy in a bunker would be more effective than an airburst.

Keep in mind that during all this collection and distillation of information, time is of the essence, but not at the expense of absolute accuracy. The FO then must concisely communicate all the necessary information over his radio via a request for artillery support, a Fire Mission, to his artillery unit. His communication must be flawless. During this process the battle has raged around him but it is secondary to his job.

Finally he waits for the artillery Fire Direction Center (FDC) to compute the data and fire the howitzers. He waits with rapt attention, staring unblinkingly at the target where his shells will soon fall, knowing that he had to have done it all without error, or in a matter of seconds, Marines may die from friendly fire.

"Danger Close" is a term used by Marines calling for artillery fire to indicate that friendly forces are within 600 meters of the target. I can't recall a single instance the term could not have been used by Marine FOs in Vietnam. It was understood the enemy was close.

They say timing is the key to everything, from investments, to falling in love, to wagering successfully on the ponies. In war, timing can be reduced to its simplest denominator — the difference between life and death.

In early December 1965 I was on the microphone in the XO pit giving the firing data to the cannoneers operating our six 105mm howitzers. Marine units south of us caught in another I-Corps ambush needed artillery support. Echo Battery was having a busy morning and an acrid cloud of burnt powder trapped in the humid air hung like an umbrella over the entire battery area. Monsoon water particles were part of the air even when it wasn't raining.

Part way through the fire mission a Marine officer I had never seen before entered the tent, then halted; his body language expressed he didn't intend to interrupt the fire mission. After the last salvo was fired he introduced himself.

He was First Lieutenant Harvey (Barney) Barnum on temporary duty to spend 60 days with the Twelfth Marine Regiment in Vietnam, an on-the-job training course for the young officer. After his temporary duty stint he would return to Marine Barracks at Pearl Harbor with lessons learned. He was to spend a few weeks with our battery then move up to regimental operations to see how the big picture was implemented. He had a calm, strong bearing about him; he moved with a quietly confident, measured quality. Barney Barnum was medium-sized and very well-mannered, a typical Marine officer and gentleman.

Meanwhile Operation HARVEST MOON was growing in size each day. Several USMC infantry battalions were seeking to destroy the battalions of the formidable 1st Vietcong Regiment which was trying to establish control in the rich farming and heavily populated area of the important Que Son Valley between Danang and Chu Lai, south of the Ninth Marines TAOR. Hotel Company 2/9 received orders to enter the large operation, and Barney Barnum was sent to fill the role of artillery Forward Observer for the rifle company.

On December 18, 1965, a reinforced Marine infantry battalion, including Hotel 2/9 was ambushed four miles east of Highway One. Hundreds of VC popped from spider holes and began firing from the flanks as the ambush unfolded in rugged terrain under a bleak monsoon sky.

The enemy spotted the Hotel Company CO when several nearby radio antennas helped reveal his position. The ambush was ignited when the first RPG round fired slammed into the company commander and his radio operator. The company was pinned down by a hailstorm of withering enemy fire and was quickly separated from the rest of the battalion by over 200 meters of open ground. Casualties mounted rapidly.

Barney Barnum ran out in the open and dragged the company commander back to cover. He then ran and picked up the U.S. Navy corpsman, who was thrice wounded tending to the fallen company commander, and brought him back to cover. Lieutenant Barnum found the company commander mortally wounded. With complete disregard for his own safety after giving aid to the dying commander he removed the radio from the CO's dead radio operator and strapped it to himself. He immediately assumed command of the rifle company and moved at once into the midst of the heavy fire, rallying and reorganizing his Marines, leading their attack on enemy positions from which deadly fire continued to come. He had been in Vietnam only 14 days.

He called in close artillery and air support to quash the calamitous VC torrent of fire. He gave ammunition conservation orders and directed fields of fire. He spotted targets for the gunships by personally firing 3.5 inch white phosphorous rockets until there were no more rockets.

As night fell the company was almost out of ammunition and was still cut off from the rest of the battalion. Barney Barnum got the dead and wounded out on choppers. He ordered everyone to drop all backpacks and inoperable weapons in a pile. He ordered the engineers to blow up the pile. Under a base of supporting fire from the other Marine units he led his company across a 200-meter open field swept with VC fire. The company rejoined the rest of the battalion and was finally out of harm's way.

During the whole encounter the commanding Marine general in Vietnam, Lewis W. Walt, had monitored Barney Barnum's exploits. Scuttlebutt insisted he was put in for The Medal the next day. Two days later HARVEST MOON was officially ended. We killed 407 VC. There were 45 Marines killed, another 218 wounded.

On February 27, 1967, Harvey "Barney" Barnum was presented the Medal of Honor by President Lyndon B. Johnson in the name of congress.

Marines return to 2/9 monsoon-drenched base camp from Operation HARVEST MOON, December 1965.

The citation began:

> For conspicuous gallantry and intrepidity at the risk of his life above and
> beyond the call of duty as Forward Observer for Artillery, while attached
> to Company H, Second Battalion, Ninth Marines, Third Marine Divi-
> sion (Reinforced), in action against communist forces at Ky Phu in Quang
> Tin Province, Republic of Vietnam, on 18 December 1965.

He was the fourth Marine to receive the nation's highest honor in the Vietnam War and the first living officer to receive it.

Barney Barnum returned to Hawaii several weeks after HARVEST MOON.
The odds of a man being in one battle, responding to all challenges, never
being hit, and living to tell how he earned the Medal of Honor are miniscule. Ironically he returned to Vietnam two years later to take command of
the very same artillery unit, Echo Battery, Twelfth Marines.

Colonel Harvey (Barney) Barnum retired from the Marine Corps in 1989
after 27 years of glorious service. He recently retired as Deputy Assistant Secretary of the Navy for Reserve Affairs. He is a past president of the Congres-
sional Medal of Honor Society. It is the hardest club in the world to join and
the Society works tirelessly to inspire and stimulate our youth to become
worthy citizens of our country. Barney lives in northern Virginia with his wonderful wife, Martha.

Second Lieutenant Jack E. Swallows came from southern California, a
golden-tanned young officer with zeal, brains, and muscle. Jack was often in
the crosshairs of the VC since his units drew some of the most dangerous
assignments south of Danang. He was an FO for most of his tour in that
place that gave FOs few second chances. He led a cat's life and his somber
approach to each day in the hot war zone belied his incredible sense of humor,
which helped him land a wonderful young woman, Ann, who went west from
the chill of Iowa to the warm California sun. Jack met her at a mixer at the
Marine Corps Recruit Depot in San Diego, his duty station after his Vietnam tour.

Google him and you will find his story about his return to an old
battlefield in Vietnam he revisited in 2003. Jack retired from the active Marine
reserves as a lieutenant colonel. He was awarded the Bronze Star for heroism
in Vietnam. The citation relates that as Forward Observer for Lima Company, Third Battalion, Third Marines, in one four-month period Jack participated in eight battalion operations, 20 company operations, and numerous
platoon operations and patrols, decisively executing his duties with skill and
keen judgment. On four occasions Jack adjusted artillery fire to within 100
meters of his unit in order to more effectively destroy the enemy, prevent
escape, and allow the infantry to assault the Vietcong positions. Jack Swal-

lows and his wife live fittingly in San Juan Capistrano where he enjoys his expanding family and travels extensively.

Second Lieutenant Robert Leo Hamel was educated at the University of Rhode Island and the University of Connecticut. His dark brown eyes gave witness to his high-energy excitement for life. As an FO, he was in constant action, asking for no quarter. Under heavy NVA and hardcore VC fire he provided close, accurate, and life-saving artillery fire support for his units. His exploits were rewarded with two Bronze Stars. One citation describes that on the moonless night of August 16, 1965, he was with the Third Tank Battalion as an artillery Forward Observer on a hill south of Danang when the Vietcong launched a probe in force with automatic weapons, small arms, and mortars:

> Fearlessly exposing himself to enemy fire, Lieutenant Hamel made a rapid estimate of the situation, determined the location of a substantial portion of the enemy forces, and called a fire mission. His target description, precise positioning of the enemy and considerable skill in adjusting fire resulted in the confirmed deaths of six Vietcong guerrillas and the complete silencing of the enemy mortars and automatic weapons.

The lieutenant Forward Observers with Echo Battery 2/12 from left to right, Jim Riordan, Franklin Cox, Bob Hamel, Dave Garner, February 1966.

The next morning it was reported that 26 VC were killed by artillery fire, but more importantly no Marine casualties were sustained due to Bob's "courage, presence of mind under the most difficult of circumstances, and his remarkable skill in properly employing artillery fire. The enemy suffered a devastating defeat."

In September 1965 Bob was at it again, this time as FO for Echo Company, Ninth Marines. The citation for his second Bronze Star relates the rifle company was pinned down from enemy fire and taking casualties.

> 2nd Lt. Hamel and his forward observer team defied the hostile fire and boldly maneuvered across 50 meters of open terrain to a position from which they could effectively call for, observe, and adjust the artillery fire. Calling in the fire and adjusting it to within 75 meters of his position 2nd Lt. Hamel was instrumental in suppressing the enemy fire, contributing significantly to the successful completion of the mission.

He was the only one of us who was an FO his entire tour. His battery commander rarely brought him back to the rear. He was constantly in shit-storms, sometimes with the ARVN Rangers, sometimes with Marine Recon units. He traveled like a gun for hire and the chance for heavy contact somehow increased with each outfit he went out with.

Even though he received wounds on five different occasions as a result of enemy contact, he does not own a Purple Heart. He defied the odds. He lives happily today back in his natural habitat, Rhode Island.

Second Lieutenant David Paul Garner, a Notre Dame graduate, was as steady and accountable as the inexorable rotation of the earth. Like all the FOs, Dave faced death often. His equanimity and heroic nature got him through the morass. He also was decorated with the Bronze Star.

On March 25, 1966, Dave was serving as FO for Echo Company, Ninth Marines, when a Main Force Battalion of Vietcong attacked the company.

> He immediately moved through "withering small arms fire and heavy mortar barrages to an exposed position where he could observe the battlefield. He then called in artillery on the attacking enemy with devastating effect. Due to his knowledge and use of the correct shell, fuse, and method of fire, the initial enemy assault was broken. For more than six hours, he called in approximately one thousand rounds on the enemy ... his aggressive and daring efforts helped to inflict heavy enemy losses, and undoubtedly prevented the Vietcong Battalion from overrunning his Company's position."

Dave was awarded the Bronze Star for his heroism. Dave became a career Marine and retired as a bird colonel. Today this American patriot lives in northern Virginia.

Second Lieutenant James P. Riordan graduated from Washington State

University. He was a gentle bear of a man with a naturally happy demeanor that even the violence his rifle company encountered could not diminish. Jim was awarded the Silver Star, the Bronze Star, the Navy Commendation Medal, and a Purple Heart. Jim retired as a lieutenant colonel after a distinguished Marine Corps career.

I was the other FO.

Jim Riordan and his wonderful wife, Sandy, hosted a reunion for the six FOs at their home near Quantico, Virginia, two years ago. It was the first time most of us had seen one another in over 40 years, yet it seemed nothing had changed.

They say timing is the key to everything, even life itself. Soon after I departed Vietnam a new second lieutenant reported for duty to Echo Battery. He followed me as the Forward Observer attached to Foxtrot Company, Ninth Marines. His timing resulted in an entirely different result than that experienced by the six of us. He had only been in Vietnam for several weeks before he was killed in battle.

Part Two — June 1962 — Quantico, Virginia — Officer Candidate Training

The Pentagon's silhouette slid under streams of thin, see-through clouds and filled my window as the DC-8 banked sharply to the east over the Potomac. It was a beautiful June Monday morning and hundreds of college men were arriving at Washington National Airport. Large, dark-green, cattle-car buses with the block letters USMC on each side waited to take us to our destination where we would spend the next six weeks. Each of us had chosen to undergo the Platoon Leaders Course (PLC) at Marine Corps Schools in Quantico, Virginia. We came from Ball State, Stanford, Stetson, Princeton, Marquette, University of Virginia, Spring Hill College, Georgia Southern, Ohio State University, San Diego State, and scores of other colleges. We all knew we were in for a challenge. But we had no clue what we had bargained for. Historically less than 50 percent of the candidates completed the Marine PLC challenge and received commissions.

The unexpected horizontal blow landed with a flat thud, whistling against the protective helmet above my right temple. I staggered a step to my left and deep-pulled volumes of oxygen from the humid late-morning Virginia air. The heavy cover of dew was now gone, sucked up from the thick grass covering the athletic field by a thirsty sun, now at a perfect angle to deliver its summer rays of heat. It had been pretty even so far, I thought. Gotta hang on. He was a little bigger than me, and I wasn't used to that. How long had we been fighting? I held my weapon loosely for a few seconds, letting my forearm muscles relax. The make-believe rifle and bayonet was somewhat thicker than a broomstick and each end sprouted thick heavy pads weighing several pounds each. It was fittingly called a pugil stick.

The semicircle our peers formed around us drew tighter. The referee was Staff Sergeant A.W. Crowe, our Drill Instructor (DI). He sensed vulnerability and screamed for the *coup de grace*, "Close and kill! Close and kill! Kill! Kill! Kill!" I took a step backward with my right foot. My opponent's eyes widened, he was breathing as hard as I, and he came forward. I stepped forward with my left foot and swung from underneath, putting as much leverage into the vertical swing with my pugil stick as I could summon. The heavy pad caught him square on his left cheek, stopping him cold.

Clocked the bastard, I thought, with the same bolo-punch swing Kid Gavilan had used to gain the welterweight throne a decade earlier.

The DI blew his whistle. It was a draw. The pugil stick match was over between the two officer candidates. We shook hands bending at the waist, each of us close to nausea, our thighs weak and shaking from the physical exertion. Each candidate in the platoon would have his turn in the ring. It was part of the bayonet-fighting course taught to all officer-candidates as part of the PLC program at Quantico. Bayonet fighting is intrinsic to the unalterable mission of the Corps. Learning bayonet fighting is learning how to kill your enemy via the bottom-up managerial style the Marine Corps employs. If you want the top-down style, antiseptic and in a vacuum, the Air Force method of killing is better suited for you.

If you had the audacity to think you could become an officer and a leader of Marines, you had to face the tests and trials of Quantico in order to learn the crafts, nuances, and military sciences the role required. We were instructed and tested in Marine Corps history, principles of leadership, basic weapons, small unit tactics, supporting arms, map reading, and other topics. In addition we were subject to the Marine Corps' boot-camp regimen of tortuous physical training, 12-mile forced marches up and down power lines, and parade-deck drill and ceremony activities on the hot "grinder" (picture a large asphalt parking lot open to the hot Virginia sun) for hours at a time. We faced full "white-glove" inspections (the platoon never passed). We ran the obstacle course until we dropped. We cleaned our M-1 rifles even in our sleep. And our sleep would be terminated by the sound of the squad-bay galvanized metal garbage can smashing up against the bulkhead before the first hint of dawn.

"Outta the racks, ladies! It's a great day to be in the Marine Corps, where every day is a holiday and every meal is a banquet!" screamed the assistant DI, a typical start to another 17-hour day.

Most of the newly-commissioned offices in the Marine Corps graduated from PLC, or the equally rigorous Officers Candidate School. The PLC course was 12 weeks long for candidates still in college, usually broken into two six-week periods in different summers. Upon successful completion, together with graduation from college, a Reserve Commission in the United States Marine Corps was offered to the candidate who somehow made it through the trials of the challenging course. With the acceptance came a three-year active duty commitment.

Three years didn't sound that bad in 1964 to me. The Marine Corps had a good haul at my college. We had no ROTC, and the Marine recruiters were better salesmen than the other services who came calling. I always planned for a stint as an officer in the service. My three uncles had been U.S. Navy officers in World War II. I was fascinated by their officer swords as a child. I had prepped at a Catholic all-male military high school in Atlanta, the Marist School. I had learned how to break down and clean an M-1 rifle in the ninth grade. But now I was going to have the best adventure of all. I was going to be a Marine fighter pilot like my all-time hero, Ted Williams. I had better than 20–20 vision, good eye-hand coordination, a quick intellect, and a healthy, strong body. I imagined how gallant I would look in my Marine dress blue uniform with golden wings.

One hot July morning after my breakfast (cereal, orange juice, bacon, toast, two scrambled eggs, and two glasses of whole milk) the platoon assembled for the day's first class. The senior drill instructor smiled and asked, "Are you slimes ready for some fun?"

Robotically we responded, "Sir, yes sir!"

"What is the Marine Corps?" he queried.

We answered in unison, 46 voices on the same page, the same answer we responded with six, maybe seven times a day.

"Sir! The Marine Corps is 187 years of blood, guts, death, hell, and destruction! The toughest fighting machine the world has ever seen! Gung ho! Gung ho! Gung ho!"

After a while you actually believed it.

"Outstanding, you clowns! It's a good thing you're so motivated because now we're going to run the hill trail!"

Oh, shit, each of us thought.... *The fucking hill trail!*

It ran for almost five miles, straight up and down, covering seven hills. The hills were slick with wet, red, summer mud and angled up 30 degrees in elevation. The problem was when you reached the top of each hill you were hanging on for dear life. Then immediately going down the hill you tried to keep your balance while your feet felt like foreign objects. With little traction, gravity was your enemy; you didn't want to lose it and start tumbling because that could lead to some of the terrible things you had seen, young candidates' legs smashed against huge oaken tree stumps, bones burst, *dear God get me through this.* Halfway through we took a break. I couldn't catch my breath. I was swimming in black nothingness and my legs swayed as I slunk into a wooden copse a few yards away just off the side of the trail. I leaned over and vomited my breakfast out through my mouth and nose. You would have thought I had pissed on the American flag by the reaction of the drill instructor.

"Who told you to puke?"

Then he yelled and fetched the platoon commander.

"How can you be so gutless as to puke? Where is your character? Are you going to do that in front of the troops?" the platoon commander asked. "You are unsat, Candidate Cox."

In seconds my nausea vanished. I slugged down half a canteen of water and my legs stopped trembling. I was ready to go I assured them. Minutes later we headed up the next hill. I didn't eat another egg for the next six months.

The biggest problem was the one in your mind — you could quit. Stone cold quit ... I'm outta here! Two little words, "I quit," and with no hard feelings the Marine Corps would release you from any duty other than a commitment as an enlisted man with little responsibility in an active reserve unit for four years. Period. No active duty ... no stress ... one weekend meeting a month, play weekend warrior (they won't call us up) ... and your military duty would be accomplished. You only had to cry uncle once, "I quit!" and the nightmare would be over. Just say it and the next day you'd be back home in the sweet summer of your college years, hanging out at the pool, grooving the chicks grooving you.

"I quit!" ... no more drill instructor with his chin in your shoulder and his campaign hat's stiff brim pressing your temple, you were a hopeless unsat candidate, he reminded you; you were unsatisfactory; you had no right to even imagine you had the equipment to become a Marine Corps officer, especially not in his Marine Corps.

You wondered, *maybe he's right. What the fuck* am *I doing here?*

Their goal was to make you quit, and over half of us did or were dispatched for unacceptable performance. You could be a great athlete but if you couldn't back it up academically you were booted out. You could be a collegiate decathlon champion with good grades but if you couldn't hack it in the leadership department when called upon to solve problems in front of your peers, you were jettisoned. The DIs went to great lengths to discover any weakness in your body or your character and exploit it to expel you, or worse, allow you to expel yourself.

The physical stress and demands at Quantico are similar to Parris Island where the enlisted recruits undergo the Marine Corps boot camp rigors. You can't quit at Parris Island, but you can at Quantico; they know it and you know it. They really try to toy with your mind — they strive to hear you say it — "I quit!" When they hear those magic words, they call it victory — they've helped the weak find his way home, no longer a threat to real Marines.

Sometimes their tactics were similar to certain brainwashing techniques employed by the Communist Chinese Army. One evening I was summoned to the platoon commander's office. The lieutenant was at his desk and at each side of him stood the two platoon DIs. It had been a very long day and I was nearing the end of the fifth week — just one more to go and I would be through the first six-week period and back home for the rest of the summer. The stress was grabbing me hard, each morning at 0500 reveille I snuck out the back door of the Quonset hut and dry-heaved. My nerves were jangled and it was a hard way to start a day that would exceed physical and psychological limits.

"Sir, Candidate Cox reporting as ordered, sir," I nervously began.

The lieutenant said, "At ease, candidate. Relax. This is informal, just you and us, not really part of the program. We want you to come to the same conclusion we have."

"Sir, yes sir."

"Would you care to know what that is, candidate?"

"Sir, what the lieutenant's conclusion is, sir?"

"Yes, candidate."

"Sir, yes sir, the candidate wants to know the lieutenant's conclusion, sir."

Conclusion to what? I wondered. I didn't even know the question. I let that thought pass. The three Marine mentors were staring at me as if I were a 200-pound green bug, totally alien to their world.

"Very well, candidate, our conclusion is you are unsat!" He really turned up his volume and when he spoke the final word he slammed his hand down on his desk with a resounding slap. I tried not to jump.

"We want you to sign this DOR form," he added softly.

DOR was an acronym for Drop On Request. Just simply say "I quit" and at your own request you would be dropped from the program, no hard feelings, no questions asked. How easy it would be to cut the cord, to end the brutal pressure and stop the physical and psychological suffering. It was so seductive; the thought of total release drew you like a moth to flame. It played with your mind, a constant temptation.

Nonetheless, declaring DOR would be an inglorious stain. I couldn't do it, no matter what trials awaited me. There was no way I would give up and throw the towel in.

"Sir, the candidate does not wish to DOR. The candidate wants to successfully complete the program, graduate with his class, and get his commission, sir."

"I don't give a shit what you want, candidate!" the DI to the left of the desk screamed.

"Look," said the lieutenant. "Face it, candidate. You are u-n-s-a-t, as in unsatisfactory. You are wasting your time and the Marine Corps' time. You don't have what it takes to be a Marine officer. You're not in shape and you're not special in the classroom. Do everybody a favor and go home."

They stared at me hard, waiting for me to capitulate. I was not going to let myself down and take the easy way out.

"Sir, the candidate will not DOR, sir. The candidate will try to become satisfactory at all levels, sir."

They continued to stare at me. I kept my eyes locked on the lieutenant's forehead. Time passed. No one moved.

"Leave. Quickly," the lieutenant finally ordered.

"Sir, aye-aye, sir." I did an about-face and trudged back to the squad bay across the road. I felt the tension melt away and drop from me like yesterday's dead leaves blown from an oak by a stiff wind. I felt exceedingly proud. I had just passed the hardest test I would face and I knew I would make it. The DI stuck his head in the Quonset hut. "Candidate Cullen? The lieutenant wants to confer with your young ass. Move out."

The following day I looked up and saw an early Saturday morning Virginia sun framed in a field of blue between the branches of a leaf-filled red maple tree on the side of the power-line trail cut through the hills. A truck passed with a white cross on its side, gingerly descending the slick, muddy slope of the hill the candidates were humping down. A forced march was underway, Marine Corps stuff, 10 miles of hell to emphatically end the week's labors. After the hike we would be rewarded with a 30-hour respite from the training.

Candidate Walter Childs grinned at me from the rear of the canvas-covered Marine 3-axle truck tugging an extension filled with hundreds of gallons of water, the elixir that could actually keep us alive when dispensed on our next break. Childs, chunking ice to his comrades, was riding in the truck. He had been placed on light duty because of a fungus. After a few weeks of harsh physical activity in the moist Quantico summer ordeal he contracted what is commonly called "jock itch."

Ignoring the onset of the irritation fueled by humidity and chafing, Childs continued to engage in the hardships the rest of his peers encountered. He had too much pride to ask for any quarter. Soon the "tinea cruris" had a life of its own, exacerbated by his thighs rubbing together during physical exertion. From the bottom of his scrotum to the tops of his knees, the full length of both thighs, his skin was red, angry, and alive with the fungus chewing past the epidermis, into the second layer of skin, producing an incredibly noxious, seeping, evil discharge. He protested when the infirmary doctor placed him on light duty. He would have given anything to jump from the bed of the truck to join his platoon on its journey. He didn't care if the misery descended to his ankles, it was only temporary after all, just please don't send him home ... unsat.

I smiled back, never before feeling a no-stress connection to the training hikes we endured, for that day I was a stretcher-bearer. There were four of us to collect the collateral human damage of the footslog. Marine officer candidates unable to move another step sometimes lay sprawled in red, wet ruts in the trail, gasping for breath, hopefully only on the brink of heat exhaustion. We were to collect the fallen. The good news for stretcher-bearers was that even though they encountered the same formidable terrain in the heat the rest of the unit was traversing, it was a psychological lift. We were at the rear, just lollygagging. We didn't have to fret about the "accordion effect," trying frantically to stay in proper interval somehow with the one in front. You could barely keep up on a level grade, almost impossible when going up the hill. Then an awkward attempt to go into low gear was required going down the next hill to avoid spilling into the candidate in front. Peer pressure commanded you to hang in there. On conditioning hikes even the DI's screams didn't seem to matter; your only thought was to make it to the barracks with your group.

With the hike finally over, we stumbled into the Quonset hut to see Childs on his bunk, legs splayed with an electric fan going full-bore, delivering its soothing breeze.

Childs smiled and wiggled next to me two days later onto a bench seat of the cattle-car trailer the platoon boarded at 0530. We were to spend the next week on the rifle range with no physical training and he knew he would be able to rectify his malady. The DI in starched, spotless utilities sprang aboard, slammed the door shut, and faced us.

"Candidates, you are now on your way to learn what the United States Marine Corps does better than any fighting force since the invention of gunpowder. We shoot truer and consequently kill more of the enemies of our country than everyone else. The rifle range is our cathedral. Therefore you will pray and practice on the sacred range. Then you will be able to eliminate an enemy 500 yards away!"

With that he distributed to each of us The Prayer:

"My Rifle — the Creed of a United States Marine" (Major General William H. Rupertus, USMC, San Diego, *Marine Corps Chevron*, March 14, 1942):

1. This is my rifle. There are many like it, but this one is mine.
2. My rifle is my best friend. It is my life. I must master it as I must master my life.
3. My rifle, without me, is useless. Without my rifle, I am useless. I must fire my rifle true. I must shoot straighter than my enemy who is trying to kill me. I must shoot him before he shoots me. I will....
4. My rifle and myself know that what counts in this war is not the rounds we fire, the noise of our burst, nor the smoke we make. We know that it is the hits that count. We will hit....
5. My rifle is human, even as I, because it is my life. Thus, I will learn it as a brother. I will learn its weaknesses, its strength, its parts, its accessories, its sights and its barrel. I will ever guard it against the ravages of weather and damage as I will ever guard my legs, my arms, my eyes and my heart against damage. I will keep my rifle clean and ready. We will become part of each other. We will....
6. Before God, I swear this creed. My rifle and myself are the defenders of my country. We are the masters of our enemy. We are the saviors of my life.
7. So be it, until victory is America's and there is no enemy, but peace!

I lay prone on the hard dirt of my firing position, the rifle butt's brass plate secured into my right shoulder. My left arm was perpendicular to the ground. My left hand cradled the rifle's polished walnut stock. Through the rear and front sights on top of the 22-inch barrel I spied the bullseye in the center of the target's matting. Gently I exhaled and slowly squeezed the weapon's trigger, keeping the integrity of the whole platform, no rush, just let it happen, the act had a life of its own, like sex, and then the report erupted and the round leaped from the muzzle at 2,800 feet per second. Dead solid perfect.

We qualified for keeps after a week of practice and tutelage. Only one failed out of 46. Childs hopped back into the cattle-car, smiling, walking normally now and clutching a brand new Expert Marksmanship Badge.

The next summer I received the thorough eye exam given to all flight school applicants. Bring it on, I thought; I had better than 20–20 vision, just like my hero Ted Williams. Alas, during the exam the U.S. Navy eye doctor detected a small astigmatism that dashed my flight school aspirations.

I had a weighty decision to make. I wasn't going to be a pilot after all, and that was why I had volunteered. I could still DOR and coast through the active reserves, fulfilling my military duty, or I could suck it up and finish Platoon Leaders Class and accept my commission and the three-year commitment that went along with it.

I went for the gold bars. Those dress blues would still look real fine on me, I figured.

I remember sitting in the bleachers on graduation day, waiting for my platoon to be called to the parade deck to pass in review. The noon sun reflected off the brass instruments and the band started playing John Phillip Sousa's *Semper Fidelis*. I had earned the right to be commissioned an officer of the Marines. It was the proudest moment of my life.

PART II

Heroes and Goats

12

A Culture Like No Other

Greater love has no one than this, than to lay down one's life for his friends. — John 15:13

I'm not intent on blasphemy, but there is another love as great as the one scripture ascribes to Jesus Christ.

And that is the unswerving code of love Marines have for their institution, their peers, and their older brothers who stood tall in the 18th, 19th, and 20th centuries, and today for those who pick up the Mameluke swords and the sniper rifles and protect America. Like Jesus — the Corps, its love and its lore — was, is, and shall ever be.

I bring you love stories about a war I have seen. They are love stories not in the traditional sense but in that special way Marines feel about each other. I write you straight from my heart. I write about Marines in the Vietnam War.

When I write about my Marines I become dumbstruck when I consider the staggering number of casualties Marine units suffer on the battlefield. Sometimes the numbers are unacceptable. But when America's elite assault force is turned loose on the enemy, it is driven by its culture. And the Corps' distinct warrior ethos is defined by intense training, inflexible discipline, resolute devotion, unflinching adherence to orders, and love by each Marine not only for the Corps itself, but for each Marine in his unit. When new Marines become knighted in boot camp they enter into the living entity that is the roll call of the glorious history of the United States Marine Corps. They acknowledge their sacred duty to pick up the shield and lance and insure that the Corps' great history continues for eternity. Pride in the Corps and its tenets are burned into each Marine's soul. So when the United States Marine Corps joins battle with the enemy of America, it does so spurred by a collective philosophy that dictates instant, aggressive response with a zealous commitment to take the objective. There are no half measures when Marines fight.

Lieutenant General John F. Kelly summed up the unique Marine mystique on the eve of the ground invasion into Iraq on March 20, 2003. A reporter from the *Los Angeles Times* pointed out to the Assistant Commander of the First Marine Division that a powerful enemy with more men, tanks, and artillery lay in wait. Then he added the possibility of Saddam's massive stockpiles of chemical weapons being unleashed.

The reporter then asked the general, "Sir, have you ever considered the notion of defeat?"

The general was sitting in the shotgun position in his jeep at the point of his division, waiting for the signal to begin the assault north. He reflected about all the Marine battlefields he had reverently visited, places like Guadalcanal, Iwo Jima, Inchon, and Vietnam. He thought about conversations he'd had with Marine veterans who fought in those places. He was taken aback by the very mention of possible defeat, a concept he had never considered in his career, which had seen him climb in rank from a private in boot camp to a general of Marines.

General Kelly turned back to the reporter and answered his question.

"Hell, these are Marines! Men like them held Guadalcanal and took Iwo Jima. Baghdad ain't shit!"

And even today, in this sophisticated electronic American age filled with creature comforts enjoyed by a blasé society, there are men who believe what General Kelly believes, that the Marine Corps will live forever.

Its reputation precedes itself, and the legend of its combat proficiency fills enemy souls with terror.

A captured North Korean major admitted in 1951 that "panic sweeps my men when they are facing the American Marines."

Later that year another Communist commander issued the following order: "Do not attack the First Marine Division. Leave the 'yellowlegs' alone. Strike the American Army." When Marine intelligence heard those cryptic words of alarm, the Marines were instructed to discard their khaki leggings.

In World War I, U.S. Marines squared off against the German army in the Chateau Thierry campaign in the gruesome battle of Belleau Wood. On July 19, 1918, first Lieutenant Clifton B. Cates sent the following message: "I have only two men out of my company and 20 out of some other company. We need support, but it is almost suicide to try to get it here as we are swept by machine-gun fire and a constant barrage is on us. I have no one on my left and only a few on my right. I will hold." Marines raced across the fields, frontally assaulting the German machine-gun emplacements and won the battle. The surviving Hun soldiers, stunned by the ferocity of the American attack, dubbed the Marines *Teufelhunden,* or in English, Devil Dogs.

In 1991, Iraqi Republican Guard commanders revealed to their troops they would outnumber the advancing 17,000 troops of the First Marine Division by a total of six to one. But when Iraqi soldiers learned they would be facing the *Angels of Death,* a nickname they had given the Marines, their morale disintegrated and they were immobilized with fear.

Recently over lunch I was shocked to hear a friend of mine, an intelligent, successful businessman, reveal that when he considered the great scope and history of America's victory in World War II he only thought of the European theater. He considered the Pacific theater to have been a second-page story punctuated by the dropping of the atomic bombs on Japan. He only had a minimal understanding of the great Pacific naval sea battles and the incredible human sacrifices the United States Navy and Marine Corps paid in the brutal island-hopping combat fought against the fanatical Japanese Imperial Army and Navy. He was surprised when I told him about Iwo Jima, an island only six times larger than Central Park, where American casualties exceeded those of total Allied casualties on D-Day at Normandy. Marine infantry battalions suffered 90 percent attrition rates and 6,800 Marines were killed in action in the five-week battle. The actual casualty numbers are much higher than the first casualty reports that were released by the American media in 1945 just after the battle ended. The Japanese garrison contained 22,000 soldiers and all but the thousand that were captured fought to the death.

My friend thanked me for the information and told me he would study the "other" part of World War II, way out in the western Pacific Ocean. His words had stirred a memory in me from a few years ago when I saw *Saving Private Ryan.* I remember the haunting opening scenes of Steven Spielberg's classic film with bullets ripping through American soldiers' torsos captured by underwater cameras and bodies bobbing in the froth of the grey breakers of the Atlantic Ocean that crashed onto the blood-drenched beach at Normandy.

"Wait a minute! Stop the film!" I wanted to scream at the theater's projection room, "this footage is high-jacked! Those men are not Marines!"

I thought the scene was obscene, not because of the visceral violence depicted, but because those scenes have always belonged to the Marine Corps, images of dead Marines in the water, on the beach, and on the battlefields of Guadalcanal, New Georgia, Bougainville, Tarawa, Saipan, Tinian, Guam, Iwo Jima, and Okinawa. I apologize for my irrational denial of the valorous United States Army landing at Normandy. But I cannot help myself. My feelings have no basis in reality, but I am biased. Semper Fidelis.

Other branches of the armed service respect the Corps. But there is nothing like the jealousy the Marine Corps engenders in its sister services. I have a friend who was a decorated officer with the 101st Airborne Division in Vietnam. He has reached the point of losing his grip when he hears another Marine war story or sees an article in the media glorifying new Marine Corps heroics. He thinks the Corps is unsophisticated, overrated, and a living public relations lie. In Vietnam, American Army infantry units would routinely fire artillery on enemy objectives before moving in, hopefully softening up enemy positions yet at the same time announcing an American operation was unfolding. Often Marine units would rapidly take the fight into the enemy's position without pre-planned bombardment, preferring instead to seize the element of surprise. I refrain from bringing up this dichotomy with my friend. No need to stir up trouble.

The truth is America loves its Marine Corps, and he is jealous.

The U.S. Army, Navy, and Air Force base their recruiting campaigns in the media upon promises about the cutting-edge technology recruits will absorb, insuring potential candidates they will become successful after they serve their time in service and have a chance to grab the American Dream. Marine Corps commercials, produced by J. Walter Thompson since 1946, are structured on reverse psychology. "We don't promise you a rose garden," is a direct challenge to the youth of America who might be cut out to become Marines.

Even better is the Marine promise: "No better friend, no worse enemy."

It's your choice.

In a perverse way Marines boast of the grim casualty numbers attached to the history of past battles. No other fighting force locks with the enemy like the Marines do who exult in this knowledge, wearing their history like a Red Badge of Courage. So the culture particular to the Corps will carry forward until the next battle call is dispatched. The corps will answer with elan, sacrifice, and courage and add yet another magnificent chapter to its history.

13

Okinawa

He was a majestic-looking bird colonel, from the brilliant shine of his rich, black leather Italian shoes, up past his patrician blue eyes to the salt-and-pepper, tightly-cropped hair crowning his lean 6-foot-3-inch frame. Vietnam would be his third war and his ribbons proved he had seen a lot of action in World War II and Korea. I was one of four lieutenants reporting to our first United States Marine Corps post after graduating from the Basic School in Quantico, Virginia.

Colonel William E. Pala was the commanding officer of the Twelfth Marines, the artillery regiment for the Third Marine Division. The colonel routinely greeted his new officers informally in a father-to-son talk session in his stylishly appointed office. The deeply polished wood of his desk and chairs gleamed like his shoes, and citations, awards, and diplomas were hung next to battlefield pictures of him at a younger age. There was one framed photograph of him on a credenza that drew our respect for the man. In it he was giving orders to two commanding officers of Marine artillery batteries on Iwo Jima.

The colonel provided his opinion of what the 13-month time-line of our tour in the western Pacific would likely look like. We would start with several months of artillery training in Okinawa, followed by a six-month cruise in the South China Sea as part of a Battalion Landing Team force in readiness, which could include up to four months in Vietnam. After that he suggested we might spend two months in Japan before concluding our tour back in Okinawa before heading home to the good old U.S. of A.

"Colonel," Second Lieutenant Jack Swallows asked, "Only four months in Vietnam?"

The colonel leaned forward and pressed the fingertips of his hands together. "Lieutenant, are you not aware we sent in a landing force of United States Marines to Danang almost two months ago?"

"Sir, yes sir. We all watched it on CBS News together in artillery school in Quantico, sir."

"Well, there you have it, son. How long do you think those wretched little yellow excuses for soldiers can hold out against the leadership and will of U.S. Marines?"

"How long, sir?"

"Son, we're not scheduled to deploy for at least two months. My fear is the whole thing will be wrapped up before any of us in this room will be able to put one foot on Asian soil."

His indoctrination was not limited to the loyalty to the Corps he expected of us along with our prompt execution of his orders. He also saw us becoming Christian soldier-poet types. You could tell he was a disciple of Christ, indeed he said so, and he imagined his officers leading Marines up the hill with a sword in one hand and a bible in the other.

I thought about singing "Onward Christian Soldiers," but instead furtively rolled my eyes, giving my buddy Jack the *can-you-actually-believe-this-shit?* glance.

"Welcome to the Fleet Marine Force, gentleman," the colonel said, initiating us into the real Marine Corps.

Introibo ad altare Deo (I will go unto the altar of God).

At the conclusion of the meeting, our first morning in the Orient, the colonel gave his new charges one last bit of local caveat.

"Beware of the native women here. They are heathen and carriers of the vilest forms of venereal diseases."

Confiteor Deo omnipotenti (I confess to Almighty God).

I know if I dared to glance at my peers I would burst into loud and irreverent laughter. Instead I stared at the colonel, thinking of an appropriate response.

Gee, Colonel, maybe we should have had this meeting last night as soon as we got off the plane. It had been a long and arduous trip, sir. We flew out of Travis Air Force Base near San Francisco, stopped for a couple of hours in Honolulu, refueled again on Wake Island where we gobbled a box lunch, and then cruised on in to Okinawa. We were of course tired but we needed to wind down after the stressful trip.

After our flight arrived, we checked into the Bachelor Officers Quarters, showered and changed, and hit the ville outside the main gate within the hour. Did you know there are scivvie houses full of prostitutes right outside the front gate here, under your very nose, Colonel? We downed shots of whiskey and chugged beers and talked up the bar girls and had a great time our first night in the Orient. Hopefully the little ladies were clean.

I held my tongue. It was still thickened from the night's abuse and my mind was cobwebbed from jet lag and hangover. By the time we left I could have sworn the colonel was a stand-in for Billy Graham.

Christe eleison (Christ have mercy).

Jack Swallows and I reported to the same unit, Echo Battery, Second Battalion, Twelfth Marines, our first Fleet Marine Force assignment as artillery officers. We began teaching classes in the garrison and conducting inspections. Then we hooked our 105mm howitzers to the truck and convoyed to the rugged northern training areas for four or five days at a time. The new lieutenants went to an observation post on the artillery range and called in live fire missions, learning how to request and adjust the powerful shells fired by our howitzers. We did it for days at a time, learning the craft of artillery Forward Observer.

That part of the island had been the stage for some of the most ferocious fighting Americans encountered in any theater during World War II. Scuttlebutt suggested there were still some Japanese infantrymen hiding in caves, old men now, still not ready to surrender. The troops enjoyed several hot meals a day prepared by field galleys. At night we were kept dry during heavy rains by large general-purpose tents. We slept well, realizing sleep would become fleeting in Vietnam.

Just before lights-out salty noncommissioned officers talked with each other about the ways of the habu, the native Okinawan pit viper whose venom was more lethal than that of any North American poisonous snake. Green troopers fresh in from the states fought nightmares of habus slithering and loose inside the tent.

It would be just a matter of time before we embarked for Vietnam. Most of the Third Marine Division was already there, including Division Headquarters. Echo Battery would deploy as the artillery component of a fully integrated Battalion Landing Team, BLT 2/9. The infantry component was Second Battalion, Ninth Marines. We would be one of the last BLTs to train together and ship out as one homogenous battalion. We trained rigorously and played hard while we had the chance

After the maneuvers in the field we returned to garrison duty. Inspections and classroom work kept the troops busy while we packed and prepared logistically for our inevitable departure. At night we gorged on steaks and swilled margaritas in the Officer's Club. Frosty mugs of Budweiser were a dime, cigarettes $1.20 per carton, and at a quarter apiece for margaritas it was difficult not to get sideways. And sideways we went, into the fleshpots just outside the main gate, knowing our available leisure time would soon be eliminated. We were hearing rumors that Marines already in Vietnam were finding unexpected difficulty.

Jack Swallows and I discovered a couple of beautiful Okinawan girls who worked at the Post Exchange. We flirted with them each time we went to the PX.

Jack softly spoke to Mitchiko outrageous sweet-nothings. "Nasan, did you hear about the famous Okinawan love story?"

"No, I not," she giggled.

He grinned at her. "It is a Number One love story about how this beautiful young Okinawan princess who works in the PX falls in love with a very, very handsome Marine lieutenant and they live happily ever after."

Her eyes got big as saucers and she said, "Oh! Jacki-san, you just big snowman!"

The young women agreed to meet us for dinner, and afterward they invited us to follow them home. Local manners required us to remove our shoes at the front porch. Hours later when we left, Jack's shoes were missing. It was raining. And taxis were impossible to find at 0300. Jack hobbled back to the base in wet socks. My Bass Weejuns kept my feet dry and I giggled all the way home.

We decided we needed dependable, cheap transportation. A few evenings later we were in the Camp Sukiran Officer's Club enjoying Happy Hour and rolling dice for the drinks. A frazzled-looking young captain walked up to the bar next to us and ordered a double Dewars on the rocks. Several hours earlier he had gotten orders from Third Marine Division Headquarters to report for a flight departing from Kadena Air Base the following afternoon. He was to report to Division Intelligence in Danang for permanent duty. He was scurrying around settling his affairs and didn't know what to do about his car, an old, run-down 1951 Ford with hundreds of thousands of miles on the broken speedometer.

I quickly glanced at Jack, furrowed my brows, and smiled at the captain; it was time to get serious.

"May we take a peek at it, sir?"

He downed his glass of scotch and told us to follow him to the parking lot behind the club.

The Ford's original coat of black paint had been worn to a dull grey after many seasons exposed to the bright sun and the wetness of monsoons. It would have made a prized target for the live-fire bombing runs made by gunships on the practice range near the Kadena airbase. We went back to the bar and ordered another round of drinks.

"Cap'n, how much you want?"

"I just had the oil changed. She's good for several more years. I'll take $400."

"No disrespect, sir, but the car will need a lot of work just to keep running. God only knows how much dinero we'll have to put into the piece of crap. We'll give you fifty bucks."

"Lieutenant, you must be joking! I don't have time for tire kickers. I gotta get this and everything else done in the next few hours."

Jack Swallows leaned forward in a friendly manner, "We are the answer to one of your problems. With such short notice I'm sure you have several others. Have you straightened out your life insurance yet?"

"Captain," I joined in, "Have you completed a new will and taken precautions that your personal gear will be shipped to the correct address in the states?"

The captain jerked back in his bars stool. "Look, you guys, I'll take $150 for the car." He was fidgeting and motioned to the bartender he needed to settle up.

"No can do, Cap'n." I said.

He looked at Jack.

Jack stuck his hand in front of the captain's wet bar napkin and unclenched his fist. In it was $50.

The captain looked the other way, then grabbed the money, and tossed the keys to Jack.

"Draw up a bill of sale and I'll sign it. I'm in Room 19 in the BOQ."

This was before political correctness existed. The first thing I did was fasten a Dixie flag plate to the front bumper. We decided to go ahead and make it look as redneck as possible for a hoot. Pigs would fly before you would see that on any officer's car today. The automobile actually gave a pretty smooth drive. We parked it in the lot between the BOQ and the Officer's Club.

The last night before we moved out from our home in Camp Sukiran for the Vietnam deployment we hit the club hard. It was margarita night. Jack and I decided we had to say goodbye to our car. We invited some other junior officers to join us and we literally destroyed the car in

First Lieutenant Franklin Cox on Okinawa just before BLT 2/9 deployment to Republic of Vietnam.

its tracks. We smashed the windows and doors and headlights with baseball bats and lug wrenches. We ripped the seats apart and slashed the tires. We poured motor oil into every crevice inside and on top of the outer surface. Then we threw dirt inside and outside and poured feathers from pillows across the oily, sticky top for the final crowning glory.

After we had been in Vietnam for a few months, we were told the colonel commanding the Force Service Regiment on Okinawa was conducting an investigation into who had defiled his parking lot and caused an expensive cleanup by leaving the unsightly car in such hideous condition. Jack and I got a great laugh out of that and our response in unison was, "What the fuck are they going to do to us, send us to Vietnam?"

On Friday nights Marine junior officers visited the palatial Kadena U.S. Air Force Base Officers Club in Okinawa. The food was as delicious as found in exclusive country clubs back in the states, cuisine like fresh crab appetizers, marbled rib-eye steaks, Bananas Foster, and excellent Bordeaux. The Air Force brass lived like kings. They got upset when we broke in and danced with their Okinawan and round-eyed American schoolteacher girlfriends. They finally banished us forever when a Marine lieutenant drove his Harley through the front door and did a wheelie on the dance floor.

A few months later in Vietnam another lieutenant and I had the opportunity to head back to the rear for a few hours of stolen R&R at the Danang Air Force Officers Club. It was the only game in town; the Marine Corps didn't provide an Officers Club in the combat zone. We walked through the front door and were immediately turned away.

"Sorry, lieutenant, Marine Corps junior officers are not allowed in here anymore. Nothing personal, sir."

I took great pleasure in trying to guess what mischief some Marine lieutenant or captain had done to banish us. I'm sure his cohorts applauded whatever prank he pulled. It was just one more reason why Marines dismissed the Air Force as REMFs (rear echelon motherfuckers) dressed like Greyhound bus drivers.

Three times we had packed up everything and headed for Camp Hansen to marry up with our infantry battalion and "flap" to Nam. The Marine definition of "flap" is to "move out with chaos." Each time in the past had been a false start, so we stood down and returned to our base at Camp Sukiran 30 miles south.

In late June 1965 we got the word to move out once again. This time the deployment seemed inevitable. We said our goodbye to our Okinawan home and headed to Camp Hansen with all our goods, including the six 105mm howitzers we towed. That afternoon the whole 2/9 Battalion Landing Team was assembled in a large theater and the battalion commander addressed us. He told us a likely destination could be Pleiku where the Vietcong had mounted a number of recent attacks against American troops. He told us the Marine Corps was not keen on the idea; the place was nearly 100 miles inland, would be extremely difficult to resupply, and impossible for tanks and other heavy equipment to get to. Another option being mulled, he related, was the Hue/Phu Bai Marine Base 50 miles north of the Marine concentration in Danang. We were told it was the only place in the world where you can stand with the mud up to your waist while the sand blows in your face. Of course we would end up in neither place.

There were 20 of us from the battery attached to the infantry, including four Forward Observer teams, each led by a second lieutenant. I had the most time in service among the new lieutenants and was designated officer-in-charge of the artillery group. I was appointed the Artillery Liaison Officer. We were billeted in a dormitory vacated by a recently departed infantry unit. Everyone was on one-hour standby, just waiting for the order to board the trucks that would take us to White Beach where the U.S. Navy ships we would board lay at anchor.

Late one rainy evening I was called to a phone in the dorm's hall. A gruff voice identified himself as the battalion duty officer. Excitedly, he told he had just gotten a message from Ninth Marine Regimental Headquarters.

"Lieutenant Cox, get your people and move out. We've just received orders to deploy."

So the time has finally come, I thought. I slammed the receiver onto its black cradle and raced into the suite next door where the four Forward Observers were bunked.

Breathlessly I told them, "This is it, guys. I just got the word! You've got 30 minutes to get your gear and your men together. We're deploying now. Shake a leg. We have just been given the green light."

There was no reply or movement. They were all under their sheets. They stretched a little, sighed, and pulled the sheets even higher.

Second Lieutenant Bob Hamel said, "Bullshit, Cox, you're just fucking with us."

Jack Swallows added, "Yeah, Frank. It's not a funny joke. Go to sleep."

I screamed at them and told them I'd be back in 15 minutes; I was going to gather my gear. I informed them if they didn't want to be locked up in the brig at Fort Leavenworth they had best get out of their racks and get their shit together. I went to my room, made final preparations, and went back to the lieutenants' room. I walked in and was dumbfounded. They hadn't budged. I screamed again.

Suddenly a familiar gruff voice sounded from under the sheets where Jack Swallows bunked.

"Lieutenant Cox, get your people and move out. We've just received orders to deploy."

Then all four of them derisively screamed, "Flap. Flap!" The room erupted in peals of laughter. The only one not laughing was yours truly. I wanted to maim and butcher Jack. I walked towards Jack's bunk.

He said "No fair hitting a guy when he's on his back in bed."

They were laughing so hard they couldn't catch their breath. Only later would I be able to laugh and admit it was a spectacular practical joke.

Four months beforehand several battalions of U.S. Marines hit Danang's Red Beach on the South China Sea, the first American units to become engaged in combat in Asia since the Korean War. We watched it on TV in the BOQ at Quantico. We cheered, hoping it wouldn't end prematurely, hopefully not before the room full of new Marine lieutenants would get our chance to see the elephant and grab the medals like all the generations preceding us had.

Cocky, young, and wildly optimistic, we assumed it would be a marshmallow war ended quickly by the awesome power of the Corps unleashed against an unsophisticated, rag-tag enemy. Sure, there would be a few casualties, but none of us would be harmed. We had grown up in theaters watching so many Richard Widmark, John Wayne, and Robert Mitchum war movies we knew we would make our own films ... if only it would last a few more months.

Echo Battery held a beach party at the U.S. Navy Base at White Beach the afternoon before we sailed for Vietnam. Uncle Sam gave us a going-away party with beer, burgers, and competitive games on the beach. The enlisted troops really came after the lieutenants in the football game, but nobody was injured because the sand slowed down the Marines.

There were many more Marines than sailors aboard the troop-carrying ship. On the first day of the six-day voyage I overheard Colonel G.R. Sharnberg, the BLT commanding officer, give instructions to his sergeant major.

"Ralph, keep these troops busy as beavers all day long until their tongues are ready to drop at taps. Otherwise they will find a way to cause trouble with the naval personnel aboard. An idle Marine aboard ship is a time-bomb ticking toward detonation. The last thing I want to explain upstairs is why one of my Marines threw a sailor into the sea."

The only possible reply quickly came, "Aye-aye, sir!"

The wardroom is the officers' dining room in a warship. Etiquette traditionally considers three topics taboo — politics, religion, and sex. On amphibious U.S. Navy warships, Marine junior officers eat with their navy counterparts. Field grade officers of both services eat together at another sitting.

The ubiquitous Filipino stewards served our first meal in the stately dining room. Until 1973 they were allowed no other occupation in the U.S. Navy. The naval officers were scattered among the Marines around the large oval table. There was a big culture difference between the contingents on the ship. The Marines officers were gung-ho with a fierce, warrior mindset. They considered the amphibious naval officers as effete, weak leaders of sailors, stuck at the bottom of the pecking order in the U.S. Navy. The young naval officers instantly decided the Marines were ill-mannered louts and boors. Each Marine officer was pleased to find his own white starched cotton napkin encased in a brass ring with his name embossed upon it.

"Well, la-di-da!" a Marine brown bar said as he pulled the napkin from the ring. "Pretty swell."

A couple of bespectacled ensigns glanced at each other and rolled their eyes.

The midday meal was a Bibb lettuce salad with pears, a delicious spaghetti dish with Bolognese sauce, and strawberry shortcake for dessert. The food was delicious, the wardroom's wood was polished to a brilliant shine, and we quickly felt spoiled in the traditional officers mess setting.

When we returned to our assigned places around the oval table for the evening meal we unfurled our napkins from the rings. We didn't know the navy custom was to use the same napkins several days in a row. We found the napkins were the same ones we had used at lunch. But now our napkins were no longer white. We had bolted down our spaghetti and wiped our mouths, lips, and chins many times at the first meal. The napkins were the color of Campbell's tomato soup. Our naval officer brothers were seated in the wardroom, giving no notice to the soiled napkins. It was business as usual for them.

Second Lieutenant Larry Cimino had been a star on the wrestling team at Villanova University. He was a brand-new rifle platoon leader with Hotel Company. He slowly lifted his napkin and dangled it in front of himself for a few dramatic seconds, placed it in his lap, and turned to an ensign across the table.

"Is the cook trying to tell us that our first meal here was the exception? That from now on food will be lousy and taste like crap so why bother with clean napkins anyway?"

He slowly looked around the table and addressed the ensign nearest him. "Or maybe you guys decided we're just dumb-shit jarheads who wouldn't know the difference."

The ensign laughed nervously and dismissed the notion, "I'm sure indeed you'll find our culinary environment excellent."

Second Lieutenant Riley Grantham was a graduate of Oklahoma State University. His powerful thighs helped his prowess on the gridiron as a halfback for the Cowboys. He addressed a nearby ensign, pencil-necked with furiously blinking eyes behind thick glasses, while he twirled his red-stained napkin with his forefinger around and around.

"Pal, I've seen Indian and white-trash folks alike who wouldn't give something this dirty to their guests. Did the laundry already run out of soap on the first day?"

The Marines giggled and the squids (Marine jargon for the U.S. Navy personnel) looked at each other for reassurance.

The ensign replied, "It is traditional in our service to use the same table linen for several days in a row. Saves wear and tear in the laundry room. We at sea must be frugal in all our endeavors."

Grantham stood up and tapped his glass. "My fellow Marine officers, if you think these linens are messy you should get a load of their underwear after a week!"

We broke into waves of laughter. The ensigns blushed and never came back to join us in their splendid wardroom for the remainder of our voyage.

Fuck 'em, we laughed. *What were they gonna do to us, send us to Vietnam?*

We held strategy sessions from reveille to lights out. Our senior officers gave us great comfort with their professionalism and knowledge. We prayed we were ready.

The next morning we awoke in Danang harbor.

14

Second Battalion, Ninth Marines Headquarters

July 30, 1965 — Song Cau Do River

Lieutenant (JG) Scott Guy, USN, was the Naval Gunfire Officer attached to the 2/9 Fire Support Coordination Center. I was his artillery counterpart. First Lieutenant Wilson Ballard was the Close Air Support Liaison Officer. We realized we needed to bond together to make the machine work.

The second afternoon in-country I searched for First Lieutenant Jim Pulaski, the XO of Headquarters & Service Company, whose responsibilities included positioning the personnel and units in the large base camp. He had a sure-fire, confident ability to make decisions and give orders. He was a billboard-poster Marine officer, clean-jawed and bright-eyed. He was also a wily leader and when he saw opportunity he took it quickly.

"Jim, where should I erect my CP tent?"

He measured me for a few seconds. A CP tent was a luxury for the infantry. He was encountering a housing shortage for officers attached to headquarters and he was flat out of tents.

"Frank, I'll find room for your tent and place it very close to the operations center for your convenience on one condition."

"And that is...?"

He parried, "I'll find room for your tent if you find room for three of our officers."

I immediately accepted his offer and went to carry the good news to Guy, Ballard, and First Lieutenant Ralph Walsh, the weapons platoon leader, my new tentmates.

Scott Guy taught me how to play cribbage, an old U.S. Navy card game played to pass the time by sailors trapped aboard ships for weeks at a time.

"Fifteen two, 15 four, 15 six, 15 eight," he would chirp, on his way to another win. I rarely beat him but enjoyed the company. When we weren't playing cribbage I noticed Scott was busy at work scribbling in a black manual.

We had both served the 0600 to 1000 watch in the Fire Support Coordination Center. A few random harassing artillery rounds had been shot just before daylight to keep the enemy honest; after that the operations tent was inactive. It had been a night without incident for the four rifle companies operating out in the boonies. The dawn broke but you could still see the brilliant white-blue tiny fires of heat tablets warming-up C-ration breakfasts for Marines starting their arduous day. It was already miserably hot and a lot of the troops had their shirts off, gambling that none of the Colonel's officers would see them disobeying his order to wear shirts at all times and flak jackets when leaving the perimeter.

After our watch duty Scott and I walked in towels carrying bars of soap to the shower area. A fast-moving, grey USMC F-4 Phantom fighter-bomber streaked low in the sky just over our position, headed south, howling a mournful modulation. It was close enough to count the bombs on its underbelly; they looked like giant insect eggs.

"Pure sex," said Scott.

"Don't talk so sweet when we're going to the shower," I warned.

Pull the rope and water falls in a splash on you from an overhead 55-gallon barrel for a few seconds. Release the rope and the water stops. Lather up. Pull the rope for a few seconds to rinse off. It feels good when the sun hits you while you are still wet. Towel dry. Done. It was a luxury; Marines out in the boondocks went weeks at a time without showers.

We walked up the hard-scrabbled path to our tent in our clogs. It was 1030 but we were coated with sweat just from the walk back from the showers. Young Marines the color of mud were filling sandbags and hoeing out small trenches around their makeshift tents made from ponchos and shelter halves to divert the rainwater that fell every afternoon.

"You are the luckiest squid alive," I teased him.

"Why?"

"Listen, Scott. You and I both know there is not an officer in the entire U.S. Navy that wouldn't swap places with you to enjoy this." With a flourish I waved my arm in a full circle, showing the panorama of a grunt Marine battalion's base camp.

He stopped and stared. "Are all Marine officers idiots like you?"

"You betcha," I replied.

Back at the tent we tumbled upon our cots for a few hours of sleep. When I awoke from a sweat-soaked nap my roommate was jotting notes in his black manual.

"What are you working on?" I asked him.

The thermometer pointed to 98 degrees in the shade of the tent. The flaps were pinned up to allow the few currents of available heated breeze to slide in.

"A detailed factual exposé."

"If it's about all the chicks you've nailed, its not factual. If the count is more than one, the one you told me about, the nasty little pimple-faced slattern who wanted to start a Marxist cell at your college, the one no other guy would even look at, yeah, that one, then you are writing fiction."

"Typical jarhead, sophomoric humor," replied Scott. He was great to be around with his marvelous sense of humor. He was also very bright. He had graduated from Underwater Demolition School before UDT morphed into the U.S. Navy Seals. So he was also a tough customer. But he had nothing else to do since the CO was afraid to employ naval gunfire that might accidentally hurl an eight-inch shell into a nearby village, and poof, there goes the colonel's career.

"Actually I'm keeping a log. I'm fascinated by all these Marine fuckups and I can't wait to see if people back in the world will actually believe these misadventures happened."

Everybody knew it was truth; the incredible mistakes, one after another, became numbing, commonplace events that befell the greenhorn battalion from the first day it landed. We were wounding and killing each other at a much greater rate than the VC were. Our very own Marines had caused most of 2/9's casualties to date because of negligence and just plain old rotten luck.

He offered the log to me.

"Here. This is just from the past 10 days or so."

JULY 18—A radio operator with one of the rifle companies loses his notebook containing all radio frequencies and call signs for the battalion. It was assumed the classified information was compromised.

JULY 20—Three Marines were injured as a result of a friendly fragmentation grenade discharge. The accident is under investigation.

JULY 23—A Golf Company combat patrol supported by artillery was to commence at 1000, postponed at 1300, rescheduled for 1500, cancelled at 1600. No explanation during whole time period.

JULY 24—On a joint patrol friendly ARVN forces opened up on a Marine platoon from Golf Company by mistake. Result—three ARVN dead, one Marine WIA, and repercussions.

JULY 26—Hotel Company sentry hears noise in front of his position and tosses M-79 hand grenade. Result—one Marine WIA.

JULY 27—For days complaints about open, deep, unmarked trenches in the battalion base camp have flooded H & S Company, the unit responsible for secu-rity. Last night a Marine staff sergeant fell into an open trench right next to the Colonel's tent, dislocating his hip. Today the trenches are marked with white tape.

JULY 27—Six Marines in a sister battalion nearby are killed by lightning strikes.

JULY 28—An H & S Company Marine PFC throws a brick and acciden-tally hits another Marine, causing serious head trauma.

JULY 28—A Foxtrot Company Marine PFC is throwing his KA-Bar com-bat knife at a tree. It bounces off and sticks in the face of another Marine.

JULY 28—Another accidental discharge wounds a Marine. This is the third in three weeks. One of the incidents saw a Marine almost kill another while cleaning his M-14 rifle.

JULY 29—An H & S Company work party removes junior officers' tents in early morning and states larger ones will be erected in their place. Heavy rain falls around 1600, as it has for the previous four days, soaking cots and personal effects of the officers. At 1700 a working party arrives to erect the new tents.

I chuckled even though I was aware of most of the misadventures. Bad luck was everywhere and it was already spooking the troops. But that wasn't the main problem. It was the enemy.

Contact with the enemy began immediately after the battalion started operations. The first few days the contact was limited to incoming solitary sniper rounds and the discovery of mines and booby traps. On July 10, 1965, everything changed. That's when the rifle companies of 2/9 crossed south of Song Cau Do River into the Tactical Area of Responsibility (TAOR) assigned to the battalion to conduct operations to find and kill the enemy.

When the last Marine units finally left Quang Nam province six years later the objective was never fully accomplished. Despite all the resolve and will the Marine Corps could summon by fully applying its assets and firepower against the enemy, NVA regular troops and hardcore Vietcong, he was never vanquished. It was his home and he knew every foot of each rice paddy, every spider-hole position he could climb into and cover with natural camouflage and shoot from after Marines walked past, every tree in each dense thicket, and every entrance into the elaborate tunnel honeycomb beneath his ham-lets. He used the same hidden fighting holes he had used for centuries, includ-ing recent decades when he battled the Japanese Imperial Army and later defeated French Foreign Legion troops. He was a history major, Summa Cum Laude. We were too busy calling in medevac choppers for our grievously wounded to reflect on the past. Of the 14,838 U.S. Marines killed in Viet-nam 6,480 died in Quang Nam province alone. For six years Marine units suffered casualties in the same villages their predecessors had in the same brutal manner. It's hard to learn from mistakes when history is thrown out of the mix.

On the evening of July 11, Companies G and F engaged in firefights with Vietcong units. The first medevac for 2/9 occurred at 1859 in the Duong Son village complex. Contact was heavy until the Vietcong withdrew.

On July 12 Division Headquarters modified the strict rules of engagement for the first time. We would be allowed to destroy dwellings when fired upon. For the next several days the rifle companies received sporadic small arms fire, sniper fire, and 60mm mortar shelling while clearing the hamlets of the complex. Tunnel systems, fighting holes, pungi traps, and trench lines were found throughout the inhospitable village complex, which was over 2,000 meters in length and was comprised of three main villages separated by flooded rice paddies. Each day a rifle company swept through one of the villages on search-and-destroy missions while two other companies were positioned in blocking positions around the village's perimeter. And on most days a medical team was dispatched to provide supplies and assistances to the local orphanage and villagers. It was the Marine Corps production of "good cop — bad cop."

We begged the villagers for their cooperation from the very beginning. We insisted we meant them no harm. With their help we would drive the communist VC soldiers out of their villages, the Marines would go home, and everyone would live happily ever after.

On July 15 Companies F and G were preparing to sweep through Duong Son (1) when a friendly psychological warfare team passed through the village. Using blaring loud speakers the villagers were asked to please go to the schoolhouse to learn why the Marines were in their village. Next a platoon of South Vietnamese Army troops showed up. Approximately 250 men, women, and children attended. The 2/9 Battalion Executive Officer addressed the villagers through an interpreter and delivered the following message:

> The Vietnamese Government has asked us to leave our homes and families to come 9,000 miles to help you and your fight against the Vietcong. Before we can defend your village we must have both your help and assurance that Vietcong are not in your village and that we will not be shot in the back as we defend the village from the outside. To give us peace of mind, we would like your help in searching your homes and your lands to destroy Vietcong booby traps, punji traps, etc. We do not want to destroy your property or homes. We do not want to kill or injure anyone, so if one person from each house will go back to his house, we will begin the search. While the rest are waiting here, we will bring medicine and trained medical people to assist and advise you with your health and hygiene problems. In addition, I want to assure you that we will

repair the damage that we have done to the graves of your ancestors and to your rice paddies. If you are ready to begin and ready to help, we are ready to go and destroy the Vietcong devices. I want you to know that your own soldiers will conduct the actual search, and we are only here to protect and defend them during the search.

The villagers then gave assistance and showed some locations of tunnels and booby traps. Accordingly, the wisdom of Marine intelligence declared the event a roaring success. But soon the Marines would discover otherwise, for when the Marines left the village the enemy filtered back in. The people would succor their loved ones — their sons, husbands, brothers, and countrymen — who also happened to be the Vietcong, by providing nourishment, shelter, and most importantly, information.

The battalion began ringing up the first body counts of confirmed VC killed. A Marine scout-sniper team using an infrared scope recorded some of the first kills. Several VC snipers were shot while perched in trees. Continuous sniper fire and hidden booby traps began to systematically add to the toll of Marines casualties. The VC quickly became adroit at isolating officers as rich targets and wounded three platoon leaders in the first few days of contact.

Each night several of my FO's requested illumination rounds from our artillery during enemy probes of our infantry units. The permission couldn't be given from my position in the Fire Support Coordination Center because of the rigid Rules of Engagement. All artillery fire missions had to be approved by the supported infantry company, and then up the chain of command to Battalion, Regiment, and Third Marine Division Headquarters. Further approval had to be granted by South Vietnamese Armed Forces District Headquarters.

Reasons given for this complex system of fire coordination included that the area was heavily populated with "friendly" natives, that there were low-level air corridors throughout the area because of the close proximity of the Danang Air Base, that helicopter traffic had to be monitored, and that there was a lack of command, control, and communication with the South Vietnamese Armed Forces. Furthermore, helicopter medevac flights for adjacent units also caused fire missions to be interrupted. The result was often an interminable wait of over 30 minutes. By then, of course, the situation had changed and the fire missions were often fruitless. It was difficult to explain those rules to the men and officers who were engaged in an up-close-and-personal manner with the enemy and vitally needed suupporting fire immediately.

Vietcong forces opened up with mortars and heavy small arms fire on Companies F and G, who had surrounded Duong Son (1) on July 17. Second

Lieutenant Jack Swallows, attached with his FO team to Golf Company, called in several fire missions with high-explosive 105mm shells fired from our host battery, Echo 2/12. Finally the enemy broke contact and several weapons and many blood trails were found. Like the Marine Corps, Victor Charlie didn't leave his dead comrades on the battlefield. That night the enemy was back, aggressively attacking the rifle company. I heard Jack over the artillery radio network.

"Sunrise, Sunrise, this is Echo 3. Fire Mission! Over."

"This is Sunrise, send your mission Echo 3."

"VC with automatic weapons and mortars, coordinates 997678, request illumination, will adjust. Over."

The battery Fire Direction Center (FDC) acknowledged receipt of the mission. Normally illumination shells would be on the way within minutes, but not with the damnable Rules of Engagement in effect. No clearance came down from above approving the mission, creating an exasperating delay. Likely some field-grade staff officer in the rear was afraid an illumination round would set a hootch in the village on fire when it fell and he would be issued a career-wrecking letter of reprimand.

Jack's company continued to be hammered by hidden VC gunners. The Marines could hear drums beating and canteens rattling in the village. Dish pan clanging could be heard east of the position. The VC were on the move and communicating. The sounds in the dark were spooky.

Finally Jack yelled into his handset, "If you don't get that damned illumination out here real quick you can forget about your FO team." Finally the fire mission was aborted.

Meanwhile, just across the old north-south railroad bed, which once ran from Danang to Saigon, and had been stripped of its rails, lay the even larger village complex of Cam Ne, bristling with a large contingent of hardcore Vietcong. The complex of six villages lay northwest of the Duong Son complex. Cam Ne was separated from Duong Son at the closest point by no more than 300 yards. The dormant railway bed ran due south between the two complexes. While 2/9 was trying to eliminate opposition in Duong Son, the Cam Ne guerrillas with their fire were having great success hampering the Marine effort. It was impossible to deal with both complexes at once. There was a small force of South Vietnamese Popular Forces (PF) in Cam Ne. They were terribly ineffective, with poor leadership and morale. At one point the PF soldiers thought they saw some VC and shot by mistake into the Marine position in Duong Son. Marine riflemen returned fire. When the dust cleared one PF soldier was killed and three others were wounded.

The northern arc of the Cam Ne complex bordered the Song Cau Do

River, which provided ability for the VC to move troops and resupply by sampan and other small watercraft. The first time Marine LTV amphibian troop carriers crossed the river to interdict the VC river traffic three of the six tractors got stuck. During the attempt to free the LTVs the Marines suffered three heat casualties. The enemy had to be laughing at Marine mistakes. Third Marine Division headquarters saw the Cam Ne complex as a major obstacle, which would have to be dealt with in a special way.

Frustration swept through the battalion and 2/9 had only been in-country for two weeks. Even though in constant contact with the VC it was rare for the Marine riflemen to have a chance to isolate and gun down the enemy. Victor Charlie was wily and furtive. And when it was known there had been enemy kills, rarely were the bodies found. After contact the enemy just vanished, along with his dead comrades and most of his equipment. The frustration due to delays in approval of urgently needed air and artillery strikes was visceral. Anger swelled in the hearts of the Marine troopers and their officers in the rifle companies.

15

Cam Ne Burning

August 3, 1965 — Cam Ne Village Complex

In 1999, the New York University Department of Journalism solicited nominations for the Top 100 Works of Journalism in the United States in the 20th century. The Vietnam War garnered four entries, including a 1965 CBS Evening News report by correspondent Morley Safer involving U.S. Marines in Cam Ne village in South Vietnam.

"It's mesmerizing! Look how slowly the green rounds appear to be moving. It's almost lovely," Lieutenant (JG) Scott Guy, USN, said. He stood next to me as we looked from our battalion headquarters post high above the Song Cau Do River we knew was flowing in the dark somewhere below us, winding in sweeping turns through the valley, a flat plain of rice fields and villages filled with Vietcong fighters.

"Scott, the red rounds are not as pretty but just as deadly. And they are all moving at close to 3,000 feet per second, which is not slow. The laziness of their flight is an optical illusion. Like they say, you never hear the one that hits you, only the ones that pass by."

Golf Company, Second Battalion, Ninth Marines, was locked in a midnight firefight with a platoon of the National Liberation Front of South Vietnam and it was high drama from our vantage point, several hundred feet higher in elevation and a mile north of Cam Ne where the fighting was a nightly occurrence. The Marine fire was punctuated by red tracers, arranged every fifth round in magazines and belts of ammunition to help the shooters guide the fire in the night blackness. The VC used green tracers. When the tracer rounds hit something they bounded away crazily from the path the other rounds took while tracking toward targets like red and green bursts of water from a fire hose in the night. The noise of the rifle bursts reached us several seconds after we saw the colored streams of the rifle and machinegun fire, and we also heard the gut-rattling concussions of grenade explosions.

"Lovely, but is it not the last place you'd want to be?" he asked.

"Negative, Bob, the last place you want to be is where those Marines are going at first light tomorrow."

The Cam Ne village complex lay enclosed in a green paradise setting. Emerald rice fields fanned out in all directions from the stately palm trees that bordered the tree lines surrounding each village. The palm fronds rustled gently in the early morning breezes before the terrible heat stilled everything.

The almost impenetrable hedgerows that traced the outline perimeters of the six Cam Ne hamlets were filled with countless booby-trapped grenades. Just inside the tree lines were two-and-a-half-foot trench systems, bunkers, fighting holes, mines, tripwires ready to spring molten shrapnel from booby-trapped mortar shells, pungi traps with sharpened spikes poised to deeply stab unsuspecting riflemen, Malayan whips with nails and pointed bamboo spike-daggers ready to spring at Marines in most bends in village trails, and gates armed with hidden grenades with quick fuses. Almost all dwellings contained underground bunkers and firing positions. All those things were accoutrements of counterinsurgency warfare that even though painstakingly avoided would still claim thousands of Marine casualties in Quang Nam province before it was all over.

The worst thing was the enemy, the hardcore Vietcong fighter, committed to driving the Marines away. He would never quit, not in a million years. His motivation was unquestionable and the South Vietnamese populace adored him. He and his comrades waited in Cam Ne with Russian SKS and Chinese carbines, 60 and 82mm mortars, 57mm recoilless rifles, and machine guns to kill the Marines when they came close. As in all the other villages under Vietcong control (and they all were in the TAOR of the Second Battalion, Ninth Marines) each villager was required to dig three feet of tunnel each day. Miles of connected tunnel systems below the hamlets allowed the VC to enjoy a will-o'-the-wisp ability to face the enemy with violence and disappear when it became advantageous. You had to live there to know how to employ the tunnel systems; the peasants had been doing it for hundreds of years against many different enemies, and Victor Charlie lived there. The tunnels were not merely shelters; they were fighting bases capable of providing continuous support for troops. Even if a village was in American hands, the Vietcong beneath it in tunnels were still able to conduct offensive operations.

Upon approaching the Cam Ne complex every Marine patrol came under fire from VC snipers and infantry units consisting of close to 100 strong. The Marines encountered booby traps or mines every few yards. Marine casualties mounted while requests for artillery and air strikes were denied. After sev-

Marines with Third Tank Battalion observe the Cam Ne Village complex in late July 1965 as Marine infantrymen prepare to attack.

eral weeks of frustration and nine Marines killed in action, the battalion commander, Lieutenant Colonel G.R. Scharnberg, visited Third Marine Division Headquarters and made the case to loosen the rigid rules of engagement to allow supporting arms immediate clearance in support of a heavy Marine assault against the VC entrenched in Cam Ne.

He must have been a helluva salesman.

That evening the colonel paged all members of the Fire Support Coordination Center to the operations tent.

"Tomorrow we awake from the dead. All you liaison officers had best get your shit together because at 0600 in the morning we will unleash all the fury we possess at Cam Ne. It better go smooth," he warned.

It was the first time I'd ever seen him smile.

At 0600 promptly on the first day of August a flight of four Marine A-4D Skyhawks roared over our position and swooped down into the valley below us and attacked the fortified VC positions with 20mm cannon fire, sending grey geysers of smoke into the first beams of daylight. Scores of high-explosive cannon rounds exploded with sharp, cracking sounds faster than you can count from one to ten. Suddenly a swarm of several F-4B Phantoms appeared with the morning sun casting dull glows off their pewter-colored fuselages. We could see the signatures of red-glowing afterburners at work sending the jets into Cam Ne. The supersonic jets made shrieking runs, firing Zuni rockets into the middle of Cam Ne (1), (2), and (3), then soared in almost forty-five-degree vertical ascents with the strange mournful sounds only the Phantom makes before leveling off and coming again, this time streaking at fantastic speeds before rising again after hurtling 500-pound bombs into the target area.

"Holy shit!" Scott screamed in my ear.

We had a fantastic vantage point on the high ground above the river and Cam Ne. We could see the brilliant quick red flashes and hear the deep blasts when the bombs exploded.

"The Big Dogs in the rear have turned us loose!" I yelled back.

Our radio operators were dancing little jigs and howling, "That's the way to deal with those motherfuckers!"

Smoke from the fires of burning hedgerows and hooches mingled with the smoke caused by the explosions of Marine armament and covered the area under a black-grey umbrella shroud.

As the three Marine rifle companies of 2/9 left the Line of Departure to assault Cam Ne the artillery 105mm howitzers of Echo Battery, Twelfth Marines, delivered fire missions of high explosive shells mixed with white phosphorous shells. The Echo Battery artillery Forward Observers embedded with the rifle companies brought in over 500 rounds during the infantry assault that was followed by a find-and-kill sweep.

The troopers on the hill roared after each exploding artillery salvo like madmen at a bullfight.

Marine M-48 tanks with 90mm direct fire guns joined in to blast enemy strongholds. Marine grunt units locked in with the enemy while Marine 81mm mortars marked targets for air strikes, adding more volume of fire to what already was an orgasm of Marine firepower.

Despite the short-term success of the Marine assault, which killed a record number of confirmed VC by the battalion to that date, things did not improve in Cam Ne.

On August 3, 1965, Morley Safer, an award-winning CBS TV war reporter, accompanied Delta Company, First Battalion, Ninth Marines, a unit that had been added to the mix, for another major foray into Cam Ne. According to Safer's filmed report the Marines came under sniper fire and lost their discipline in front of the camera, creating the first divisive incident of the Vietnam War. The report on TV in America during dinnertime showed the Marines burning down dwellings in Cam Ne with Zippo lighters and flame-throwers.

Safer reported, "Shortly after the sniper fire, one officer told me he had orders to go in and level the strings of hamlets that surrounded Cam Ne village. And all around the common paddy fields [camera focuses on a roof being lit by a flamethrower] a ring of fire. One hundred and fifty homes were leveled in retaliations for a burst of gunfire. In Vietnam, like everywhere else in Asia, property, a home, is everything. A man lives with his family on ancestral land. His parents are buried nearby."

Safer did not present the Marine Corps account of the Cam Ne televised incident. Marine intelligence revealed a hardcore VC company of approximately 100 men initiated contact with Delta Company with intense fire. The fierce battle lasted over five hours. Most of the structures were burned by Marine 3.5-inch rocket fire directed toward hostile fire from the huts. Others were destroyed by flamethrowers or grenade action used to neutralize VC positions.

The televised rebroadcast of the Cam Ne events created an irreparable rift between the press and the American military leadership in Vietnam that smoldered for the rest of the war. To make matters worse for the public relations–conscious U.S. Marine Corps, the cover of *Time* magazine featured a picture of a young Marine rifleman torching the roof of a Cam Ne thatched roof with a Zippo lighter.

It was a terribly bad-luck month gone wrong for the battalion; strange events that could never have been forecast happened so often that the unbelievable became believable.

At the start of the Cam Ne operation the battalion CO rode into battle in an M-48 tank that promptly got stuck in marshy lowland. He got out and proceeded on foot.

In the initial assault LTV troop amphibious tractors tore up rice paddies, angering the peasants the Marines had been sent to help (financial restitution became commonplace). Mines destroyed some of the LTVs, some just broke down, others got stuck in the mud and rice paddies, and a few sank in the tidal rivers. Marine commanders finally decided the LTVs could not be counted on in that kind of terrain.

In just over a three-day period, a series of bad-karma events befell the leathernecks of 2/9.

Hotel Company received incoming rifle fire from nearby Golf Company.

A speeding Marine 6×6 truck struck a Vietnamese peasant and sped off, prompting a "hit and run" investigation.

Hotel Company got stuck in a rice paddy at night. "Cannot read map," was the explanation from one of the officers.

VC snipers killed two young riflemen.

A defective 105mm howitzer round fired by Echo Battery fell short into Hotel Company, ironically killing a member of the artillery FO team and wounding eight other Marines. "Thank God for flak jackets," the company commander added in his radio message about the event.

Lance Corporal Walter Strother with Foxtrot Company was shot through his left arm and the round exited his back, caused by an accidental discharge by another Marine's rifle.

PFC Richard C. Toll with Echo Company was accidentally shot and killed by another Marine in the fire team who dropped his rifle on a run to a water hole.

A Marine tried to replace the safety on a trip flare and the grenade ignited, causing second degree burns to his face, hand, and arm.

The battalion was forced to change all radio frequencies when an Asian voice repeated over and over across the net, "What's your name? I want to talk to you. I want to fuck you."

A Marine PFC with Echo Company threw a grenade at a suspicious noise just outside his position at night. It did not explode. The next morning he went with a group to find the dud. He picked it up and it blew off his right hand.

A rifle company commander and three riflemen crossed the Song Yen Ne River, just northeast of Cam Ne (3), in a small boat borrowed from the village chief. A Marine accidentally dropped his M-14 into the river under sniper fire. The small boat sank during efforts to retrieve the rifle. The village chief demanded 3,000 piasters in Vietnamese currency. The next day the M-14 was not found in the 20-foot-deep river with a swift current during search efforts. An investigation came to no conclusion.

Mortar attacks targeting Marine positions were launched from inside the Cam Ne complex, including a successful coordinated night attack with VC sappers against the nearby Marine tank park. Marine activity became feverish to pacify Cam Ne as 2/9 casualties accelerated in its first month in Vietnam. In one two-day period 2/9 took more than 45 casualties from snipers and booby traps and recorded not one official VC KIA.

On August 31 several episodes typified the month's history. At 1225 a Vietcong sniper killed an 18-year-old lance corporal with Golf Company with a head shot. Other Marines fired at the sniper and saw his body fall out of the tree. The sniper's body was not found after a search. At 1535 two Marines were badly wounded by a booby trap while carrying the dead lance corporal's body back to the company commander's position. Later two HU-1E gunships fired rockets in support of a patrol from Foxtrot Company. Seven VC were seen to fall by the helicopter crew chief during the Huey attack.

No bodies were found. The choppers were fired on from five different positions.

The Marine riflemen became entranced with the bad luck and soon believed it was meant to be. Our sister battalion, First Battalion, Ninth Marines, wandered resignedly into the same traps so repeatedly she became known as the "Walking Dead."

Reaction to the inflammatory CBS Cam Ne report was instant and powerful. The CBS switchboard lit up like a Christmas tree with calls critical of the negative portrayal of the Marines. Early in the morning after the film was broadcast, CBS President Frank Stanton was awakened by the telephone

"Frank, are you trying to fuck me?" yelled a voice.

"Who is this?" asked the president of CBS.

"Frank, this is your president," answered Lyndon Johnson, "and yesterday your boys shat on the American flag."

16

The Loser

I could not look on death, which being known,
Men led me to him, blindfold and alone.
                    —"The Coward," Rudyard Kipling

September 2, 1965 — Second Battalion, Ninth Marine Headquarters

The four Marine rifle companies in 2/9's domain, Companies E, F, G and H, continued to seek and find trouble from Victor Charlie on a daily basis. After Cam Ne, the ubiquitous enemy contact occurred against smaller groups of guerrillas. The artillery Forward Observers with the rifle companies continued to actively request artillery support. The first stage of approval took place in the operations shop of the battalion's Command Post. Captain Marvin Sterne was the S-3, the battalion operations chief of 2/9, one of the most heralded Marine infantry battalions in the glorious history of the Corps. Its nickname was "Hell in a Helmet."

Captain Sterne had excellent credentials. The son of a Marine general, he had earned a regular commission in the Corps after graduating from elite Amherst College. His mother's family tree consisted of generations of educated, privileged WASPs. He was in line for promotion to major.

The captain was also 40 pounds overweight (it was rare indeed to encounter a fat Marine in Vietnam), terribly moody in the darkest of ways, petulant, incapable of making decisions under fire, which is the prime task for the head of operations of a Marine infantry battalion, and an incomparable bully. Fat spilled from his cheekbones to his pelvis to his calves. The fact that he was 6-feet-3 inches in height didn't in the least mitigate his corpulent appearance. He had a florid, fresh-meat tinge to his complexion, and his entire visage was topped off by an out-of-a-bottle, canary-yellow buzz-cut.

If you were unlucky enough to be involved in conversation with him you noticed that his left eye wound to the left as his right eye remained in its normal gaze locked in your direction. The whole thing produced a gargoyle effect; you felt creepy and wanted to break any eye contact, but of course you could not. I had been attached to Sterne's shop since its arrival in Vietnam. I was the Artillery Liaison Officer — the link between the artillery and the infantry. I had noticed when the shit hit the fan and it was time for command decisions the good captain was prone to panic attacks.

The young Marine enlisted personnel in the S-3 shop, radio operators, jeep drivers, and clerks (but by definition all riflemen), could not help but notice he rarely ventured into the field to personally investigate the situation. He remained rooted in the rear CP snapping at PFCs and sending Lance Corporals trotting off on constant errands to insure his creature comforts. They made bets with each other as to how long he would remain in the rear, out of the danger zone where the rifle companies operated. It was painful to see a Marine officer earn the disrespect of enlisted men under his command, but Captain Sterne quickly became adept at it. His incompetence was matched by his repulsiveness and he was reviled by the young enlisted men.

He would race to the chow tent for lunch at first call, not heeding the age-old unwritten Marine tradition: enlisted men eat first. His knife and fork ripped the meat *du jour* apart, he engulfed platters of reconstituted mashed potatoes, and beware if you were between him and the occasional ice cream bucket in the headquarters mess tent. He voraciously gorged and grazed, hinging and unhinging his jaws with his mouth open, slowly licking his fingers one at a time between bites. Afterward, drops, driblets, and crumbs garnished his "Old Corps" herringbone utility shirt. Finally, suitably stuffed, he rewarded his morning efforts with an early afternoon siesta as the Asian heat poured ultraviolet rays onto his tent in which he sweated and snored on his cot. Both his underlings and his peers loathed him.

Suddenly, early in the afternoon of September 2, 1965, a cry for artillery support came over the radio net, jolting everyone in the sultry bath of sweltering heat inside the vast operations tent to full attention. Golf Company had strolled into a cauldron of Vietcong fury and was pinned down near the Cam Ne village complex, cut off from avenues of escape. I heard my friend Second Lieutenant Jack Swallows, the Golf Forward Observer, deliberately communicate his fire mission: "Coordinates 974692, VC with automatic weapons, friendly WIAs, will adjust, over."

A perfect scenario would put the howitzer shells Jack needed to help his Marines survive on target within several minutes.

But as the natives throughout Asia say, "Nebber hoppen."

The rules of engagement were in effect, which meant the artillery request had to be approved up the chain of command before the cannons could deliver their artillery shells. The reason for the stringent burden of proof to get permission for artillery was to insure no friendlies in populated areas were accidentally hit by American fire. This is when the term "collateral damage" crept into the lexicon of mainstream America. The Vietcong was a savvy student and actually calculated for the artillery delay into his timeline.

In this case Jack had called fire upon an area not connected with any village, as a quick map inspection revealed, so no friendlies were in the neighborhood. Seconds turned to minutes. Vietcong fire was pouring into Golf Company, its troops seeking cover behind rice paddy dikes alive with black ants.

Jack repeated with insistence, "Will adjust, over!"

The III Marine Amphibious Force Headquarters issued a Standard Operating Procedure (SOP) that ordained initial clearance had to be given by the parent battalion's operations center. In this case it was Captain Sterne's shop. He was not on duty and his substitute would not make a decision. I raced to the large tactical map and pointed to the exact coordinates Swallows had described. His target was not near a village. Still, no approval came.

The radio buckled with the demands for artillery from Golf Company's commanding officer.

"Where is the fucking artillery?" he screamed into his radio.

No answer came. The S-3 officer in charge was staring at the huge map as if it contained an answer to the whole enigma, which it did, but he would not pull the trigger. He kept wetting his lips as his eyes shifted from the radio blaring cries for help to the map and back to the radio.

Young Marines in the tent manning nearby radios muttered barely audible phrases, "Them are Marines, goddamnit. Give 'em the arty. What the fuck are you waiting for?"

We could hear mortar rounds impacting in the valley below us, in the vicinity of Golf Company. I decided to end the stalemate, even though I did not have legal authority. I based my decision on a means-to-the-end rationalization.

I grabbed the S-3 radio operator's handset, got on the artillery net, and granted permission to Echo Battery's Fire Direction Center to shoot the fire mission. Jack adjusted the first Marine howitzer shells slightly, and then ordered the kitchen sink. After that the enemy broke contact. The fight was over.

Within seconds Captain Sterne roared into the operations center and discovered it was I who had granted permission to fire. He stared at me, his cheeks billowing, turning scarlet with anxiety; you could see the wheels in his mind turning, "*What will Regiment think? What will Division think?*" he wondered. Could this incident be the one that drove a stake into his career ambitions?

"Lieutenant Cox, how could you have given permission? You don't have the authority. Did the arty hurt any friendlies?"

"Oh, it wasn't hard, sir. The situation required me to do so since no decision appeared to be coming from your people."

The troops were enthralled and some were stifling giggles. The captain's eye machinery was in meltdown mode as his panic, welling up in him, became visible.

I said, "Sir, Golf Company was vulnerable. We were taking casualties. The artillery was ready. Your company commander was screaming for it. My FO has been 100 percent accurate. We've had enough fucking Marines die for no reason. It seemed like a good idea at the time."

That final sentence must have done it. Sterne became enraged, spittle flecks fell to the deck as he shouted, "You are hereby relieved, Lieutenant Cox. You are confined to your quarters until you receive notice otherwise." He turned to his first sergeant, "Top, please escort Mister Cox to his tent."

On the way to my tent the senior enlisted Marine gave me a firm handshake and congratulated me.

"You gave him the truth, sir."

"Hell, Top," I said, repeating the refrain heard from every young enlisted PFC in Vietnam, "I wasn't going to make a career out of this green motherfucker anyway."

For two full days I lived a life of leisure, playing cribbage with my tentmate Scott Guy, the Naval Gunfire Liaison Officer. The Statler Brothers serenaded our tournament via Radio Vietnam. They were counting flowers on the wall while playing solitaire with a deck of fifty-one. Scott was dominating me so much I asked him if our deck only had fifty-one cards.

"The Colonel asks that you report, sir." The commanding officer of Second Battalion, Twelfth Marines, my artillery parent unit, had sent his runner for me.

I stood up, flipped my cards over, and informed Bob, "I win, squid!"

He protested, "Bullshit!"

I shuffled across the expanse of the battalion base camp. Past the Marines filling sandbags in the thermal heat, north of 100 degrees. Past the Headquarters Company command post where the gunny sergeant was instructing his charges, who would soon assume the night vigil defensive outposts. Past the burning latrine fire sluicing sulfurous clouds, remnants of human waste. The Corps burned its shit in many ways.

"Lieutenant Cox reporting as ordered, sir," I spoke as I rapped on the colonel's command post bamboo door.

"Enter," replied Lieutenant Colonel Randolph L. Knockel, my boss. He sat at a makeshift desk set upon pallets that had once borne cases of C-rations. Several neat piles of correspondence and maps lay upon his orderly desktop. Tightly cut grey hair clasped his head. He gestured politely to a chair next to his desk. He was always patient, always listening, always a true Marine officer and gentlemen. The colonel had met the challenge in Korea as an FO and responded brilliantly. He led by example and intelligence. His cannons put the steel on target, on request, with great accuracy.

"Frank," he started, "looks like we've got a little problem."

"Yes, sir."

"I received a call today from the 2/9 S-3 shop asking for an artillery liaison officer."

"Yes, sir."

"I informed Captain Sterne he already has one." His eyes twinkled.

"I understand, sir. Thanks for the vote of confidence."

"That will be all, Frank."

I stood, thanked him, and was making my exit when he added, "Lieutenant, it would behoove you to lay low for awhile."

"Yes, sir," I responded.

I made straight for the 2/9 S-3 tent. Sterne was assessing his maps, listening to the situation reports radioed in by his rifle companies. The young Marines in the tent stood and smiled. It was business as usual.

Two months later the list of officers in the Marine Corps who had advanced from captain to major was released. Sterne's name was not among his peers. His career was shot. He was dead meat, a regular officer having been passed over for advancement by the clairvoyant wisdom of Headquarters Marine Corps while his peers moved up the ladder. He was relieved in late November and replaced by Major Archibald Peay, who in two weeks rectified the deferred maintenance caused by Sterne. The Corps usually gets it right with its leaders.

17

Disaster

October 16, 1965 — Combat Patrol Radio Report — West of Danang Airbase

Part One — The Basic School —
Quantico, Virginia — December 6, 1964

Captain Brewster K. Clark pointed to a tactical map next to the podium. "Common sense and constant awareness are the infantry officer's best companions," he said. He was in heavy camouflage and into his role as counterinsurgency instructor. He had just returned from a stint in Vietnam as an advisor attached to an ARVN unit. We could tell he knew volumes about stealth, concealment, and death. The classroom was filled with over 250 newly commissioned Marine second lieutenants in my Basic School Class (TBS 2/65). The green officers, who soon would be sent to Fleet Marine Force units as platoon leaders and forward observers, were fed a steady dose of instruction on the art of combat patrols. Within a year or so over 30 percent of us would have faced enemy fire as the guerrilla war magnified. The captain got our attention the first day of class when Marines dressed in Vietcong black pajamas sprang from behind the curtains and opened fire on us with blank ammo.

"Gentlemen, you must be constantly vigilant. Rule one: secure your position! Err on the side of caution. Become aggressive only when you are locked in battle with the enemy. Then destroy him quickly," he advised.

Second Lieutenant Felix Lincoln, from Belleville, Illinois, sat two seats to my right. We were less than two months away from graduation. We were undergoing the traditional six-month course new Marine Corps officers undergo after being commissioned. The Basic School curriculum fine-tunes officers, gentlemen, and infantry combat leaders.

Early into one of Captain Clark's final classes I noticed Lincoln's head slowly bow, then spring up immediately. Minutes later I glanced to my right again. His eyes were glazed, his lashes slowly closed, his eyelids flickered one more time, then his head drooped as he slid down into slumber.

Part Two — Danang Airfield, Republic of Vietnam — October 16, 1965

In late September 1965, 2/9 was awarded an early Christmas present. We moved back to the sprawling Danang Air Base to replace 3/9 as the Air Base Defense Battalion. U.S. Marine and Air Force warplanes were stationed there to support the ground troops in the countryside fighting the Vietcong and make launches up north to attack North Vietnamese vital ports and factories. Because of previous successful attacks against the airbase by Vietcong soldiers and sappers, U.S. Marines had originally been landed in March 1965 to provide security for the base.

It was softer duty for the battalion after the previous rugged several months down south in the dangerous Cam Ne/Duong Son territory. The four rifle companies stood guard duty and manned listening posts in the night while running patrols just outside the perimeter in the daytime. The enemy contact was minimal and the troops had to pinch themselves when they were given liberty to make beer runs and hit the bars in the local ville called "Dogpatch." After 10 brutal weeks of operations in the bellicose area south of the giant air complex, the battalion was relaxing in a pleasant space. Hot chow was plentiful, the paradise of China Beach was just down the way, and willowy, attentive young women doled out pleasure in the seamy slums outside the base. It would be the easiest duty we would see and we knew it. The living was easy for those of us in the operations shop. We stood leisurely watches in the nerve center and monitored situations that could possibly affect the battalion's defense of the airbase.

In the early afternoon of October 16, 1965, country singer Bobby Bare was moaning on Armed Forces Vietnam radio about his tribulations in Detroit and how he just wanted to go back home.

It had been a nice nap in the jumbo GP tent I shared with five other junior officers. From the top of the tent hung parachute cloth, trapping some of the blistering Asian heat above it. It shimmered as shrieking F4-B Phantoms ignited afterburners rolling past us on takeoff down the runway 50 yards in front of our tent, metal hell strapped under their wings, presents for our ubiquitous home-grown enemy. Snores whistled from two other lieutenants asleep on sweat-soaked cots after pulling their watches. I opened the screen door and headed for my 1400 watch in the battalion S-3 operations tent, the life-support system for the infantry companies. Inside the S-3 shop background noises of communication warped together — intermittent pops, hissing, steady static, and dull situation reports from units in the field related in monotones.

An oversized map straddled one side of the op center, graphically showing the current position of each Marine unit in I-Corps. Our PRC-25 radios monitored all other battalions' networks, gathering intelligence and providing backup information.

Division intelligence tried to put the fear in us, continually predicting a whole-scale VC attack on the airbase. The III Marine Amphibious Force commanding general, Lewis W. Walt, issued a personal warning to Marines of Third Battalion, Third Marines, on a visit to Hill 22, several miles southwest of the airbase in December 1965.

"Men, our intelligence estimates there are 10,000 Vietcong troops within a one-day march of the Danang airbase and that they intend to attack the airfield soon. If they do they will come right through your area of operation and it will be the job of you Marines to stop them. Have a Merry Christmas."

After a while we dismissed the warnings as implausible. Even the fearless Vietcong wouldn't risk a massive frontal assault upon such a heavily defended base. Nonetheless, 24-hour vigilance was required of the Marines manning the perimeter and patrolling the villages adjacent to the airfield. At a minimum you could always count on Victor Charlie to probe and snipe and chip away while planning bigger mayhem.

The monotonous situation reports coming into the communication center were suddenly interrupted. A platoon from Third Battalion, First Marines, several miles west of us was being torn to shreds. Helplessly we stared at the radio, hearing the calls for reinforcements, for fire support, for anything. Muffled sounds of battle could be heard when the platoon leader's radio operator keyed his handset. Spellbound, examining the map, I soon learned the platoon leader was Second Lieutenant Felix Lincoln.

It was a routine combat patrol in the early afternoon. Just a week prior, another 3/1 unit had swept the same area and encountered no contact. Contact had been light for several days in the western Danang Marine TAOR. Marine intelligence sources assumed the Vietcong were probably massing in the mountains to the west, preparing for the soon-approaching monsoons when our air power would be neutralized by diminished visibility. The heavy rains would mercifully drop temperatures but present new challenges, including creature discomfitures and tactical dilemmas.

The platoon had come upon a large open field. At the other end was a thick tree line some 200 yards away. The field was about 100 yards wide, a near-perfect rectangle. On each side dense hedgerows created a border up the length of the field stretching all the way to the far tree line.

Lincoln motioned to the first squad leader to take a direct route, angling toward the corner where the far hedgerow met the tree line. The platoon advanced across the flat field in one long column, 36 Marines, each following the footsteps of the man in front. There was no flank security put out by the lieutenant. There is speculation that Lincoln gave an order to his platoon sergeant to establish flank security and the order was ignored. Rumors insist the noncommissioned officer often second-guessed Lincoln. In any case there was no cover available on the field. The only things on the hard-scrabbled earth were ankle-high stubbles of old crops, bending in the gentle, mid-afternoon breeze.

The point man was within 20 yards of the far corner of the field when SKS carbine rounds lifted him into the air. An accurate, devastating cone of high-velocity rifle fire raked the platoon from two right angles. The crossfire was precisely interlocked and the ambush had been rehearsed repeatedly by the Vietcong to inflict maximum havoc. The platoon leader had directed his Marines into a perfect "L"-shaped ambush. Rocket-propelled grenades tore into the platoon just as landmines with thousands of shards of blazing metal were command-detonated by the VC infantrymen, stunned even themselves by the damage they were inflicting so quickly.

Back at our op center at the airbase we felt the explosions viscerally ourselves, coming to us straight from Lincoln's radio. The transmissions bore unrealistic reality — we weren't there but we experienced it real-time, like violence junkies who get off on live police radio bands.

A clerk-typist asked the battalion intelligence officer, "Lieutenant Pitt, why hasn't he requested any airstrikes or arty support?"

"There wasn't enough time."

A radio operator asked, "Are we sending a reaction force?"

"Yeah, but they won't get there in time to be of any help and they'll probably get hit while they're at it so they better watch it," answered Pitt.

It was over in minutes, an unredeemable situation, the Marines who lived to talk played dead as the enemy swarmed through the platoon's position. Lincoln had his radio handset in his hand. We could hear him breathing irregularly over the radio, suffering from wounds. The last thing we heard was the report from Lincoln's Colt .45 pistol, sending a round into his skull, fired by the VC soldier who had ripped it from the lieutenant's grip.

The Lincoln saga became part of the curriculum at Marine Corps Schools. Nonetheless, for many years after, Marines died in the same zipcode, repeatedly ambushed. We learned from our mistakes, but Victor Charlie would mutate. He had a lot of different ways to kill.

18

Gooks

Danang City — Christmas Eve, 1965

I had a jeep, but not because I needed one. The official Table of Equipment provided one for my job. I was the Artillery Liaison Officer; therefore I had one at my disposal. It was irrelevant that if I put it in gear and moved 200 yards in most directions from the relative safety of Echo Battery's position the vehicle would become ensnared in jungle or mired in the water buffalo dung and swampy mud of a cultivated rice paddy. Actually the rice paddies in I-Corps were like the eighth sea or the sixth ocean — they were the main mix — water and human labor and nature working together. The other 10 percent of the steamy terrain consisted of villages protected by the thickest of jungled tree lines. They formed an archipelago in the vast paddy-marsh that stretched from the South China Sea to the Annamese Cordillera, often called the Central Highlands. You never wanted to be in either the villages or the mountains, the result was the same, choose your pleasure, an NVA well-rehearsed ambush in the mountains, instant unsuspected incoming, or a miniscule trip wire in a tree line thick with primordial vegetation, so hard to see. If you accidentally brushed against the trip wire the personal carnage from a booby-trapped grenade could be as destructive as a B-52 strike on your position.

No, the jeep had an infinitesimal easement, an ex-railroad bed, the rails long gone, pilfered by the Vietcong for more important things. The road went north for five miles to Danang City or south to certain doom.

It was Christmas Eve 1965 and the Roman Catholic Cardinal from New York, Francis Cardinal Spellman, "The American Pope," was preparing to celebrate Mass at the Second Battalion, Ninth Marines, base camp. A few days earlier two of my junior officer pals and I set up plans to take the jeep to Danang and treat ourselves to an afternoon of liberty as a special Christmas present. When the other lieutenants showed up we piled into the vehicle and its tires took hold in the muddy battery area adjacent to 2/9. We were excited to steal a few hours of recess from the war.

Lance Corporal Randolph Cassidy, my radio operator and occasional driver, was at the wheel when he involuntarily jammed the brake pedal hard, facing a dilemma, at a crossroad. Boston Irish-Catholic and transfixed by the scene, he pointed to the large field to the right of the road where hundreds of Marines had assembled for the Magic Show. Already the Cardinal himself could be seen with his crimson hat, making his way to the raised makeshift altar. Sweeney's eyes looked at the religious scene, then to me, then up the road straight ahead to Danang.

"Which way, sir?" the 19-year-old Marine begged.

I answered, "To the party, Randy!"

He pressed his right foot hard against the accelerator, jolting us toward Danang. The sun's rays blistered into our necks. It had been almost cool the previous few nights, but today the thermometer would bubble again.

The population thickened as we neared the city, its numbers swollen by thousands of refugees fleeing the countryside. The aroma of sun-dried fish heads hung over the river. Peasant mothers scrubbed the clothes of their children against the rocks on the bank. The downtown streets were crammed with old cars and new motorcycles, with chaos and carbon monoxide. An occasional tank would lumber past, its metal treads grinding up the remnants of the street, spewing diesel fumes and unbearable decibels in its wake. Tiny specks of dust fell, framed by afternoon sunlight streaming between large branches on century-old trees. Our khakis were already sweat-streaked.

We grabbed an outside table on a sidewalk adjacent to a main intersection. I held up three fingers and the waiter brought us each a lukewarm bottle of "33," the strong Vietnamese beer.

Beggar children swarmed around us, their deep brown eyes hollowed out with desperation, crying for cigarettes. Old men with terrible wounds from earlier wars limped past. Carmelite nuns with brown scapulars steered children to a library. Young, honey-brown bar girls in red miniskirts walked to work with quick, short steps, their thighs bound by the tightness of their skirts.

More beers came. Heat caromed off the sun-torched pavement, spreading the fragrance of the urine-splattered gutters.

We saw street freaks, ARVN soldiers with jelly spines holding hands, black-market peddlers of every commodity, corpulent swine-faced American civilian workers, American Military Police smacking night sticks into their palms, and U.S. sailors off their ships for a few hours of liberty. The only people that looked our way were the swabbies with their white bell-bottomed trousers, tossing glares at us.

Black-toothed women heated coals in a nearby alley, cooking rice, and the camphor smoke curled in the still air like incense at High Mass. Children stooped and defecated just steps from the fire.

We switched to whiskey and ginger ale.

The cycle driver approached our table in dirty white pajamas, smiling conspiratorially. Immediately the image of an age-old Asian pimp scene in a grade-B movie jumped to mind.

"Hey you numba one wootenant maline, you want boom-boom?" he asked. You could bet we had already planned on that part of the afternoon's entertainment.

He claimed to know the most beautiful young women, some of whom he said, "Mebbe virgin."

We got a big kick out of that one

"Mebbe fifteen dollah, wootenant," he volunteered at his spiel's end.

"Mebbe we only pay $10, no more," said one of my buddies.

The Vietnamese man wiped the sweat from his face with the back of his hand.

He smiled and said, "That okay." He added that for a small stipend he could have us there in minutes.

"Mebbe you take us to scivvie house now!" I ordered.

We ordered drinks to go and each of us hopped into our own cycle-carriage. The drivers' steel-muscled legs pumped furiously, hurling us down the streets, racing each other, cutting the angles off intersections. We went right down the middle of the streets, encouraging the pedicab drivers to race each other while whooping at Vietnamese peasants scrambling out of our way. We were never good with the hearts and minds theme anyway. The searing sun sent feral cats under shadows cast by bonsai trees. Just as well, I thought. We'd heard the gooks would eat anything alive with a hint of muscle. Protein replenishment is hard to find in a third-world zone.

Ten minutes later we stopped at the door of a concrete hovel, old and poorly maintained like the rest of the nearby structures. Pigeons scratched the grassless dirt of the yard strewn with clumps of wet wastepaper and torn Styrofoam. An almost empty old tin bucket of brackish water with mosquitoes scuttling up its side leaned against the side of the house. The driver rapped on the door. An old Vietnamese woman cracked the door open and sized us up, then flung the door open with a flourish and a curtsy. Maybe she learned the body language from French actresses when the French Republic ruled Southeast Asia. Three young females entered the small front room, one for each of us. In seconds negotiations were concluded. Mine grabbed my hand, brushed a thin curtain aside, and led me down a dark corridor through a large room to a corner cubicle with a small smudged window. Yellow soiled sheets separated the cubicles. I heard muffled moans; the room had other unseen tenants.

Suddenly I heard the unmistakable rebuke of an upset young woman. One of my buddies had done something to send her into a tirade.

"You no scivvie-honcho! You no act like wootentant, you act like P.F. Shee. You numba 10,000 wootenant!"

Mine was very young but at the time I wasn't into ID checks. I stripped off my khakis and slid back on the cot. The last thing I saw before I closed my eyes was a lizard, tracing across the windowpane, looking for a way out.

Later I tried to stop gagging while lacing my boots. I became overcome by the odors in the shack. My sweat turned my khakis into drenched cotton and when I staggered back outside the strange smells of the city assailed me. I told my friends we needed to *di-di-mau* in order to get home before dark, and even though the war lay in wait, we would somehow feel safer.

Its 43 years later but the sounds of their voices still sets me on edge. Diphthongs snarled, vowels squeaked, the dissymmetrical pitch of their language makes me want to cover my ears like a hound when a high-pitched frequency is picked up; it's still an assault to the wiring in my brain. Political correctness was just being birthed in our nation's consciousness then, but in this case it's an impediment to the truth. After a few months in the country, when the Vietnamese spoke, I tuned it out. How could I not? Would their words have rushed at us with such negative vibes if we were winning their hearts and minds?

And the drama! If a child was superficially injured or a structure damaged in any way when Marines were in the vicinity the cries of the village women rang with discordance to the heavens, as if a disaster of unbelievable horror had occurred. They became the greatest of salesmen in the finest traditions taught at Harvard Business School. We taught them well; they combined our plaintiff-oriented legal system with another American trick, entitlement, and threw it back in our laps, demanding the final denominator, the U.S. dollar.

And we couldn't pay enough as quickly as possible, blood money to shut them up; after all, we were winning their hearts and minds, General William C. Westmoreland told the world. The commander of Military Assistance Command, Vietnam, also said after the Vietnam War was lost that the United States "won every battle until it lost the war."

It made no difference the VC had torched the thatched roof of the complainant; he claimed to be an American sympathizer, and if we were providing a better life, why was there no electricity to set off water-sprinklers? It wasn't hard for even the least intellectually gifted Marine to comprehend after just a few operations that our cause was flummoxed.

Their kids were cool, which meant the traditional Vietnamese family structure was still providing social fiber, even though not many dads were hanging around the village. After our arrival, and the compendium of violence we brought to their landscape, the mere fact they remained basically sane is a tribute to their tenacity and to the historical traditions of a proud and indomitable people.

There was no Captain Kangaroo or Big Bird for the children. The United States Marine Corps provided the daily double feature in Technicolor, red-faced burly men in green uniforms with horrid body odor (no fish in our diet, just Korean War vintage C-rations, canned meat and peanut butter). We brought them 3-D live movies with canisters of napalm skidding across the land for a few seconds before igniting, sending scores of gallons of billowing red flame forward for hundreds of yards and plumes of black-as-crow-eyes smoke to the heavens. When the fighting was over we gave them Snickers and tiny, soft, beige teddy bears and smiles of encouragement. How could you not be torn up inside by the savagery to which they were exposed? Forget the tales about the grenade suddenly flung by a 10-year-old or the Coca-Colas for sale by kids with slivers of glass in the bottle ready to sever your larynx. That was the stuff of urban legends.

They sought our advice and solace, squatting nearby with huge, bright brown eyes and brilliant smiles, watching and listening, just like the kids we once were. Their innocence captured the hearts of the young Marines who would do anything for the children. When it was time to do the work, they fearlessly hopped on the backs of their half-ton water buffalos, like conquistadors, and drove them into the green tilling fields.

While dealing with the enigmatic two-headed mandate — win the hearts and minds while ringing up body counts — we got confused, then detached, then pissed. Finally we felt an abhorrence for the whole Vietnamese universe, the doleful village women whining and moaning after a firefight while still casting disdainful lightning bolts into our eyes (it's hard to deal with a mom when you're seeking to destroy her son), white-goateed pap-san zipperheads denying knowledge about the whereabouts of our enemies (their sons and nephews), yellow-peril farmers sending information to their comrades while we strode through their neighborhood into the next ambush; how had they alerted them — ESP? So we actually began to hate them. We wanted to waste their hovels, their filthy pens with swine, their rice supplies after harvest so Victor Charlie would have no sustenance, and their water wells (after incoming, a trooper occasionally dropped an M-79 frag-grenade into the bowels of the village water well).

We especially wanted to eliminate the creepy smell of their habitat that was always noxious to our North American olfactory sense, but sorry about that; the earthy, smoky, rotting smell of I-Corps would haunt us for years.

More often than not we quelled those vindictive emotions. We were Marines and, despite our resentments, we extended the olive branch to provide the villagers with a fair shake.

We felt no kinship whatsoever for the ARVN soldiers of the South Vietnamese allied army. They never earned our respect. They were too busy avoiding any possible contact with Victor Charlie, their dominant alter ego, who called out "*Who's your daddy?*" The ARVN never answered; leaderless with no *esprit de corps*, they were like dead reeds of winter stalk blowing in the winds of defeat in their own land. They would provide little defense for the certain outcome of what was truly a civil war.

And how the young Marines hated the South Vietnamese army troops! They were shiftless and undisciplined, stealing livestock from those they were protecting, disengaging from first contact with the enemy, giggling at night like faggot prep-schoolers under conditions any Boy Scout inherently knew required noise discipline. Our allies were slack-jawed anti–American cowards shirking duty in their own fatherland and laughing about it, occasionally and always accidentally wandering aimlessly and pridelessly in their black U.S. Keds into ambushes which required American forces to intercede with certain casualties a result. Marvin the ARVN excelled at thievery, snitching chickens and pigs and rice from the populace, and C-rations and Marlboros from Marine supply positions.

Very bad things happened to Marvin if he got caught red-handed by Marines. If nothing else was going on you still might hear a sudden and quick rattle of rifle fire in the base camp. The next morning you would hear a trooper say, "Marvin had best keep his hands to himself. Sorry 'bout that."

The irony is how much we respected and were actually enthralled by the courage of Marvin's brother, Victor Charlie, our enemy in black.

19

Meltdown

New Year's Eve, 1965 — Echo Battery, Twelfth Marines,
near Duong Son Village

He was a mustang, one who rose above enlisted rank to become a commissioned officer. In late November 1965 he took command of Echo Battery, Twelfth Marines. The battery was busy firing multiple daily fire missions as requested by its four forward observers in the bush. Some officers had a bias and felt a subtle snobbery regarding their mustang brethren. We hoped fervently that Captain Benton Rice would be a winner. Lives depended on him.

I wrote my mother on November 5, 1965, "A Captain Rice has just been named our new Battery Commander. I'll reserve any comment on Rice at this stage." I had observed him in the field back on Okinawa and I had not been impressed.

On November 26, I told her, "Rice is not the type of Commanding Officer we have come to expect. Oh well, you can't hope for everything."

You needn't have been a shrink to see he was psychologically unfit. Angular and horse-faced, his physical presence and strange responses to mundane situations, those easily solved by even the greenest of grunts, gave the troops little confidence. The sound of a solitary sniper shot 2,000 yards away would send him sprawling to the deck, remaining immobile. The officers under his command felt concerned, then outraged after observing his skittish behavior in his first few weeks at the helm. We realized our skipper was a living, walking, talking time bomb. Panic welled up in him at the slightest hint of enemy contact. Fear sprang from the battery commander and grabbed his troops by the throat.

The battery officers searched each other's eyes for a confirmation of each of our own conclusions, that he was an unstable hazard.

I looked at the battery executive officer.

"I'm not being mutinous here, but do you notice our CO is not squared away?"

The XO answered, "We don't want to leap to any conclusions, but yeah, I think he might be *dinky-dao*."

The first sergeant added, "I don't want to be a sea lawyer but I think we have a Section 8 on our hands."

We agreed to watch him carefully and to blow the whistle when he either became a danger to the unit or a threat to wreck the morale of the troops.

On December 29th I wrote my mother, "For the last few days, Captain Rice has shown himself to be a striking parallel to Captain Queeg, the paranoid skipper in *The Caine Mutiny*. I feel he is terribly unbalanced, exhibiting psychosomatic tendencies bordering on paranoia. And mother, as much as it disgusts me to say it, he is simply a coward."

Contact with the enemy had bloomed exponentially that month. Our battery was based on a huge salt flat seven miles south of the Danang airbase. Our howitzers spat fire missions supporting Marines in the midst of the VC's home, the murderous I-Corps province of Quang Nam. In villages surrounding us firefights suddenly ignited, and gunfire bursts erupted as furious as in the movies, then were just as quickly ended.

We prepared strong defensive positions for the battery, readying beehive rounds, so named for the very distinctive whistling buzz made by thousands of flechettes flying downrange at supersonic speeds and intended for use in case elite Peoples Army of Vietnamese troops mounted a night assault against our position. The North Vietnamese Army was now actively conducting combat operations in our sector. Marine casualties were mounting daily in the nearby countryside, caused by well-concealed VC ambushes, by misfired American ammo booby-trapped by an ingenious enemy, and tragically by other Marines because of error or carelessness. The dirty little war was no longer little.

Historically the Marine Corps won the battlefield, often against incalculable odds, by successfully relying on its ultimate trump card, heroic leadership. The officer corps' swagger led such a ferocious, unexpected assault into the German army's fortified positions at Belleau Woods in June 1918 the Krauts dubbed the victorious Marines "Devil Dogs." The United States Marine Corps even today maintains one definable essence, 234 years of the finest heroic leadership in recorded warfare history.

At noon on New Year's Eve Captain Rice asked, "Frank, how long will it take a reaction force to get here when we get hit?"

The infantry battalion's headquarters was across the dirt road 400 yards to our left rear.

"Most riki-tic, Skipper, maybe 10 minutes. Not to worry," I answered.

The battery's highest enlisted noncommissioned officer, First Sergeant

Echo Battery, Second Battalion, Twelfth Marines, advertises help for Marines from other units.

Harry Sturm, cut his green eyes at me. The universal nickname for a unit's first sergeant is "Top." We were in the Command Post, a heavily sandbagged tent, headquarters for the battery and also the captain's home. We speculated we were more secure than any other Marine artillery battery in Vietnam.

Rice suggested we add more listening posts outside our perimeter that night. I was duty officer for the night and acting Executive Officer.

"Sir," I began. "We've got 360 degrees of triple concertina wire, interlocking fire from our machine guns, artillery support from elsewhere, a grunt battalion across the street, Huey gunships on call, over a hundred pissed-off Marines, and "Top" here. Sir, no gooks are getting anywhere close."

Jesus, I thought, *the troops don't get enough sleep as it is.*

Rice then suggested, "I think we should send a large ambush patrol a few hundred meters outside our wire tonight."

We had ample security in all directions. It was an incredibly dangerous suggestion. I thought the top sergeant would blow a gasket.

"Captain," he sugarcoated his response, "our mission is to blow the shit out of the zipperheads with accurate artillery fire, while protecting our position. We are squared away on both counts."

He changed the subject. "Now, what can we do for the troop morale? It's mighty sour."

I chimed in, "Sir, could you beg a few more R&Rs this month? The troops are really restless."

Harry Sturm was the embodiment of the "Old Corps." Indeed he had been a China Marine, just before World War II.

"Lieutenant, we had crabs crawling through our eyebrows there was so much slant-eyed pussy in China," he informed me.

His glance swept across the sandbags, the howitzers, and the razor-sharp concertina wire triple-canopied like giant bristling Slinkies in front of the large guns.

"The Corps today ain't much better than the U.S. of A. horseshit army," he said with disgust as he looked at some of his young cannoneers tossing a football back and forth on the brilliant white sand after chow call.

Harry Sturm was as salty as they come, hopelessly in love with his Marine Corps. He put the fear into his young troops with a gravelly voice that delivered his profanities with a west Texas accent. The first day I reported for duty to the battery on Okinawa, fresh in from Quantico, I walked into his office. Reaching across his desk to accept my orders he eyed me head to toe, looking for weakness.

He read aloud, "Hmm, let's see ... Second Lieutenant Franklin V. Cox, USMCR."

As he sounded the letter "R" he spat upon the gleaming floor next to his desk and locked eyes with me, defiant, defending his Corps against a fledging, a reserve officer at that. I let it pass. But a week later I caught him in an error. So I jumped him and called him down hard.

Respectfully, he responded, "Aye-aye, sir."

We were simpatico forevermore.

He was the scourge, father figure, dictator, and alpha-dog honcho for the enlisted troops in the battery. He was constantly on their asses; he firmly believed an idle Marine would find trouble as surely as water seeks its own level.

A theoretical cease-fire existed on New Year's Eve 1965. Beer rations had been extended to the troops. The officers and senior enlisted men were playing five-card draw, jacks-or-better to open. Excellent scotch was being sipped in the well-supplied bar in the NCO tent.

"Where the hell did you get this Johnny Walker Black?" I asked the gunnery sergeant. The resourcefulness of Marine senior noncommissioned officers to trade for (or steal if necessary) goods and equipment for their units is legendary and is a singular point of pride.

"Lieutenant, those Air Force pogues (desk-bound soldiers) in the rear will trade anything to get their soft little hands on a Marine Ka-Bar combat knife. Can you believe we got a whole case of this good scotch for one Ka-Bar?"

"Gunny, you once again have outdone yourself. Happy New Year!"

We toasted each other, all the way around. We were all looking forward to the day we would return to America, to the almost unimaginable world of green lawns and fast cars and ice and girls with round eyes and golden hair and silken thighs.

Armed Forces Radio was beaming Sam the Sham; he was after Little Red Riding Hood, a lustful bad wolf intent on having his way.

At first dusk I went to collect the firing data for what had become a nightly ritual. Each artillery unit fired Harassing and Interdiction fires (H & I). It was the assignment of the battery's Executive Officer, after consultation with his artillery liaison officer embedded with the infantry, to determine the most likely place to kill, or at least disturb, the nightly activities of the enemy by shooting howitzer rounds at the best-guessed places he might approach or inhabit. Current intelligence and a careful study of maps determined where the shells would land. The targets were described up the chain of command for approval. We avoided any place where civilians may have been or where Marine ambush patrols had been set up.

All night long, each night, each Marine battery desultorily fired H & I fires, one round at a time. The chances were less than slim the enemy would be hit — it was a big world out there; the chances were greater you could have tossed a watch up into the gales of a hurricane and have it drop back into your hands, but each night it was *de rigueur*. God forbid that the cannoneers may have gotten some quality rest. Usually the shells exploded harmlessly into rice paddies or onto an intersection of unoccupied trails. Occasionally they struck sleeping peasants in their thatch-roofed homes or penned-up water buffaloes tied up in a nearby corral. A wounded beast of burden makes horrific noises in the darkness. Sometimes the H & I shells unfortunately fell on Marines, and afterwards there was hell to pay for those who approved them. H & I fires were part of the reason that after 10 months in Vietnam Echo Battery had fired 22,200 rounds of 105mm shells. Multiply that number times the scores of artillery units up and down the country and you get a sense of the magnitude of the firepower we threw out. We had the firepower but the Vietcong had the people's hearts and minds and the perseverance and patience to face our might.

But it was New Year's Eve and, because of the cease-fire, all was calm. There were to be no H&I fire missions.

The madness began shortly after 2200. I was at my post inside the XO pit, from which the data to fire the cannons was given via microphone over wire to each gun. I was sharing a delicious cheese spread from home with some troops who had a batch of vodka mixed with Hawaiian punch. A landline call for Captain Rice rang from the artillery battalion operations officer. I went to his command tent to fetch him.

Sturm came outside and said, "The captain is in bed again with chills," accentuating the word "again."

As I glanced into the CP tent Rice first appeared normal. But after a closer look at his face I saw the wild fear in his eyes. I could almost see the spiders creeping through the folds of his soul, and could almost grab the snakes twisting through the plasma of his mind. The battery clerk and the CO's radioman looked at me, spooked out of their minds. I told Sturm to stay vigilant and went back to the XO pit. I got back on the landline and told battalion headquarters I was in charge. The officer at the other end accepted that; he had a hunch about Rice, having served with him a few months beforehand at regimental headquarters.

He then issued a warning order, "Be prepared to move your battery out in four hours to provide artillery support for a possible imminent operation. Will advise ... out"

I instructed the first sergeant to begin preparations to move out if necessary.

At midnight it happened. The first tracer rounds bisected the battery area, approaching like a stream of slow red bees then gaining supersonic speed as they raced by. I knew the enemy's tracer rounds were green. Illumination flares turned night to day, popped by our nervous sentries. From our right green-star clusters rose from the village where an ARVN company had set up shop. From across the abandoned railroad bed to our left, red-star clusters made the black sky turn scarlet and M-14s jumped to life in the Second Battalion, Ninth Marines, base camp. Hand grenade explosions from all directions accompanied the panoply of colors with a symphonic noise. Rounds from our own infantry snapped overhead. Rounds from the ARVN's M-1 carbines could be heard passing through our area also, headed for the infantry position.

The two friendly units were shooting at each other and we were in the middle. As I looked back toward Danang airfield the sky was lit with hundreds of American flares. I shouted, "Cease fire, cease fire!" Ten yards away I saw a young Marine, his shirtless torso bathed by silver moonlight, taking careful aim at our infantry behind us muttering, "Fucking grunts.... I'll fix 'em."

I dove and left my feet, leading my shoulder into his left side, knocking him and his rifle to the earth. I cursed him and told his squad leader to put him on report.

There was no attack; there was no enemy activity. It was all over in 10 minutes. It was an undisciplined "mad-minute" New Year's Eve celebration by young Marines, letting off collective steam. As I wrote my mother, "What else would you expect the kids to do? It's New Year's Eve and they've been cooped up like this for months with very little liberty."

I repeated my orders to the platoon sergeants to cease-fire. Soon everything was cool. I went to the CP to check on the captain.

It was sickening and way beyond unacceptable. Rice was cowering behind the sandbags in front of his CP tent, so terrified he could barely move his lips to speak

"Frank, do something!" he babbled. "The gooks are inside the wire. I saw 'em! We're getting overrun!"

The first sergeant stared at him and sadly shook his head.

I said, "Captain, relax, everything's fine. There are no VC. We didn't get hit. Just itchy, friendly trigger-fingers. It's all over."

Rice screamed in angst, "Call in air, Frank! We're getting overrun!"

The troops had gathered around the CP, shaken and shocked by the meltdown of their commanding officer before their very eyes. I grabbed Sturm and instructed him to immediately order all the troops out of the CP area and to take charge of Captain Rice's weapon and stuff him on his cot under watch for the night.

The next day Rice was admitted to Charley Med for hospitalization, never to return to the unit. He was not communicative. They found his Colt .45 pistol under his pillow in the hospital and confiscated it. He was medevacked to the states. His malady was diagnosed as NR (neuro-psychiatric).

On January 4, 1966, I wrote my final words about the captain to my mother.

"Queeg is gone, evacuated to the states on a Section 8 ticket. He is a goddamned nut."

Eleven months later I ran into Rice in the Officer's Club at Camp Lejeune, North Carolina. He was sporting fresh gold oak leaves, having been promoted to major. Sometimes even bad deeds go unpunished.

20

The Disappearance of First Lieutenant James T. Egan, Jr.

January 1966 — Recon Special Ops, Operation DOUBLE EAGLE

It had been terribly hot on the high ground the afternoon of January 21, 1966, where the Marines had been sequestered since the morning. The mission for the 14-man reconnaissance patrol was to gather information for a major operation the American command was preparing to crank up, Operation DOUBLE EAGLE.

For the Marines stealth and silence were their accoutrements. They had not been dispatched to assault. They were many miles from the closest American units, ensconced in the heart of the territory of the enemy. They were to find out how many Vietcong and North Vietnamese Army battalions existed in that environment of hilly jungle and vine-infested terrain, full of deep ravines with dense, almost impenetrable, outlandishly thick growth between sheer jungle ridges that sapped the strength of the Marines. The Marine scouting party's mission included discovering what weapons, supplies, and support the enemy owned. The Marines were to find out where the enemy was going to attack next by observing his activity, up close. The reconnaissance patrol had to do all this and more while remaining unseen. Discovery meant certain disaster.

In early January 1966 Marine Amphibious Force intelligence concluded a malevolent confluence of enemy forces had formed together in southern Quang Ngai province. Task Force Delta, commanded by Brigadier General Jonas M. Platt, was assembled to find, engage, and destroy the enemy amassing in a 500-square-mile area twenty miles southwest of the coastal capital of Quang Ngai City. General Platt's intelligence assets estimated enemy strength numbered over 6,000 regulars, including the elite 18th and 95th NVA regiments and the 2nd VC Main Force Regiment.

Task Force Delta comprised four Marine infantry battalions, including mine, Lieutenant Colonel William F. Donahue's Second Battalion, Ninth Marines. An artillery group with a total of 26 pieces ranging from 4.2-inch mortars to 155mm howitzers would provide fire support. Also attached would be a provisional reconnaissance group, an engineering company, an amphibian tractor company, and a shore party group. The Marine concept of operations called for three distinct phases: reconnaissance, landing, and exploitation.

The reconnaissance stage would be the kickoff for the largest American operation in Vietnam to date. The First Cavalry (Airmobile) Division committed four infantry battalions into the battle area south of the Marines near Bong Son. The Marine First Force Recon Company at Chu Lai was ferried several miles inland to the Ba To Special Forces Camp to send out creep-and-peep patrols beginning on January 12.

On January 21 the 14-man recon patrol, led by First Lieutenant Richard E. Parker, Jr., reached Hill 829, approximately 4,000 meters northwest of the Ba To camp. Parker and an advance party reached the top of the hill at 1400 and halted for the day because of poor visibility. First Lieutenant James T. Egan, Jr., and his artillery forward observer team were positioned slightly lower on the southern slope.

Jim Egan was an elegant young Marine officer with brilliant blue eyes and a charming Irish smile. He had been a classmate of mine at the Basic School, class of February 1965, at Marine Corps Schools, Quantico, Virginia.

He and I were among 31 in our class of 250 lieutenants designated to become artillery officers. After the six-month Basic School Course we immediately underwent a quick three-week Artillery Officers Orientation Course, also at Quantico. Jim Egan was an excellent student and consistently ranked high in all his courses. More importantly he had this charismatic charm you could almost touch. You could just see he had "it."

He had prepped at the Pingry School in his hometown of Hillside, New Jersey, just west of Manhattan. Some of the school's famous alumni include Michael Chertoff (ex–Secretary of the Department of Homeland Security), Mark Donahue (1972 Indianapolis 500 winner), William Halsey (World War II Fleet Admiral, U.S. Navy), Richard Tregaskis (author of *Guadalcanal Diary*), and Thomas McCarter (CEO of Public Service Corporation).

Egan entered Notre Dame University in September 1960 and enrolled in the Naval Reserve Officers Training Corps. It was there he met David Garner, who later became a fellow officer with me in Echo Battery, Twelfth Marines, in Vietnam.

Dave recently told me, "At Notre Dame Jim was a quietly effective leader and the nicest guy in the world. He was obviously a smart guy; friendly, sincere — he would give you the shirt off his back. His senior year he was a midshipman company commander. His company won the 'Best Company' award one semester. He was president of the Glee Club his senior year."

Egan became engaged to a young woman from Saint Mary's College. They had met at Notre Dame on election night in November 1962 when both had volunteered as poll workers. They decided to spend forever with each other.

At Quantico, Jim shared with me the aura of Saturdays in South Bend in football season played out on a green meadow between arching stands packed with Notre Dame disciples. Each week we recapped the previous game as Notre Dame raced to a 9–1 record in 1964. Touchdown Jesus, a 134-foot tall mural that looks upon the gridiron, had just been dedicated the previous May. I was proud to tell Jim the captain of the team was Jim Carroll, my old teammate from Marist High School in Atlanta.

After artillery school Jim was assigned to the Third Battalion, Twelfth Marines, based at Chu Lai. It is an implausible coincidence that the first tent he came upon when he initially reported was inhabited by another Marist chum of mine, First Lieutenant Robert Rowe, the unit's communications officer.

Recently Rowe wrote me, "I remember looking up as Jim walked in and said hello. He was a brand new freshly-scrubbed brown-bar and a great guy. A few days later I took him by chopper to Hotel Battery in the highlands. I remember how beautiful it was to fly through the clouds and drop straight down in a tight spiral to avoid giving a good profile to the VC. Hotel Battery was nestled in a small valley surrounded by mountains."

On October 9, 1965, Jim wrote a letter to Larry Clayton, one of his best friends at Pingry.

> My spot is Chu Lai which doesn't have much in the way of liberty. I've been assigned as the Forward Observer for Delta Company, 1st Battalion, 4th Marines, and for the last two and a half months I've been on almost all the platoon, company, and battalion operations. We've been lucky though, the VC are poor shots and usually fire from too far away — mainly because they are afraid of Marines. At present we are on Ky Xaun Island northwest of the airfield at the mouth of a river — our very own South Pacific island a la Vietnam. The local VC Chamber of Commerce stopped by to throw a few rounds at us the first few nights but I think they've become discouraged with their lack of success. We are resupplied by chopper and get hot meals twice a day. Rumor has it we'll be headed back to Okinawa in November — I'll believe it when I see it. I've been here since May 19. See you for a cool one soon.

As fate would have it when Jim linked up with Delta Company he found a Notre Dame classmate, First Lieutenant John L'Estrange, who was an infantry officer with the company on the same remote island.

L'Estrange had this to say about his former college pal: "Jim Egan was a very close personal friend. I knew him very well before either of us joined the Corps. It was pure coincidence we both ended up in the same rifle company. Jim was a very courageous Marine. As the FO he was always with the forward-most element of Delta Company whenever we were on an operation. He was also a great guy."

The recon patrol had furtively departed the Ba To Special Forces camp January 20, 1966, at 0430. At noon they stumbled upon a deserted pungi-stake factory. The patrol crossed several rivers, then reached and began climbing the mountains, breaking through heavy brush, climbing higher and higher, tripping over hidden inch-thick vines, slashing with machetes and Ka-Bar knives jungle clumps of primal vegetation for minutes at a time just to gain a few yards of progress. No sign of the enemy had been seen when they took a mid-afternoon break on an escarpment with a vantage point that allowed good visual inspection of the country below them. Across the draws from them in several directions were freshly cut trails etched into the sides of precipitous hills.

That night they set up on a long finger of a promontory that allowed them to see the expanse of the vast valley below. Insects attacked, seeking the essence in the Marines' blood. White-winged magpies screeched into the darkness that enveloped and swallowed first the mountains and then the whole valley below.

Heavy, moist clouds dropped torrents of rain, inches of it atop the mountains, with such volume that in the valley below new rivulets joined and formed frothy racing surges. Creek beds with quiet trickles became furiously alive in the monsoon season. Soaked to the bone, the patrol lay in ponchos, searching for any sign of the enemy. Each man was allowed to collapse into a few hours of trance-like REM sleep.

Success of reconnaissance patrols is dependent upon remaining undetected. Detection often occurs because of a chance encounter with the enemy, often surprising both sides, and often demanding quick fighting followed by immediate withdrawal. Plans allowing for the possibility of the separation of the patrol must be specific. Separated men are to "evade" (move like an escaped POW in a hostile land) to a previously designated rally point.

The next morning the patrol saddled up and moved out, headed for the next objective, the top of Hill 829. They crossed a wide valley flourishing with rice cultivation. Starting up the hill the Marines found the climb muddy and slippery from days of rain torrents. Their green utility uniforms became brown-black rags, drenched by their sweat and the rain and muddied by the slime they slipped upon.

The thickness of the vegetation reduced the visibility to 30 feet. Up the hill they labored, into clouds and freshly sun-stirred fog that strained visibility even more. Trees were thick and 50 to 60 feet high. Elephant grass sprouted out of the soil on the slopes between the trees. Finally in the early afternoon the patrol stopped near the top to await better visibility. The summit of the mountain loomed a half-mile higher than the valley floor. Lieutenant Parker kept the FO team on the southern slope and placed the rest of the patrol on the north, west, and east slopes of the mountain.

At 1505 Vietcong forces violently and with total surprise attacked the patrol from the south.

In an official statement later, Corporal Lewis B. Oberhaus, a member of Egan's FO team said, "I saw Lt. Egan receive one round in his mid-section, and clutch his stomach and fall to the ground. When hit we were close to a large tree with the roots protruding from the ground. After Lt. Egan was hit, he crawled toward the tree where he had his gear. I stood up and fired a burst of rounds at the Vietcong, who turned and ran back down the hill. The Vietcong were approximately 50 feet from my position when I opened fire on them. After opening fire, I chased them approximately 150 feet down the hill. I then returned to where I last saw Lt. Egan and found that he was gone."

Parker and the rest of his men raced toward the fight.

In his official statement, Parker said, "Lt. Egan was missing. This whole action took only a couple of minutes. I sent out teams to search for him, and especially to search for tracks, which would be observable in the mud had he moved another way. He was not found, nor was any traces or signs of movement in another direction found. I searched until dark (with great hazard to the patrol since these VC had certainly gone to inform larger VC units in the area of our presence) and then moved the patrol north a few hundred yards for the night. The following morning we were attacked by about 50 VC. In any case it is certain that he did get his rifle and move away from the scene of the incident under his own power. In such a case — being separated — he would begin to return to our rally point. Since he did not return, I believe he was probably captured or killed by the VC in trying to do so."

Corporal Phillip M. McIntyre, another member of the recon team, responded in his statement, "I later heard from one of the members of the FO team that Lieutenant Egan had immediately run toward the shots. Egan was then seen to clutch his stomach as if hit. Lieutenant Egan was not seen again. The rest of the patrol, in the meantime, pulled back about 40 meters and formed up. About three or four minutes later, seven or eight members of the patrol began a systematic search-assault. We found nothing — no blood, no traces of what had happened, or anything. The patrol then moved about 200 meters away and set up a perimeter. Drums were heard all that night. The next morning we established an OP overlooking the suspected site of a Vietcong hospital and R&R area. VC located on the high ground behind us spotted us and opened fire. Our position became untenable. We withdrew, moving down the steep side of the hill, led by Lieutenant Parker. We regrouped and set up an ambush position and called artillery in on the hill from which we had received fire. A platoon was sent by helicopter from Chu Lai for support. As soon as the helicopters could get through the fog, we were lifted out. On arrival back at Ba To, only two members of the patrol were still found fit for duty."

At first light, Egan's battery commander and the First Force Recon company commander did an aerial search for any sign of Egan. A few days later a ground force of 50 Marines was choppered into the area where Egan had been last seen. All searches were negative; not a sign of Egan was found anywhere on the mountain. He had vanished.

The hard-luck patrol was meeting disaster at every turn. During the chaotic fighting the next morning while searching again for Egan, another Marine was captured. Lance Corporal Edwin R. Grissett, Jr., from San Juan, Texas, became separated from his unit and was captured by the Vietcong. He normally weighted about 190 pounds. According to fellow POWs after two years in captivity he weighed only 125 pounds. He suffered particularly from dysentery and malaria, and in his weakened condition, begged his fellow POWs not to tell him any secrets because he found it difficult to resist the tortures of the Vietcong. Near starvation in late November 1969, Grissett caught and killed the camp's kitchen cat. Fellow POWs watched helplessly as guards beat Grissett for the crime. He never recovered. A returned POW testified that Grissett died on December 2, 1969.

Jim Egan's disappearance was gruesome news for those of us in Vietnam who knew him. The logical conclusion was he was wounded in the brief firefight and the Vietcong quickly abducted him and spirited him away. Any conclusion at all was guesswork, and rumors became part of the story.

I initially heard he had been dragged through village after village, the VC making the ultimate example out of him ("see what happens to you if you are not with us?") until finally executing him by crucifixion. No one could assert whether any of it was truth or fiction. Only one fact was infallible: he was gone, somewhere. Later there were random reports by South Vietnamese soldier POWs claiming to be in the same prison with Egan who witnessed he was shot to death for defying orders. Those who knew him didn't doubt that for a minute. Rumors turned into urban legends. Only one acceptable fact persisted through the years: he had vanished. Jim was officially listed as MIA.

Months became years, and new stories of escape and death replaced earlier ones. The missing lieutenant became a captain. The war continued on its inexorable, hideous path. The fiancée waited for her heroic knight to return. His parents, Mr. and Mrs. James Egan, Sr., kept unflinching faith in his existence. But still, there was no sign. There had not even been enough evidence to list him as a prisoner of war. He was listed in the quiescent limbo of "MIA." The missing captain became a major, advancing in rank with his peers.

On March 30, 1975, almost 10 years after U.S. Marines first landed on Danang's Red Beach, 100,000 South Vietnamese soldiers surrendered Danang after being abandoned by their commanding officers in the face of 40,000 attacking NVA troops.

On April 30, 1975, at 0835, the last Americans, 10 Marines from the U.S. Embassy, departed Saigon, concluding the U.S. presence in Vietnam. The last chopper rose from the embassy's roof and flared slightly, providing the Marines aboard one final glance at the surreal scene below as NVA soldiers hoisted their flag in the courtyard. Then the chopper sprinted to the east and the U.S. Navy fleet in the South China Sea.

Still, even at the end of the war there was no sign of Jim Egan, dead or alive.

The Department of Defense officially declared Major James T. Egan, Jr., dead on February 3, 1978. The description is a chilling litany of emotionless words: Died While Missing ... Ground Casualty ... Body Not Recovered ... Religion — Catholic.

His name is etched on The Vietnam Wall in Washington on Panel 04E, Line 081. Next to his name is a cross, a special designation for MIAs. To this day scores of people still wear his MIA bracelet.

On January 1, 1976, at Notre Dame, the battalion of midshipmen gathered to remember Jim at a special Mass in Sacred Heart Basilica. The Notre Dame Glee Club sang in memory of its former leader. Dave Garner, Jim's old classmate and my old battery mate, arranged the event. Dave, at the time, was the Marine Officer Instructor for the NROTC unit on campus. I have a picture of Garner kneeling next to a "memory" marker dedicated to Jim Egan in the Arlington National Cemetery.

A street was dedicated to him in his hometown on his birthday in 2004. His fiancée from Saint Mary's College, 40 years before, was in attendance. The announcement of their engagement had been published on January 17,

1965. The announcement's final sentence said the wedding would take place "next summer." It preceded Jim's disastrous encounter on the mountain by a year. Somehow fate got in the way of a storybook marriage, and the children Jim and his fiancée had dreamed about creating and raising remained just dreams.

21

Twenty Minutes of Terror: Night Sapper Attack

February 21, 1966 — Echo Battery, Twelfth Marines — Le Son

Driblets of rain fell from the bunker's timber roof, which bore several layers of sandbags. The steady trickle did not form a puddle at the base of the two-man outpost because the battery position was in a vast, open salt flat. Eons ago that land had been the base of an inland saline lake. Now it was a sprawling stretch of hard-packed brilliant white sand, a virtual island surrounded by oceans of cultivated rice paddies and hostile villages resting on jungle pads. The rain quickly bled into the limestone below the surface. Pale fog clouds swept past the bunker under a moonless sky, limiting visibility to less than 50 yards.

Lance Corporal Jose Mendez, a 20-year-old artilleryman from Abilene, Texas, surveyed the landscape before him but there was nothing to be seen past the few visible yards of white sand just in front. He and another Marine were positioned in Outpost Number 3, which straddled the extreme southwest point of the battery position. He knew the open expanse of the salt flat ended about 400 yards to his southwest, where a dense tree line provided a shield for the northern hamlet of Le Son. Marine infantrymen had swept the unfriendly Le Son village complex, which extended to the south for over a mile, for months but failed to eradicate the determined Vietcong soldiers who always returned after the Americans left. An eastern breeze suddenly stirred the fog blanket into tiny rising whorls.

I can't see shit. A whole gook battalion could be out there getting ready to take us out ... maybe just 100 yards or so out there ... and I'll never fucking see 'em 'til it's too late.

Mendez breathed warm relief into his chilled fingers, cranked up his land line connected to the battery Command Post, and whispered a desultory situation report.

"Echo 5, this is OP 3. Situation the same ... no enemy activity. Out."

He chided himself to remember to bring the gloves in the footlocker back in his tent the next time he had sentry duty out on the perimeter. He thought about the girl he had never seen who had originally become a pen pal when her Christmas card sent to an anonymous Marine fell to him by happenstance a few months before. Now, after a series of letters back and forth, he felt the two had feelings for each other. She was a Phi Mu at Texas Tech, and when he mentioned her to Lieutenant Chuck Blakely, the battery's Executive Officer, he was told the girls in that sorority were fancy, well-bred young women, usually rich, and flowers of the Lone Star State. Mendez was mostly Mexican-American mixed with a few drops of German and Comanche Indian blood. His father toiled as a carpenter at Dyess Air Force Base, and his mom took in ironing for the field-grade officers on the base. His favorite subject in high school had been shop; his eyes glazed over when he was forced to study the humanities. On his 17th birthday he begged his parents to grant the permission necessary for him to join the Marine Corps. They relented and off he went to the San Diego Marine Corps Recruit Depot. He had flourished in the Corps, first as the top recruit in his Series Class and later as a consummate small-unit leader. He assumed the college girl's father was a lawyer, or a doctor, or maybe he owned the construction company that was building the new shopping center with a Dairy Queen as the anchor. They hadn't discussed parents yet, and he hadn't brought the subject up. He knew she had blonde hair and hazel eyes, loved to swim, and drank rye and ginger. She was excited about the upcoming football game next Saturday when her Red Raiders would host the hated Texas Longhorns. He tried to imagine what she looked like naked.

An illumination flare fired by a nearby infantry unit burst in the sky to the east and slowly descended, casting supernatural shapes through the thickets of fog. Two mortar shells impacted beyond the illuminated area. Dense air muffled the reports of the explosions and the rattling of rifle fire. Then there was no sound, anywhere.

Mendez glanced at his cohort on duty in the two-man outpost. Private First Class Gerald Downing's M-14 rifle was nestled in the right-front corner of the bunker, easily within reach of the nineteen-year-old red-headed Marine who at the moment was getting some much-needed shut-eye, slumped against the sandbags that formed the bunker's wall. Downing grew up in Juliette, Florida, between Ocala and Orlando. His father owned a general store and there was always plenty of food on the table for him, his two brothers, and a sister. The best thing about his father's store was his unlimited access to live bait — red wrigglers, minnows, and crickets. He used the bait to pluck trophy bass and shellcrackers from the looking-glass waters of the spring-fed Rainbow River. When he dared to tease himself and imagine his homecoming he always imagined sitting with the family in the dining room, smelling the freshly-sizzled fish on the table while grabbing a steaming, crispy hushpuppy full of slivers of spring onion. The Floridian was a better-than-average student and a solid linebacker but he had gotten into a little bit of trouble his senior spring semester in high school. The local benign magistrate gave him a choice: a tour in the Marine Corps or six months in the county jail camp. He planned on enrolling at the University of Florida when he left the service.

The two young Marines, who trusted each other without reservation, volunteered for bunker duty so they could serve together on their own little dangerous island. That way they wouldn't have to worry about the other's performance should the battle come their way. There were a few in the battery they weren't so sure about. They were both short-timers. They had arrived at the battery from the states within the same week and were both in the final month of the mandatory 13-month tour for Marines. Because of mutual trust, they took turns sleeping. The two young leathernecks were members of Gun Number One crew. The battery normally bristled with six 105mm howitzers to deliver accurate and timely barrages of powerful artillery shells against the enemy. Each cannon position had an ammo bunker just behind which also provided shelter for its gun team. Gun Number One had been pulled out of action the previous day and sent to Force Logistics Support Group for its required six-month maintenance service. So the CO decided the gun crew would man Echo Battery's three outposts for several nights in a row and earn future stand-down sentry time.

Mendez only had a little more than half an hour before he would awaken his buddy, who would take over the second half of the midnight to 0400 watch. Then he heard the sound that only occurs when mortar rounds leap from the barrel after being dropped down their tubes and hit the firing pin.

First Sergeant Harry Sturm was the senior enlisted man of Echo Battery, Second Battalion, Twelfth Marine Regiment. He was a swaggering old salt who had been a China Marine, having served in Shanghai as a young PFC in 1939. He had just blistered a few of the staff noncommissioned officers and lieutenants in the latest of a series of five-card draw poker games that were held on occasion in the NCO tent, which had the best-stocked bar in the southern Danang Marine sector. After the game he had completed his entries to the day's journal for the battery, which memorialized and accounted for the disposition of men and equipment and all relevant events that had occurred in the previous 24 hours.

Green-eyed with a face of tanned leather, salty, profane, and all-powerful, Sturm put the fear of the Lord in the heart of each enlisted Marine in the unit. He used his flat west Texas drawl like a weapon, cajoling and threatening the young Marines, insuring their service was outstanding. He looked like an uncle that would like to kick your ass without much provocation, and he instilled the principles of the "Old Corps" into the newest members of his beloved Marine Corps. His relationship with the troops was purely based on fear. He was ingenious in creating new work projects when he found idle Marines. He went out of the way to bully them, played favorites, and held grudges. He even tried to intimidate new lieutenants when they initially reported to the battery. Many of the young Marines truly despised the crusty old top sergeant.

He was proud he only had downed two Jack Daniels on the rocks during the card game, he told his battery clerk. He was really working on cutting back.

"A top sergeant of Marines must keep his head about him," Sturm instructed the clerk. His jowls shook when he spoke. He had developed a pot belly and his once-robust biceps had lost their shape. Lack of exercise and a steady diet of whiskey will do that to a man's body.

After he checked with the XO pit to get a recount of the latest situation reports from the three perimeter outposts, he headed to his rack. Harry Sturm had just snuggled onto his cot, pulled a blanket against the February chill, and closed his eyes when he heard a sound he immediately recognized ... the *whoosh!* noise of incoming enemy rocket shells.

At 0129 in the wee morning hours of February 21, 1966, the well-rehearsed Vietcong attack against Echo Battery was unleashed.

Just seconds after Mendez heard the launching of enemy mortars, two warheads fired from within 40 yards by Vietcong rocket launchers slammed into Outpost Number 3's sandbags with earsplitting fury, crumbling the makeshift bunker's left side and blowing away that side's timber and sandbag roof. Simultaneously the enemy fired rockets at the other two outposts. Mendez saw a brilliant red-white flash and heard a startled scream from Downing as the first explosions of mortar rounds impacted just behind his outpost. Then he lost consciousness.

Sturm heard the sounds of incoming rockets crashing into the battery's outposts followed seconds later by a series of mortar shells exploding, starting at the southwest corner of the position and moving continually in a line to the northeast. Then Vietcong small arms fire crisscrossed through the area from two different positions. He knew what was next and informed the battery commander.

"The shit has hit the fan, Skipper! The gooks are going to try to breech our wire and attack our gun line!"

The Vietcong mortar gunners worked their tubes to perfection and walked the murderous shells in two parallel lines from one corner of the position to the other corner across the battery for 10 minutes. Forty 60mm mortar rounds rained down on Echo Battery. Green tracers from two sets of Vietcong riflemen, one of them located 300 yards east of the battery and the other 200 yards south, interlocked and grazed through the artillery unit. The gun team leaders had aroused their men and the Marines were stumbling out of the six ammo bunkers, loading their rifles and trying to establish fighting positions. But the enemy fire was everywhere. In the chaos most of the men ducked back into the bunkers.

An illumination round fired from a sister 105mm howitzer battery lit up the south and southeast area of the battery minutes after the VC attack was sprung. But the 300,000 candlepower-light arc became morphed in the fog and low clouds spilling crazy-quilt bounces of light and dark shadows

105mm howitzer position at Echo Battery 2/12, south of Danang, September, 1965.

throughout the landscape. The man-made illumination only added to the surreal sounds and images that haunted the cannoneers of Echo Battery.

The enemy's execution and coordination of the attack had been flawless. While delivering harassing small arms fire from east of the battery another VC element also hosed a steady stream of rounds 400 yards to the northeast into the headquarters of the Second Battalion, Ninth Marines, the infantry battalion that Echo Battery supported. In the immediate confusion the Marine infantrymen returned fire, and some of their friendly bursts snapped over the beleaguered artillery unit under attack. Victor Charlie had brazenly sneaked into an area of cover between the two Marine units and increased the madness.

As the final mortar round exploded, as if on cue, the VC sapper team of 10 slashed through the outer perimeter wire and swarmed through the concertina headed for the line of the battery's six howitzer emplacements brandishing Russian sub-machineguns, satchel-charges filled with high explosives, and antipersonnel hand grenades. With their tennis shoes crunching onto the hard-packed sand, under the cover of a raven-black sky, they split into three small squads and made a beeline for the cannons of Echo Battery. They had rubbed charcoal across their bodies for camouflage. It was 0140 when the sappers stormed the gun positions.

Mendez lifted himself from the floor of the bunker. A sandbag had smashed into the left side of his helmet and stunned him for several minutes. He shook his head and heard his friend cursing.

"Downing! Man, are you okay?"

"Yeah, just got the breath knocked out of me. How 'bout you?"

Mendez squinted through the back of the bunker and scanned the breadth of the battery as the last mortar rounds fell. Incandescence from a sputtering illumination flare displayed a brilliant picture of the battlefield for a few seconds. He saw figures in black sprinting toward the guns.

"I'm cool, my man, but we got a bunch of gooks in the wire!"

The band of enemy sappers had split into three groups, each headed for a specific howitzer. They had strapped satchel charges to their chests. They had spent many hours rehearsing the scenario. Time was of the essence. They wanted to commit their mayhem and bolt as swiftly as possible amidst the confusion the incoming mortars had created. The sudden surprise of the attack momentarily immobilized the battery's ability to provide a stiff resistance.

The Vietcong assigned to destroy the Number One howitzer didn't blink when they gained access to the position and discovered it was not there. One of the VC immediately improvised and placed a 15-pound satchel charge against the gun's ammo bunker, which sent chunks of bunker timber reinforced with corrugated metal 30 feet high.

Gerald Downing was fully recovered by the wallop to his outpost. Man-made daylight from an illumination flare displayed a man in black moving quickly to the east from the Number One gun position toward the other howitzers. The young Marine from the Sunshine State became one with his M-14 rifle, breathed deeply, aimed at the figure's torso, breathed out slowly, and pulled the trigger. The target fell.

Downing screamed to his partner Mendez, "Man down! I just wasted a slope!"

Three other VC had just gained access to the Number Two howitzer. Two of them fired bursts of sub-machinegun fire at the ammo bunker 18 yards behind the howitzer and at the bunker on the northwest side of the perimeter. The other guerrilla, the explosives expert, strategically placed and set off a satchel charge under the carriage of the cannon which ripped off both wheels, the right brake drum, and the right equalizer, rendering the powerful weapon useless.

A member of the Number Three howitzer position who had low-crawled out of his ammo bunker saw the sub-machinegun firing to his right. He isolated a target with his rifle and picked off one of the VC sappers. Several other attackers were seen to fall.

Several sappers chucked hand grenades at the hard-backed tents behind the gun positions where the rest of the troops of the battery were housed.

Then in an instant it was over. The enemy band dragged their wounded comrades with them and vanished, perfectly executing their exit plan. They vanished into the gloom like zombie ghosts as the last scene of a science-fiction movie fades away. But the events of the previous 20 minutes had been no movie. The VC left no trace of their visit to the Echo Battery position except for three distinct blood trails through the sand.

Seven wounded Marines were collected for immediate medical evacuation, including Harry Sturm, the most severely wounded of all. He lay in a bloody heap, in critical condition from shrapnel wounds caused by a grenade explosion next to his feet. Private First Class John Arthur Garrett, Jr., a popular 21-year-old from Maryland, was manning a corner bunker M-60 machinegun when an incoming Chicom rocket shattered the outpost with a direct hit. Garrett was the only Marine killed during the bold attack. The official Marine enemy casualty report stated one VC was killed and three others wounded.

At 0430 an Echo Battery squad patrol found a satchel charge, a rocket launcher, several hand grenades, and various blood trails just outside the wire at the south side of the position. A request was made for engineers to destroy the explosives. A photographer was needed by first light.

Five days prior to the attack I had departed Echo Battery with my artillery Forward Observer team to join Foxtrot Company, Second Battalion, Ninth Marines, which was being inserted into a major operation against VC and North Vietnamese Army battalion–size forces operating in the Bong Son area, over 50 miles to the south. Even though Operation DOUBLE EAGLE was the largest operation in the war to date, we encountered only light contact with the enemy. We returned to the infantry base camp the night after the sapper attack. The next morning I took my FO team back to the battery. Another twist to the enigmatic war had just occurred. We had gone on a dangerous mission while leaving the relative safety of the battery position. Funny how things work out.

Mendez and Downing were breaking open a case of artillery fuses to stack in the ammo bunker. They were enjoying the warmth of an early-morning sun without their utility shirts. The sun hadn't been out for weeks, it seemed.

"Glad you studs made out okay the other night," I started.

Downing responded, "Lieutenant, you won't believe the shit they brought down on us the other night. Holes in the tents as big as silver dollars!"

Mendez added, "Sir, glad you came back to where the real war is. You gotta stop pussy-footing around with the grunts out in the bush where nothing happens. Victor Charlie is right here in this neighborhood."

Downing grinned at me like he had just opened up the greatest of birthday presents.

"Really terrible about what happened to First Sergeant Sturm and all, ain't it Mr. Cox?"

Then he turned and winked at his buddy.

22

Random Chaos

Artillery brings dignity to what would otherwise be just a brawl.—
Anonymous

April 10, 1966—Hill 327—Quang Nam Province

Because I was commissioned before the other new lieutenants in the battery, I had more time in grade and drew the responsibility of Artillery Liaison Officer to help coordinate the artillery's mission to support the infantry. I was attached to the Second Battalion, Ninth Marines, headquarters as part of the Fire Support Coordination center when the unit landed in Vietnam.

When the infantry unit was in a static position, I was allowed to spend a lot of time with my parent unit, Echo Battery, Twelfth Marines, which was conveniently positioned 400 yards to the west. It made it easier to discharge my additional duties that were not full time but were traditionally given to junior officers.

Because I had attended Emory University Law School for a year, I was named Battery Legal Officer, and my name was placed into a pool available as defense counsel for accused Marines facing court-martial.

The most common and serious charges were brought under Article 113 of the Uniform Code of Military Justice (UCMJ).

Misbehavior of a Sentinel or Lookout:

Any sentinel or look-out who is found drunk or sleeping upon his post, or leaves it before he is regularly relieved, shall be punished, if the offense is committed in time of war, by death or such other punishment as a court-martial may direct, but if the offense is committed at any other time, by such punishment other than death as a court-martial may direct.

This was primal to the Corps' existence — honor, duty, country, and discipline. If the men on watch, assigned with the task to safeguard the lives of their brethren, broke down, the Corps would break down.

It was very serious business and the Marine Corps considered it a major transgression. Troops could die if sentries fell asleep in combat. Vigilance was vital. If no one was minding the store, Victor Charlie could have his way and the result would be more dead Marines. The Marine Corps command ordered examples be made of those found guilty, though the ultimate punishment, death, was not given in Vietnam. Those convicted were looking at a lifetime bad-reputation sentence, a Bad Conduct Discharge. If they were really unlucky they would get six-six-and-a-kick (punishment consisting of six months forfeiture of pay, six months hard labor, and a dishonorable discharge).

I met the accused, Private First Class Logan L. Whittington of Ames, Iowa, 45 minutes before his trial. He seemed like a good kid, he had just turned 20, and, like a lot of riflemen after a few months in combat, his nerves were shot. Seconds in a very bad place — forget the minutes, hours, days or weeks that would follow — dealing with the whole violent combat scene was enough to take the youth away from anyone. And after the psychic toll of heavy contact, back at the base camp, the body-wrenching mundane daily rigors — carrying heavy crates of off-loaded mortar and machine-gun ammo, digging holes in the hard-packed earth to create foxholes to dive into to escape incoming mortar shells, filling sandbags in the 105-degree, Hades-like heat, after a while a fellow just got drained — his mind told his body, "*Relax.*"

And that's when he may have fallen asleep, he said, at 0200, half a football field in front of his company's wire, manning his listening post, having been awake for 21 consecutive hours in a combat situation (sometimes waiting for the initial contact was even worse than the combat itself, but he didn't think so).

The witness for the prosecution, Staff Sergeant Reggie Thompson, said in the initial investigation he had called for a situation report from Whittington and received no response over the land wire. Therefore PFC Whittington was charged under the UCMJ of violating Article 113.

Just before the court-martial began I told him to level with me. "Private, tell me in your own words exactly what happened that night."

"Mr. Cox, I'm not gonna go to sleep on my buddies. But who ain't tired in this shit, all day and all night, no rest and no fuckin' sleep? I didn't hear his fuckin' call. It's scary as shit out there; nobody wants any noise. Why didn't the cocksucker himself crawl out to see if I was okay, or at least awake? So he just says I was sleeping. Fuck him."

I saw his point.

Each side of a formal court-martial is given the basic outline of procedure to follow, line-by-line; just follow the script in the manual, justice for dummies. Both sides were following the script when suddenly I saw daylight.

The time to make a motion for a summary judgment (in this case a dismissal for the accused) arrived and I went for it.

"Where is the evidence?" I asked the panel.

The prosecution had rested its case on the sole testimony of Sergeant Thompson with no other witnesses. I didn't question the veracity of the sergeant. I just reminded the panel he might have become confused in the darkness. I reminded the members of the panel that a summary judgment required an immediate decision requiring them to decide whether or not to dismiss the charge for lack of evidence.

The members of the court stared at each other. Justice is justice, but the marrow of the Corps has always rested on the unswerving devotion, fidelity, and veracity of its noncommissioned officers. I had created an enigma. How could they disregard the testimony of Sergeant Thompson, a respected non-com? Still, what's right is right. They conferred and declared PFC Whittington innocent of all charges.

Sergeant Thompson and his commanding officer stared at me with daggers in their eyes. If looks could kill, I'd have been six feet under. I couldn't help it when I shrugged and softly smiled at them.

For the next several months I was assigned other cases to defend and the results were the same. My clients were all declared not guilty. Soon my unit was deluged with requests asking specifically for me to represent Marines facing court-martial. It wasn't my primary duty, and my battalion commander deleted my name from the list of available defense counsels. Marine brass wanted convictions. My courtroom appearances were eliminated. It had been a lot of fun to stick it to the man.

A good thing that resulted from performing additional duties was that you got to enjoy the luxuries that existed in the rear. And the greatest of these was hot meals. I was starving after Private Whittington's court-martial.

The Marines lined up in an orderly queue carrying their mess kits, waiting for lunch in the rear at Second Battalion, Ninth Marine, headquarters, a place between the nightmare space where its four rifle companies encountered daily battle and the escape hatch and security you could hold onto all the way back in the rear at Third Marine Division headquarters in Danang.

A minority of the staff officers in the rear who were field-grade career aspirants, senior majors and junior lieutenant colonels wanted no part of the boonies where the fighting was taking place once they got used to the relative safety of the rear. They were too busy saving their asses and avoiding making tactical decisions in case a wrong move wrecked a career. Sometimes they were the same ones who bellowed, "Thank God for Vietnam. It's the only fucking war we've got!" but it was all show, they had become cowards and wanted no part of it. An officer in an antiseptic environment looking at a large-scale map miles from the action does not have the same passion as a grunt facing an enemy 25 yards away trying to take his life. The Marine generals were like they had always been — inspirational leaders and fearsome warriors. The junior officers in forward area carried out the day-to-day responsibility of providing the on-the-spot leadership required to conduct the war. The lieutenants and captains with the rifle companies and the artillery batteries were the ones who made the crucial life-and-death decisions under fire.

It was lunchtime in the rear and I had just finished a tray of soupy whipped potatoes and a strange cut of beef laced with gristle, my first hot meal in several days. I was grateful and sated. A commotion arose a few yards away in the open area between the mess tent and battalion headquarters. A Marine had slumped to the deck, and a cry for "Corpsman! Corpsman!" was heard.

Why here? I asked. Then I saw. A Marine on the deck had just been hit in his neck by a spent bullet. He was hurt and dazed, but not dead. It was impossible to know where the round had been fired from. In any case it missed its intended target and then gravity took control. Was the bullet theirs or ours? It was so random you couldn't place any mathematical probabilities on the proposition. The event was a good morale booster. You felt safer because it could never happen again at the same exact place, never in a thousand years. You could actually see everybody's face in the area brighten up.

More than one Marine muttered, "What an unlucky fucker.... Thank God it wasn't me."

Field artillery is called the "King of Battle." It was Napoleon himself who answered the question, "Whose side is God on?" He said, "God is on the side with the mightiest artillery." But it is a very dangerous business.

Everyone feared the "short round," the friendly artillery shell that for some terrible reason fell on American troops, killing and maiming our own, falling short before reaching the enemy. Usually the culprit was human error, wrong coordinates radioed in at the scene of the accident or wrong information fed to the guns. Sometimes it was just a mechanical problem, maybe bad powder, maybe really old fizzled-out ammo, and the worst of luck if it got you. A lot of careers were wrecked by misdirected artillery fire. Scapegoats were usually found for each error even if the incident was attributable to the fog of war, miscommunication, confusion, or just plain bad luck. Events don't always go according to Hoyle in combat.

The Second Battalion, Twelfth Marines, consisted of four firing batteries. Batteries D, E, and F fired 105mm howitzers and the Mortar Battery employed the Howtar, a 4.2 inch mortar mounted on a howitzer carriage (that is, according to the book *United States Marine Corps—Table of Equipment*).

But in early 1966 the Marine Corps supply system was functioning at a low ebb and the Mortar Battery had to pack up and leave Vietnam. It just couldn't hack it as an effective, dependable unit capable of placing supporting fire for the infantry on the money. U.S. Navy vessels deposited the men and equipment of the battery in the very spot they had sailed from for the war five months earlier, the White Beach Naval Facility, Okinawa.

The retreat was not because of any failed leadership or execution by the men and officers of the battery. Indeed, it was a band of exceptional artillerymen and Marines. It was not the personnel that made the unit noncombat operative.

It was the system, the flawed, archaic, broken-down system that was the United States Marine Corps Supply System. Sometimes the system caused more problems for the Marines than the Vietcong snipers.

For example, the artillery battalion had a severe shortage of communication wire the day it offloaded from naval vessels at Danang Red Beach. Also the radio batteries that had been stored in the Okinawa supply depot were found to be old, moldy, and damp. Communication (comm) wire was used to lay and employ land lines for communication between the firing batteries and the battalion Fire Direction Center, between different batteries for smooth coordination, and on occasion between the Forward Observer (FO) and his battery's Fire Direction Center. There were many other uses for comm wire but its best use was to provide the equivalent of a telephone system.

When an artillery unit runs low on comm wire it must resort to radios for communication. When the unit almost runs out of comm wire it must rely on radios even more. Radios use batteries. Warfare demands constant communications. Radio batteries become scarce. The next thing you know the batteries in the radios go dead. And then the FO can't communicate with his artillery unit when he needs to. His infantry unit is caught in a VC ambush but the artillery FDC can't hear his fire emission requests because his radio has gone on the blink. It is dead, as will be Marines soon. Sorry 'bout that.

Ironically the motto of the Twelfth Marine Artillery Regiment is "Shoot, move, and communicate."

Headquarters Marine Corps has always aimed to come in under its annual budget whether in war or in peacetime. At Quantico, as young officers at the Basic School, we were warned by our instructors the Corps made it a practice to return part of its annual budget to the Department of Defense. We were instructed to rely on the uncanny ability of the senior NCOs, our Gunnery Sergeants and First Sergeants, to steal, salvage, gerry-rig, and improvise when the inevitable shortages cropped up. Marine leadership has forever suffered from a long-term case of paranoia, assuming enemies in the other armed forces and in Congress want to eliminate the Corps. One way to blunt the attempts against its very existence is to show it always comes in under budget because of provident and frugal leadership. The Marine Corps boasts about its ability to improvise, tactically and economically.

But it is the Marine in the field and in the fight who must endure this self-imposed Spartan economic philosophy handed down through the generations. It is a dark and cruel little joke the leathernecks suffer and in a perverse way the troopers take pride in being on the short side of the supply system. But sometimes the result of supply shortages is a terrible one — another dead Marine.

In the case of Mortar Battery, 2/12, the failure of the supply system got down and dirty — and unacceptable. The battery limped back to Okinawa in early January 1966, according to the Command Chronicle Report of its parent, "To be reequipped and resupplied." The unit had been denied its lifeblood — comm wire, batteries, and a sufficient amount of high-explosive mortar 107mm shells. Just to hear the resounding crack of them hit the target would make you happy to be a Marine.

The Command Chronicle Report further declared, "Of the 700 requisitions submitted by this unit, approximately 15 percent have been received. Because our requisitions have not been filled it would be almost impossible for this unit to maintain itself on a deployment to a war zone."

The Marine Corps' Vietnam War decayed supply system had so failed its mission in this case it couldn't provide supporting fire for the brave infantrymen locked in battle with highly motivated Vietcong and North Vietnamese Army elite warriors just across the rice paddies and the ridgelines. Once again, young Marines paid the price.

There is never any wiggle room when heavy artillery is employed. If any member of the process involved in firing artillery makes an error, Marines may die. In Vietnam it became a constant worry. Mistakes with artillery were freaking everybody out, from generals at III MAF Headquarters to grunts in the boonies.

The absence of radio batteries caused FO's request for fire missions to be relayed from one unit to another until finally the definitive, specific, everimportant language sent to the FDC could be utilized so the ferocious rounds of the howitzers, fired from five, maybe ten miles away, could land on the enemy target 200 yards in front of Marines, hopefully interdicting the enemy trying to kill U.S. Marines. Sometimes the terrain itself forced similar radio relays. Too many parties in any communication chain can create disastrous results. Sooner or later mistakes occur with numbers passed from one radio operator to another to another. Specific information in the transmissions got mixed up and morphed into calamitous requests. A word changed here, a number misunderstood there and the next thing you know, artillery shells impacted on friendly Marine positions rather than on intended enemy target coordinates, and Marines died.

FOs sometimes read maps wrong and accidentally called shells in on friendly positions, and Marines died. A 200-yard misread can take out half a Marine platoon.

In the early stages of the Vietnam War the Marine Corps was busy inserting battalion after battalion into the enemy stronghold of I-Corps. It especially needed infantry platoon leaders and artillery forward observers. In the past Marine artillery officers had been sent straight from the Basic School at Quantico to the U.S. Army Field Artillery School at Fort Sill, one of the finest military schools in America. But for us that were picked to be artillery officers in February 1965 that was not to happen. Instead of Fort Sill we attended a short Artillery Officer Orientation Course at Quantico. It was there we learned the basics of artillery, a crash course where we were prepared to face the sudden decisions required of us in combat. It was a half-measure, and a few short months later young Marines paid the ultimate price.

One morning a rifle company from another battalion stopped at our battery position, headed for a multicompany operation. I spotted an old friend from Quantico, the company's FO, and I called out his name. It took him several steps to recognize the greeting. Startled, he turned and looked at me. He slowly responded, processing the immediate environment, like an animal haltingly leaving the safety of its cave, looking, smelling, and twitching. He simply said, "That you, Frank?"

His face was a dirty bronze hue. Hours-old brown dust clung to the remnants of threads of sweat cooling his body, caked even into the tiny wrinkles now carved at the corners of his mouth.

He simply said, "Have you heard about it yet?"

"No," I responded.

"I screwed up so bad you won't believe it," he said. "We got hit ... rockets and automatic weapons out of nowhere. It was 10 days ago. I called in a fire mission, in a hurry. I called in my own coordinates by mistake. The adjusting shells took out part of the first platoon. I hit some of my own Marines." He looked away, his eyes scanning the ridgeline of Hill 327 as if looking for an answer.

None came.

"We've been out in the field for so long I've lost count," he finally said. I could only speculate about what he had lost count of.

"Oh my God, I'm so sorry," was all I could squeeze out.

After he told me his story that day he joined his company for a hot meal. A short time later they left, sweeping in a long column formation to the southwest toward an enemy dressed in black, already setting ambush positions. My friend's steps ploddingly hit the dirt, sending orange plumes of dust ankle high.

It was the ultimate fuckup — Marines killed in action from friendly fire. It became a mantra for the Marine maneuver battalions in I-Corps.

Officers in the Fire Direction Center occasionally made plotting mistakes. Consequently cannons fired at friendly positions, and Marines died.

After getting the calculations from the FDC gun teams manning the powerful weapons sometimes accidentally put the wrong dope on the guns, which made them fire out, and Marines died.

Old ammunition and powder to propel the shells on their way malfunctioned, causing shells to fall short ... the dreaded "short round" ... on friendly positions, and Marines died.

A short round from artillery or errant gunship attacks on friendlies both meant the same grim thing: American youths were killed or maimed by miscommunication, or worse, negligence. The count went on, and the worst year was in 1969, when 4,716 GI casualties resulted from friendly fire (National Archives). The military's official term for death by friendly fire is "misadventure."

There were a total of 7,458 American Vietnam War deaths caused by "nonhostile" reasons, almost 13 percent of our deaths in the war. There are a lot of ways to get killed other than by the enemy when there is stress on weapons and equipment and men. Vehicle crashes killed 1,187 GIs. Families of 842 American servicemen were told their loved ones died from "accidental self-destruction," while another 382 died from suicide.

Surprisingly only 234 American combatants were killed due to "intentional homicide." You would think with all the madness and terrible leadership that existed, from the top down, and all the talk about "fragging that bastard," there would have been many more murders.

U.S. Department of Defense language can be unsympathetically austere. How do you find closure when you are officially told your son died in that group of 1,371 names under the heading "Other Accidents?"

Just to the west of the strategic U.S. airbase at Danang was the highest ground in the vicinity, Hill 327. If you looked east from its crest you could see the twinkling blue waters of the South China Sea. The airbase nestled between the hill and the sea. Just northeast of the base was the city of Danang, South Vietnam's second largest city.

U.S. Air Force F-105D Thunderchiefs were executing Operation Rolling Thunder, taking off from the airbase's 10,000-foot runways and then streaking up to the industrial cities of North Vietnam to blast targets with bombs. U.S. Marine F-4B Phantoms used the same airfield to provide close-air support for beleaguered Marine infantry units in the surrounding countryside.

Far to the west dark blue ridgelines jutted into the horizon, part of the major mountain chain that further south was called the Central Highlands. Crack division of the North Vietnamese Army swarmed down the Ho Chi Minh trail from the north to fight the Americans in South Vietnam. The trail snaked through thick jungles and forests in those mountains. The scenes from the top of Hill 327 were breathtaking, so peaceful and lovely it was hard to recall there were Asian and American youths trying to kill each other in the land below.

There was a Marine unit with HAWK ground-to-air anti-aircraft missiles stationed on top of Hill 327 to provide air defense for the airbase. A Marine rifle company was based in the vicinity to provide security for the anti-air unit. HAWK is the acronym for Homing All the Way Killer. It was one of the most highly technical and sophisticated weapons systems found in the Corps.

One morning I accompanied Second Lieutenant Jack Swallows and his FO team on a trip to the summit of Hill 327 to conduct specific artillery fire registrations. The site was selected because of its superior vantage point.

At one point during the morning, Major Ellington Black, the commanding officer of Bravo Battery, First Light Anti-Aircraft Missile Battalion, showed up and I introduced myself. The missiles themselves looked formidable enough; most were arranged so they sat on their sleds facing north at an empty blue sky. The CO looked at his bristling missiles like love objects. You could tell how important he thought his mission and command were to the American war effort. Jack and I had seen his type in the rear before, however, all hat and no cattle.

"We are ready and anxiously awaiting for the appearance of enemy attack aircraft," he informed me.

I asked, "Sir, does intelligence expect an air attack?"

He answered, "Just let those commies send some of those gook pilots down here to hit our airbase. Just let 'em, goddamnit. I'll tell you what we'll do, by golly. My Marine gunners will blow the piss out of 'em, that's what."

I decided not to tell him the North Vietnamese generals weren't that foolish. They wouldn't commit any of their MIG-17 fighters to what would be a certain suicide mission. The total inventory of their air force consisted of 36 warplanes. I decided not to tell him I would be stunned if one single HAWK missile was ever fired from his position (upon its retirement from the arsenal in 2002 not one HAWK was ever fired in anger by the United States). There were too many American interceptors and other air assets available not only at the base but also out in the Gulf of Tonkin on aircraft carriers. North Vietnam knew better than to tangle in the air with us. Later in the war they finally committed their MIGs, and the results were disastrous when they faced American aviators.

The major's unit was much more susceptible to attacks from Vietcong sapper teams than from supersonic MIGs. The war was rudimentary in South Vietnam, fought by men with guns and bayonets. There were no weapons using stealth technology, except for one. And he wore black pajamas and worked mostly at night.

"Could you imagine a pair of jets coming straight at us from that pass over there?" I threw at Major Black.

My friend Jack slowly rolled his eyes, waiting for the inevitable answer.

The CO's face lit up and he said, "Lieutenant, I ask God for that challenge every night as I kneel before my cot. I beseech Him to allow them the folly of attacking us." He looked out at all the space and sky off that mountaintop and prayed the bogeys and bandits would come.

The first Marines to arrive in Vietnam went initially to provide security for the massive U.S. airbase at Danang. Shortly thereafter the Marine maneuver battalions moved out into the nearby countryside to further thwart the enemy. That countryside consisted of villages, where the population lived, including the enemy, and terrain in between the villages. That terrain contained many wide rice paddies in the low coastal plains surrounding Danang. The rice paddy fields were wet, slippery, and muddy, and so were the few roads and trails across dikes that connected villages. Wide, full-flowing rivers insured an infinite water supply. In the monsoon season everything just became wetter and muddier.

Jeeps were impractical in that quagmire of terrain. There were few built-up roads to navigate. So imagine how immobile the M-48 tank that weighed 52 tons was in the swampy land. Marine Corps expeditionary combat teams did not have *à la carte* parts. When a Battalion Landing Team arrived all its parts came with it, including tanks. So the tanks had to be put to use somehow, even though the battleground was unlike the plains of Europe and the deserts of the Middle East, places more suitable for tank warfare.

The official military nomenclature for these steel monsters is "armor." At Quantico, nearing the finish of our long, six-month training program at the

Basic School, and just weeks before we were to be sent to Fleet Marine Force units, we were required to list our top three job preferences. A second lieutenant friend of mine had listed armor as his top choice. He was losing sleep at night obsessing which MOS (Military Occupational Specialty) would be assigned to him. When he did sleep he said he often dreamed about his exploits as a tank company commander, riding in the lead tank, spotting the enemy set in defensive positions, and directing his tanks to fire at will. He wanted armor all the way. The official USMC definition for the MOS is:

> Military Occupation Specialty, MOS 1802 (Tank Officer): Summary. Tank officers command, or assist in commanding tank units. Provide recommendations to the supported unit commander for the tactical employment of tank units. Tank officers, as maneuver unit leaders, must be able to evaluate intelligence and the operational situation. Additionally they formulate, coordinate, and execute operation orders.

It had always been the opposite for me. I could never see beyond that grim black-and-white scene inside the hull I always imagined when I thought about armor. It was the instant after an armor-piercing shell had hit the sweet spot and exploded inside the tank, sending waves of hot ragged metal in all directions. The result was always the same. Several death-masked charred bodies spilled out of the inferno from the hatch, one of them with a face that looked suspiciously like mine.

My first choice was air-ground liaison officer, so arcane that my buddy Second Lieutenant Grant Conley and I were the only ones in our Quantico class of 250 officers to list it. We figured we had found a sweet niche. It had a little glamour to it, and we would get orders to Fort Benning to attend jump school right out of Quantico. We would avoid the messy job of being in or attached to the infantry. It also would be more exciting than the mundane option, motor transport officer, or worst of all, an embarrassment in front of your peers, supply officer.

But the Marine Corps, if nothing else, was and always will be about the infantry. And in 1965 the Corps had a special need for young officers in Southeast Asia. We both got artillery and ended up with the grunts.

The morning of February 15, 1966, Foxtrot Company was preparing to kick off an imminent search-and-destroy operation. As the artillery FO I was discussing options with the company commander, Captain Carl Reckewell. Suddenly I received a last-minute call from artillery headquarters. After we had broken contact with the enemy (it was highly likely we would have a skirmish with the VC) I was to call and adjust an indirect fire mission from the Third Tank Battalion, just to see how it worked.

Reckewell looked at me. "Are you serious?"

I told him it was a request from high places.

Tanks have direct-fire cannons, much like the guns on U.S. Navy warships, which deliver shells on a flat trajectory with no room for error. Artillery howitzers fire at high angles. They lob their shells with a lot of hang time, over hills, and the rounds fall accurately on the target. The data fed into the calculations from the artillery FDC even include the rotation of the earth. Somebody had a cockamamie idea to experiment and try the tank cannon as an indirect fire weapon. Marine brass in the rear wanted to justify the existence of tanks in the swamp.

Several hours later, we had worked our way across two rice paddies and through a large quiet village. The captain and I were with the lead platoon and the other two platoons were following us in a column. After clearing through most of the last village on our mission we received a large volume of rifle fire from a tree line 200 meters to our east. I was low in the brush at the edge of the village on my belly staring at the tree line.

The skipper was on his radio, coordinating with the two platoon leaders to our rear. He cut his eyes at me and motioned at the tree line with his left arm. I called an artillery fire mission into the tree line's coordinates.

I repeated loudly over my radio, "Roger, on the way!" when the howitzers fired the shells. I always added extra volume to warn the grunts nearby that artillery was in the air and on the way.

Next to me my radioman looked at me the same way he did each time he heard that warning. His face was nothing but freckles and wide blue eyes. He looked like Huck Finn. He smiled; he had comfort in my ability to read the map accurately.

Fifteen seconds later we heard our shells pass just over us, making the air moan with brittle harsh noises. The 12 explosions from the volley cracked and roared in a strange coordinated rhythm, 1 ... 2-3-4, 1 ... 2-3-4, 1 ... 2-3-4. The tree line danced in orange and black colors as Marine artillery shells exploded 20 meters above the ground and flung shrapnel down through the trees and the jungle growth and even into the earth itself.

We watched the target and waited for a few minutes. There was no more VC fire. The captain and I looked at each other, satisfied, end of problem, no Marines hurt. The quick fight was over, and we took a short break. The slopes had broken contact.

We were about to do a quick damage assessment when my radio delivered an insistent order from artillery headquarters.

"Shoot the tank mission."

Captain Reckewell shook his head but acquiesced. The extra mission was anticlimactic, superfluous, and dangerous. Besides, Luke the Gook was long gone, headed home for the night. A couple of colonels had bees in their bonnets somewhere in the rear so we had to conduct the fiasco.

I called in the same coordinates for the tanks I had just used to call in the accurate artillery fire. I specified white phosphorous shells, Willie Peter; even a blind man could see the incandescence from them.

"On the way!" the Third Tank Battalion radio operator informed me 15 minutes later.

Captain Reckewell joked, "Better late than never."

I waited, watching the tree line across from us. Nothing happened. Finally, far to my right, almost out of my peripheral vision, I saw the spotting round impact, sending a brilliant white plume of smoke up into the royal blue afternoon sky.

I wasn't sure I could calculate the error in deflection. I looked at the captain. The tankers were off-target by half a mile to the right.

"Here goes," I told him. I radioed my adjustment to the Fire Direction Center. "Left 800, repeat range."

The next spotting round was almost out of my left peripheral vision. This time the tankers were off-target a half a mile to the left. It had been a good day so far; Victor Charlie had harmed no one.

The captain looked at me and snarled, "Fuck it! Shitcan this clusterfuck of a fire mission!"

Over the radio I said "End of mission ... out."

Later, back at the base camp, the tank intelligence officer had the nerve to ask for a damage assessment.

In a separate incident months earlier, Company A, Third Tank Battalion, left its static position near the Danang airbase to provide support for Marine infantry units involved in a search-and-destroy mission just to the north of Danang. The executive officer was in the lead tank with seven other Marines aboard, including a few infantry troops. While executing a routine fording of a small river the M-48 tank unexpectedly pitched into a hole. The powerful tracks of the heavy vehicle spun helplessly across the slippery slime of the river bottom, churning up the spongy mud but losing friction. The noise was shrill as the giant diesel engines were redlined. Then the hole became deeper. The tank sank helplessly, a victim of its own massiveness, in over its head in a prison of mud and water. Three Marines escaped. The rest drowned.

PART III

Hopes and Dreams

23

Her

Love is my sin and thy dear virtue hate,
Hate of my sin, grounded on sinful loving
— William Shakespeare, Sonnet CXLII

1966 — Quang Nam Province

She was not there, and how deeply we missed her and all our women back home, true-love girlfriends, life-giving mothers, and even kid sisters. They fueled our resolve to somehow endure and make it back home. They wrote often and dispatched parcels filled with little things we missed as posta-dolescents (most of the Marine troopers were 18 to 22 years old). The care packages from home contained things like cookies, bibles, earmarked paper-backs, good-luck charms, family pictures, Kool-Aid, home-town newspapers, Little League baseball trophies, bars of Ivory soap, flip flops, half-pints of Ancient Age bourbon, bottles of Aqua Velva aftershave lotion, posters of Elvis, Raquel Welch, and Johnny Unitas, treasured comic books, white t-shirts dyed green, mosquito repellant, Tabasco sauce, and Hershey kisses, instead of the ones we dreamed about. The grunts threw away the underpants sent from home. They weren't worn out in the jungle, once saturated with sweat they would rub your thighs raw.

Lance Corporal Brady Gillespie rushed into the XO pit as I pulled off my headset with a microphone wired into each of the battery's six howitzer positions. I had just given the data to the cannoneers to finish a fire mission. He had a huge smile on his face and a box in his hands.

"Lieutenant," he started, "look what Maggie sent me!"

I looked closer. It was a round cereal box. A Quaker man on a blue back-ground smiled at me.

"It's from my mom," he boasted. "What a gal!"

What was the big deal about oatmeal, I wondered?

"Mother's Oats, dig it, sir?"

He then opened the box sent from Philadelphia, plunged his hand into the oat cereal and pulled out a pint of good Irish whisky. He was wild about his mom, Maggie, who wrote or sent him things daily. She had sent a similar present 15 years earlier to her kid brother in Korea, also a Marine named Brady.

"What a great Irish family we got, sir," he bragged.

He opened the bottle and we both hit it hard once. He slumped in the chair next to me, smiling, remembering his folks back home in the City of Brotherly Love. He had a month left on his tour.

"Twenty-nine days and a wakeup, sir, I'm so short I could trip on a dime. I'll catch a foul ball for you at Connie Mack Stadium and send it to you."

He leaned back, holding the cylinder of cereal, knowing that 30 days in-country could be an eternity.

We dreamed about her constantly, the one back home. We all had a sweetheart, maybe real, maybe imaginary. It didn't matter because we needed someone to obsess about, temporarily escaping the reality of war. Our souls needed relief, and any form of denial worked.

For more than three years she had been mine. She really had me; I was as addicted as if a genie had taken her essence and mainlined it straight into my cerebral cortex. I had never gotten enough of her, and even in the middle of a war I couldn't get her out of my mind for more than a few hours at a time.

She curled near me, both of us sleeping on a cot in the cold, monsoon night with waves of rain slashing the sides of the tent. Giant 155mm howitzers were positioned just behind us, and the shells roared just overhead, headed downrange, but I could relax with her arms around me. The rain slowed to a trickle of drizzle. I smelled her perspiration rush at me like perfume. I touched her and brought my fingers to my face and smelled her essence, and I placed myself into where my fingers had been and slowly stirred around inside her until she moaned sweetly. I became very still, not wanting to rush this most wondrous of gifts.

I drifted in and out of the dream under my mildewed blanket that I pulled over my head to block the world out. My green cotton utilities had not been changed for days and felt like a damp cloth wrapped around me. Yet I felt blessed to be on a cot and relatively dry in the deluge of the incessant monsoon rains while my pals were out there in the blackness with their rifle companies, under no tent at all. Then the rain came again, this time coming down with a vengeance. I breathed deeply and imagined her kneeling between my legs. I exhaled the bad stuff from the war that kept me awake, like releasing trapped birds from a cage, until I was as asleep as the dead.

Just before dawn I heard the quick report of grenades exploding nearby, answered by the hammering of a machine gun.

I was awake for good now. I picked back up on the same dream-thought about her and shifted back a few years. We had just gone to confession on a chilly Saturday evening at the cathedral. The nuns convinced her she must try to be chaste and a handmaiden of the Blessed Virgin. She desperately wanted to be a nice Catholic girl. After our contrition, in the dark cathedral parking lot, I switched the engine on and smelled her precious fragrance and glanced at her looking back at me. Her eyes were twin blue beams of passion. I reached over and kissed her softly and quickly she was facing me on my lap, her gorgeous ass swirling against the steering wheel. We made love in the shadows of the sacristy. Afterward she sobbed as we left the church's parking lot, bemoaning her sin. Religion can be a bitch.

A few weeks later I thought I spotted her up on the ridgeline of a steep trail we were ascending in the Que Son foothills, U.S. Marines hot after North Vietnamese Army snipers. I could see glimpses of her incredibly blue eyes and her wide, outrageously promising mouth through the thick brush of the green jungle as we raced toward the peak. She was wearing a snowy white t-shirt and pale blue shorts and she waved at me, encouraging me to reach the summit no matter what, as the sunshine played a song in her blonde tendrils swaying in the mountain breeze and highlighted the golden down of her thighs.

Deep in the forest at night in the heartland of the VC, I'd try to get a few hours sleep on my poncho on the ground; *please, Lord, let this be an uneventful night.* I would resurrect a time sequence spent with her, remembering everything, her slight frown, her quick reads about people, her gasp of breath when I touched her, her delicateness, her animalism. As long as she held me in her arms I could sleep, and sleep was the best denial of all.

I tried to avoid the inevitable bad-vibe montages ... *with the smile of a kitten and her eyes locked into his, she slowly unbuttons her blouse, the whiteness of her fine breasts showing below the tan line, and strokes and teases him.*

No need to go there. And the troops exploited that fear with each other, tormenting their comrades, the same ones they would unblinkingly die for.

"Hey, shitbird. It's Saturday night. Wonder who Suzie's humping now?"

Those were fighting words for sure, but were accepted as good-natured cruelty. The violence around them stole away their youthful innocence.

It mattered not that 18 months before, just after the car hop at the drive-in restaurant brought our lunch on a tray and attached it to my car window, she gave my ring back. She was sorry, but someone else had entered her life, and she thought she would marry him. The pain in my stomach felt like a stiletto had been shoved into it.

That's okay, I told myself. I rammed a small white lightly oiled patch down the bore of my M-14 rifle. We were getting ready to head back into Indian country in an hour. I'd fix it all with her when I got home; you could bet on that.

I would run into her somewhere and she would see me and be dumbstruck with the realization that she really did love me and that I was the only one for her. I whispered her name softly, just as I did each night with each breath, until I drowned into sweet sleep.

24

Short Timer

I would go without shirts or shoes,
Friends, tobacco or bread
Sooner than for an instant lose
Either side of my head.
— Rudyard Kipling, Chapter 8, *Kim*

April 18, 1966 — Echo Battery Base Camp

"Lieutenant," he began, "the most terrible mistake I ever done was the day I took the oath to join this green motherfucker."

The reference was typical of the young enlisted Marines in harm's way who accomplished the thankless mission of the U.S. Marine Corps in Vietnam. Other synonyms for the Corps included "the crotch," "the green machine," "leathernecks," "gyrenes," "grunts," and especially "jarheads." The young men in the infantry units were always miserable. They knew no other American units in the war faced as much violence, daily horror, and outrageous casualty rates. So they morbidly accepted their role with a swagger and took pride in being ruthless fighters. Their squadmates were rendered lifeless next to them suddenly and unexpectedly, and always incomprehensively, by a variety of violent means. There were 58,193 Americans killed in the war. The bell tolled 25,481 times for those 18, 19, and 20 years of age, too young to legally buy a Pabst Blue Ribbon in most states back in the world, but certainly old enough to give it all for Uncle Sam. They reserved the right to refer to the Corps disparagingly. The loathsomeness they held for the other American armed services, the squids, the air-dales, and the doggies, was palpable. Their disdain for pogues who worked in rear-echelon areas was manifest.

Lance Corporal Rory Gilcrest continued to describe his dissatisfaction. He was a cannon-cocker with Echo Battery, Twelfth Marines. He was convinced the cool recruiter, the salesman-sergeant in the dress blues back in Macon, Georgia, had seduced him.

"Lieutenant, he told me I'd learn engineering. He told me I had a good shot at college after boot camp. He looked me square in the eye and told me what the split-tails would do for a dude wearing this uniform. I trusted him and thought he was giving me the real skinny."

He reached down and tossed some of the brilliant white sand from the salt flat where his battery was positioned into the air. Silvery silicone particles drifted back to the ground.

"Shit. The only engineering I've learnt is how to set up a claymore mine."

His tour was almost over.

"I'm so short I could sleep in a matchbox," he added.

He would be back in sweet Georgia soon, and he planned on catching up on his pastime, bass fishing.

Then he said, "One thing I ain't never doin' again, sir, and that's sleeping out in a tent in the woods. Fuck that."

He already had suffered too many bad-vibe dreams for that, he said.

He had been awakened, and then wounded, when from nowhere a swarm of VC sappers on a moonless night invaded through the wire and chucked satchel charges and grenades into the battery's cannon and tent positions. Tiny grenade fragments splattered his arm as he and his pals drove the enemy away. It was tough to really sleep after that, he said; he was happy to get three straight hours of slumber before the fear awakened him.

He stood watches from 0400 until 0600. By 0800 if he wasn't performing maintenance with his team in the Gun Number Four position he was ordered to join one of the working parties whose tasks included filling countless sandbags with heavy shovelfuls of the salt-flat sand, hoisting 90-pound ammo boxes from trucks to gun positions, riding shotgun on resupply convoys sent to fetch chow or ammo or fuel back in the rear on the only available road, which also harbored snipers and mines. All the chores were done under the umbrella of heat in the neighborhood of 105 degrees Fahrenheit. He weighed 158 pounds, down from 181 after ten months in Vietnam. He became more nervous with each day as his tour neared expiration. He was given to involuntary spasms of dry heaves each morning as he spewed any remaining sustenance onto the sand. He watched it evaporate in seconds, bending over, wiping the nausea-induced sweat from his forehead.

One morning we saw a Marine rifle company leave its base camp behind us and swing past us, headed for the danger awaiting its search-and-destroy operation. As bad as he had it, he knew there were worse jobs.

"Thank God I ain't a grunt," he said.

Rory's 21st birthday, three months away, would be celebrated with a barbecue in the National Memorial Park that bordered the muddy Ocmulgee River in Bibb County, Georgia.

"Sir, you can catch flathead catfish just off the river bank there."

I told him to hang in there; he'd be living off the fat of the land real soon.

"Aye-aye, sir. 'Preciate that."

His mom raised him and his older brother in a trailer park somewhere between Macon and Perry. She had a job that required her to be away from the trailer from 0800 until suppertime as a short order cook in the café in the Bibb Company textile plant. Ample supplies of cotton in the loamy fields surrounding Macon insured a thriving textile industry.

The trailer home became more peaceful after his father deserted them years earlier. There was no more kicked-in doors or beatings in the home, acts of violence committed by a bewildered father who one day announced he was headed west to the oilfield country in the Permian Basin to make his fortune. He promised to send more money back to them than they had ever seen.

Gilcrest wasn't sure if his father was still alive, and he gave it no thought; that part of his soul was dead and buried. He revered his mom and was rude to the occasional drunk male worker who telephoned asking to speak to her.

In his junior year in high school he was a terror at the plate, driving fastballs to deep left field and curveballs over the right field fence. His coach told him he had a lot of promise on the diamond. But his mother acquiesced when he begged to join the Corps on his 17th birthday.

He squired a girl named Wanda to the Junior-Senior Prom.

"She looked real prime, Lieutenant. She was the best-lookin' gal at the dance and she smelled so fine when we slow danced it really got to me."

He remembered her dress was the color of cinnamon and the soft skin of her arms and shoulders was beautiful. She wrote him frequently, and when he returned home he intended to pursue her.

Though his grammar was poor, he was intellectually gifted; his IQ had to be north of 120. I suggested he apply for Officer Candidate School. I would write the letter of application for him.

"No thanks, sir. I don't dig nothin' about this green-weenie no more. You know what they say — eat the apple, fuck the Corps. But thanks just the same, anyway."

He was tapped out, nothing left to give except for the most precious thing of all. He was counting the seconds until he left for home, just below the "gnat line" in middle Georgia.

Enigmatically his best friend was from the Bronx. Lance Corporal Jesse

Turlington had loads of personality and was one of the prize physical specimens in the battery. He was a clear-headed leader and a problem solver and was graced with a charismatic, engaging persona. He said he couldn't wait to get back to the Bronx and teach weapons classes to the Black Panther posse in what was left of his neighborhood. I smiled at that one, and he broke into laughter, knowing he hadn't fooled me.

They worked together on the same gun team and forged the unit into the most efficient in the battery. Each earned the other's respect by performing daily duties well with a modicum of complaints. They teased each other gently and with almost child-like innocence.

"Rory, you gonna take me home to Macon to meet your white dudes?"

"That's affirmative, Jesse. But you gotta show up carrying a watermelon in one arm and a bucket of Kentucky Fried Chicken in the other."

"My guys would love to entertain yo' redneck ass and your chucks [black slang for white Marines] in New York fuckin' City," laughed Jesse.

The troops found ways to amuse themselves when there was peace and quiet. After all, they were just kids. It was never hard to find volunteers to ride in the supply truck sent to the rear to fetch ammo, chow, and mail. When time permitted there were unscheduled stops during the resupply trips at local scivvie houses. At one point over 20 percent of the enlisted Marines in the battery had contracted gonorrhea.

Rory had punched out a white Marine a few months earlier who had disparaged Jesse with the epithet, "splib" (white slang for black marine). Back in Okinawa, before the battalion went to Vietnam, racial differences were a *fait accompli*. On weekends small racial squalls were frequent. There was very little mixing. In Vietnam it had become elemental to bind, no matter the demographics.

Rory was a natural-born leader; his peers looked to him for solutions and answers. He never showed his fear to them, always displaying calmness with a no-sweat attitude. But he bared his soul to me. I was his father confessor, his confidant, and his sounding board.

"When I get home I will drop-kick the first peacenik prick I see," he threatened.

"Skip it, fuck 'em," I responded.

It got quiet; it always did when he considered his next delivery in a conversation.

"Okay, roger that. But I *will* get some of that college-girl tail I've seen in your pictures from home."

"Cool," I smiled and responded. "But first you must be able to diagram a simple sentence. College chicks aren't into retards very often."

He had already applied to the state university system and it was certain he would be taking remedial English in a few months on an oak-treed campus with tan-legged sleek coeds in shorts striding to late summer classes. He smiled back. The only girls he'd ever really known lived in trailers.

"What are those college girls really like, Lieutenant?"

"It's embarrassing, Rory. You can't take 'em anywhere. All they want to do is fuck."

He enjoyed the humor, shook his head buried between his hands and implored, "Dear God, get me home."

25

Irony

April 29, 1966 — Ha Dong Bridge

Forty-three years sounds like a lot of time. As a unit of time it is longer than the average lifespan of all men who ever existed. The past four decades have witnessed more innovation and change by man than seen in any single century beforehand. Yet for those of my generation the time has passed so quickly that without photographs you'd swear a lot of it never happened, like a chrome-tinted wavy slide show attached to memory cells, frames rushing by like haunting images passing the fogged windows of a limousine in the night darkness, flickering past and disappearing, bringing to mind a past moment of laughter, a long-ago spasm of love, an image of someone not seen for decades, popping up from nowhere into your consciousness; now you see him, now you don't.

Yet everything did happen. Otherwise there would be no YouTube, sheep-cloning, Starbucks, terrorists, same-sex marriages, or even Rodeo Drive tanning salons.

In late April 1966 the commanding officer of Echo Battery, Twelfth Marines, brought me in from the infantry to spend the final days of my 13-month tour in the relative comfort of the battery position to make preparations to rotate home. I said my goodbyes to Captain Reckewell and the members of his rifle company and returned to the battery, ending my billet as Foxtrot Company's FO. My duties for the few remaining days would be to assist the CO and XO with daily battery routines. I was looking forward to a very special event, a one-way ticket "back east," from Vietnam to America, compliments of Uncle Sam. I was really short with my tour down to its last few days.

It was a luxury to be back inside the wire after operating with the grunts out on the battlefield. The good life included showers and soap, hot meals, sleep taken on green canvas cots inside hard-backed tents with wooden flooring rather than on an earthy bed under a black canopy of sky sometimes splashed with orange flickers and bursts of light created by B-52 strikes miles away. You knew it was an Ark Light mission when the ground's trembling made your inner organs move. We would never face anything as manifestly terrible as that. If they can take that, they can endure anything, I thought. But the NVA kept coming in droves inexorably down the Ho Chi Minh trail by the tens of thousands for years. They had been into nation building (their own) for centuries, successfully driving all foreign threats away. Vietnam has forever had the most powerful weapon when measured against the strengths of her enemy — the weapon of patience.

It was time to call in the dogs and piss on the fire. Serenity filled my soul; I was so thankful I was actually going to make it. Like every other FO who'd been with a rifle company for months I was proud of my performance and my response to the challenges of my station in such a violent world ... Semper Fidelis. But now, I was letting it all ooze out, ready for the rest of my life in America. The feeling was like the rush of excitement on the final school day of the year in grammar school — three months of sunshine and baseball and movies lay ahead. It was the feeling of a great escape, of no more high-stress responsibility, of tranquility and security interwoven.

Visions of smiling round-eyed girls tanning lazily in the sun enticed me. I could almost see the curls of smoke and smell the fragrance of imaginary T-bone steaks sizzling on phantom Weber grills. Each day I would stare at the cover of the automobile magazine on my footlocker featuring a new Pontiac GTO burgundy convertible with a 389cc power plant under its hood and a four-in-the-floor shifter that was geared so tightly you could blow the doors off everybody else, even 'Vettes. There was one just like it parked in my mother's driveway, resting under a tarpaulin, waiting for me. I couldn't wait to get in it, to run through the gears, mere seconds to 60 mph, a steel stallion, the first of the true muscle cars. My first stop would be the world's largest drive-in restaurant, the Varsity. Months of sterile C-ration meals had me primed for the chocolate shakes and chili dogs I had enjoyed during my childhood and teenage years. I couldn't wait to see my family and old friends and make new ones.

But mostly I tried to imagine what it would be like to feel safe. There would be no sudden, unexpected noises at night wrecking what was at best restless sleep, no incoming, no outgoing, no explosions, no illumination flares eerily lighting the darkness and making alien woeful sounds while drifting to the earth. I tried to imagine what it would be like to actually relax. There would be no reason to make sure my radio operator had extra batteries, no reason to create preplanned artillery fire missions, no reason to predict likely enemy ambush positions, because there would be no more combat patrols. Relax, relax, and relax. Would it really be possible?

Each of those final mornings I mumbled a quick *Hail Mary* and leaped from my cot to embrace the day. Soon I would be on a plane headed for the real world, hopefully in a window seat allowing me one last glance through its pane to see the green coastal plains glimmering, to see the Danang smoke-filled rancorous metropolis meet the cobalt blue of the South China Sea. And just as the plane moved across the coastline I would look below and wonder which method the fishermen in the bobbing sampans would choose to catch their fish. Would they use hooks with live eels dangling, or would they use nets?

My first leg would be to Okinawa for final processing for a few days. There I would collect my personal items and grab the first available seat to Travis Air Force Base near San Francisco. Finally I would fly to Atlanta, crossing over the pink-brown Painted Desert, feeling the sudden bump of an air updraft above the Ozarks, seeing the winding turns of the Mississippi, then skimming above the lower Appalachians dotted with lusty purple May-blooming rhododendron to finally reach home with a gentle landing. After enjoying a long R&R leave at home I had orders to report to my next duty station with the Tenth Marine Regiment based at Camp Lejuene, North Carolina.

On April 29, 1966, two days before my projected departure date, I entered my tent to clean my weapons for the final time. I would be turning them in soon to the battery armorer.

First I cleaned the M-14 rifle I opted to carry in addition to my standard Colt .45 M1A1 pistol, which was issued to all officers. I field-stripped the rifle and cleaned all its elements and applied light oil to key operating areas. I separated the rifle's two black phosphate magazines I had taped together and extracted all the remaining 7.62mm rounds from the magazines and wiped them off and cleaned the dirt out of the magazines. Next I tested the springs and reloaded each magazine with 20 rounds of ammunition. Then I placed the clean rifle to the side and reached for my pistol.

I held the pistol's handle with my right hand and pulled the slide back with my left hand and released it. It was stuck, and I tugged the slide forward in one motion with no finger on the trigger.

An unexpected enormous flat thud sounded as the shot rang out. My ears were filled with a ringing, high-pitched noise and became numbed. I couldn't grasp what had happened in the first few milliseconds that followed the discharge. I tried to deny the throbbing feeling I had in my lower left leg. Instantly the throbbing turned to white pain. I looked down, and saw blood seeping from my calf through the green cotton of my utility trousers.

Dear God, what in the hell just happened? I asked.

As I stood up and tumbled down the wooden steps in front of the tent I knew the answer. I felt bewilderment and embarrassment as I lay in the sand watching a corpsman dashing for me.

Jesus God did this just fucking happen? A lieutenant of Marines blows a hole in his leg while doing the rudimentary thing a Marine must do and that is clean his weapon so it will function and fire when it's time to grease the bad guys. It is impossible to screw that task up! I know I didn't have my finger on the trigger but it went BOOM! anyway and the feeling in my leg tells me this is no fucking dream and worse the opposite exists. This is really happening and it will be a living nightmare! Fuck me.

It was not going to be the return home I had so anticipated. The bullet entered the right side of my left calf. Luckily it just missed the tibia and passed out the other side of my leg, causing a severe flesh wound. A vehicle took me to the Charley Med facility where I was hospitalized for a few days. A week before the accident I encountered difficulty with the slide stop on the weapon and took it to the battery armorer to get it serviced.

Captain James H. Kirkham was named to conduct an investigation of the incident on April 30, 1966. He was given a statement from the chief of individual weapons at Force Logistics Service Group at Third Division Headquarters, who inspected the weapon and noted the slide stop was broken. The last Finding of Fact in Kirkham's report of the investigation states, "that Lieutenant Cox's injury was due to accidental discharge of his pistol U.S. Cal. .45."

He stated in his opinion my action was in the line of duty and not a result of any misconduct on my part. Nonetheless I received a letter of reprimand for negligence.

I wrote my mother, "How ironic. Four days before I go home and this happens. Been in a lot of firefights with the VC — never scratched. Guess my luck just ran out."

The large transport plane, a C-141 Starlifter, lurched forward and lumbered down the Danang airbase tarmac, gathering speed and airlift and then vaulted into the Southeast Asian sky. Gaining altitude the plane banked and fanned slowly to an eastern heading. Below were soft green mountains and turgid olive rivers and small villages everywhere dotted amongst submerged fields of jade-colored grasses of rice. But it was impossible for a lot of the passengers to see the landscape below. There were very few window seats on the aircraft. The occupants were wounded or injured U.S. troops, mostly Marines, and most of them were confined to the stretchers and bunks they lay upon. Flight surgeons and nurses began tending to their patients as the plane leveled and crossed the eastern shoreline of Vietnam. Intravenous bags were strung, medicines delivered, bandages changed. The burn victims had it the worst.

The trip back home was nothing like I had dreamt about for months. There was no exhilaration, just a joyless homecoming. Despite the fact the official investigation found the event was accidental, I remained terribly embarrassed. The main damage was to my pride. We live with our mistakes. The good news is I wasn't on a career path. Life goes on.

A few days later I ended up at the U.S. Naval Hospital in Charleston, South Carolina. Six weeks later I reported to the Tenth Marines and became the Executive Officer of a 105mm howitzer battery. The final words of my last fitness report from Camp Lejeune read, "Lt. Cox's growth potential is considered excellent."

Forty years later I told Bob Hamel about the accident. We had served together as Forward Observers with Echo Battery. He replied via email the same day:

> Sent: Monday, February 13, 2006 8:26 p.m.
>
> Subject: Re: Accident
>
> Frank, you're one lucky SOB. That round could have taken your leg off. Probably the only assholes you caught shit from were people who had never seen any real shit like you did. Man, that sucks. On your way out and you take a round from yourself. Glad it wasn't worse.
>
> Semper Fi, Bob

For years I have had a recurring dream. I have been called back to Vietnam for a second tour. I am wary but confident my past experience will serve me well. I am just off the plane from the United States at an overnight way station next to the Danang airbase runway, and the next morning I will go up into the mountains to take command of my new unit. I set up a small tent, complete with a clean, clear plastic floor. It is the only tent in the area. I am the only Marine in the area. I dig small trenches just outside the tent flaps and the rain begins to fall. Everyone else, the sailors, the army soldiers, and the airmen, become soaked trying to erect shelter. I remain dry. In the background there is a lot of noise from rifles and rockets, sheets ripping and trains roaring. But nothing impacts in my area. The war is still going on, not even a pause after four decades. I feel dread but take solace in knowing I've only got 13 months left.

26

Residuals: Denial, Anger, and Risk-Taking

After three years in the Corps I came home and started a real life with a job and a new bride. I expunged everything about Vietnam from my short-term memory.

Aroint thee.

When I got out and rejoined the real world in the late 1960s nobody talked about the Vietnam War except in desultory fashion; its entire scope had become unimaginable. I was more than happy to take the whole folder of information and place it way back, deep into my subconscious; *not even going to think about that shit anymore.* Sometimes when you repeat the same lie to yourself over and over you actually begin to believe it.

The war raced on, brought to us by Walter Cronkite at dinnertime, described in days-old, mottled grey film footage with the voice-over provided by Dan Rather's breathless accounts of battles. After a few years the footage looked the same for all the firefights, showing no beginning and no end. CBS could have saved the network a lot of expense money by simply repeating the same tape stock over and over, and no one would have known the difference, or sadly, cared. It was easy to see we had no way out.

LBJ's mournful heavy-heart declarations morphed into Richard M. Nixon's reassurance he would end the nightmare quickly. With his blue growth of beard, his eyes maniacally jumping around, his hands gesticulating with no rhythm, Tricky Dick said he had it all figured out. He would stop the red tide threat soon with no more American casualties. But the beat went on, and on, for years.

Meanwhile the Revolution consumed every facet of our society. Grandmothers burned bras; black-power brothers thrust fists to the heavens, grew huge afros, and dared The Man to look them in the eye; psychedelic music, film, and fashion commandeered the arts; middle-class young women in t-shirts filled with untethered breasts announced fucking was fun and went for it with gusto. Dagwood and Blondie, Ozzie and Harriet, bowed from the stage. Jimi Hendrix electrified the audience, which had down-to-there hair, shoulder length or longer, maxing the music volume. Joan Baez and her sisters appeared on an anti-war poster with legs provocatively crossed and promised, "Girls say YES to boys who say NO." Silicon-chip-enhanced hand-held calculators made it easier to count how many hours of creativity we began wasting while staring at the idiot box in our new family rooms. The quaint family den, with all its domesticity, vanished, shoved out the back door by the revolution. And with it went the nation's innocence.

The military-industrial complex kept pumping out the napalm and grenades, meeting the requests by our leaders in Washington, who became hopelessly mired in a reactive funk. Our country's leadership was fed a steady diet of strategic and tactical misinformation from the Command in Vietnam and was trapped in a fog of indecision, arrogance, and lies.

Scenes of red, white, and blue-draped coffins being delivered out of the bowels of C-141 transport aircraft at Travis Air Force Base were as common as beer commercials on TV. Just a few miles away the peace children of Berkeley were lighting candles of incense while at the same time tossing wine bottles with burning USA flags wrapped tightly around them at Marines, just back from Vietnam, visiting the Presidio.

For seven years American troops died and choppers fell like metal rain. The American persistent headache became a collective heartache for the ages. The war had created its own universal existence, like Hal in Kubrick's *2001: A Space Odyssey*. But unfortunately Vietnam wasn't fiction.

It spelled defeat. In 1971 U.S. Marine patrols were running into similar ambushes with the same dire consequences in the very same villages they had six years before. It was madness, and finally we just left.

Perversely, I couldn't wait until the weekly casualty figures were released by the Department of Defense, usually on the CBS Thursday Night Evening News. As the count of our bloodied Americans skyrocketed weekly, then yearly, I took comfort in the chilling numbers pouring antiseptically from the screen and celebrated the fact my friends and I escaped the same fate in the war earlier. The higher the toll, the greater the thrill became, like doubling down in blackjack and winning large when the only card that could have produced an impossible-odds victory miraculously appeared.

Denial became an ally of mine while serving in Vietnam, and I brought it back home unconsciously. One day in a hot tent on a Vietnam salt flat, a friend race in with some news.

"You heard what happened to Egan?"

"Nope, what?" I asked.

Second Lieutenant James Egan had been in our Basic School Class at Quantico. He was commissioned into the Corps after graduating from Notre Dame University and was one of the most popular lieutenants in the class.

"Gone," my friend answered. "He was the FO for a mission down south. He was on the high ground with a small Marine recon unit. A company of VC discovered them and jumped them. During the firefight the VC captured him. They say he was dragged through village after village as a trophy. Finally one day a week or so later they took him to the center of a large village and actually crucified him to death."

Jesus, I thought, too many possibilities, too much information to assimilate. Only part of the story was true, and it went unsaid because no one knew the whole story. He was never seen again.

"My God, how horrible," I said.

Then we looked at each other and the inevitable phrase jumped out of both of our mouths. I would hear the same words over and over during my tour.

"Thank God it wasn't one of us!"

Another thought always came to mind, left unsaid: *Better him than me.*

Basic survival instinct made you distance yourself from cold facts so you simply dismissed the truth. That way it couldn't happen to you, so fuck it.

Even today I disconnect with the harsh fact of the death of someone I know. I may even see the body in repose in the casket at the visitation in the funeral home. But later, I forget.

When I saw an old high school friend recently I asked about the whereabouts of a childhood pal of ours. He studied me closely for several seconds. "I thought for sure you knew he was dead. It must have happened four or five years ago. He went quick ... an embolism."

I dropped my eyes from him, feigning surprise. I'd forgotten. You *can't* forget something that basic about someone you once knew closely. But I did and still do.

When it happened before your very eyes in combat, your acceptance of it was absolute; there was no denying it, and you would always remember the circumstances. The dead had to be recovered on the battlefield. The wounded had to be collected and dragged back despite the cost; there was no wiggle-room about that in the Marines. It was Rule Number One.

For over a decade I blocked recollections about Vietnam. The main carryover was my involuntary response to unexpected noises, a dropped platter in a restaurant, a blown speaker hurling unexpected high-amped decibels, car tires hitting a curb unexpectedly. I practically leaped from my skin, often startling those nearby to similar reactions. Then everyone would have a good laugh.

Anger has always been at home with me. When I recollect the earliest memories of my childhood, I hear the gut-wrenching sound of my angry father's voice followed by my mother's moan after his ear-splitting slap found her head. I hear each wooden door in each room she had sought shelter behind being kicked in; the lock was useless against his assault, and she was defenseless as he went after her again and again.

I see him removing his thick, leather belt. He told me I was to receive 10 lashes, and if I cried he would deliver 10 more. I didn't cry, but he delivered the extra 10 just for good measure.

"I told you not to go over to that goddamned yard next door," he yelled while beating me.

After all, those neighbors were Yankees. My khaki shorts had become grass-stained as we played "King of the Royal Mountain" that late April afternoon. There were seven of us. The cardinals and wrens were chirping and skipping from limb to limb in the dogwoods that shaded us with white blossoms (that crimson cross on the blossoms was the stigmata, the nuns informed us) from the afternoon's west sun. The game had begun on a slope in my front yard. We wrestled and writhed and tossed each other to gain the advantage. The pile slid a few yards, into the yard next door. My father pulled in our driveway just as I had gained the summit. He was home early. I'd forgotten the country club was closed on Mondays. Since no golf or cards could be played, he went home to his family.

I smiled at him from top of the heap as he got out of the car in grey linen slacks. He crooked his finger and beckoned me to follow him into the house. I looked and saw our game had ended in the yard next door, the yard owned by Yankees. Slowly I followed him, knowing what lay before me.

His father and uncle founded the first Chevrolet dealerships in South Georgia in the early part of the 20th century. After immense success in peddling cars to crackers who had somehow established a new lease on life, despite the debilitating loss to the Yankees in the War of Northern Aggression, Cox Motors established the first Chevy dealership in the Bradenton, Florida, area. The cash registers sang with sweet music in the pay window at the dealership all through the Great Depression. The family chieftain, my grandfather, James Cox, saw the value early on of making loans to subprime customers. He reckoned in the new America everyone needed a car. Each of his five children, including my father, got new Chevy convertibles and packets of $100 bills when they matriculated as freshmen to the University of Florida. Before college the children had to endure Sunday morning fire-and-brimstone Baptist services. Once on the free-wheeling campus in Gainesville, they studied well and partied on the weekends with the best of the hell raisers. Ultimately all five of the children of James Cox became irredeemable alcoholics.

My father was an exceptional student at Florida and a handsome son-of-a-bitch. After college he entered Emory University Dental School and courted a beautiful Atlanta debutante. Tall and gallant, well-dressed and impeccably polite, he cut a fine figure upon entering the Atlanta social scene. My mother couldn't help herself. She fell for him. To boot he had a helluva golf game. So my other grandfather saw to it he received a membership into East Lake Country Club, the home base for the legendary Bobby Jones.

My mother's parents had met and married in Denver. Her father was given the opportunity to take an executive job with Western Union in Atlanta in 1915, which he quickly accepted. Mr. and Mrs. Clyde W. Carver, a Catholic couple, raised their family of five children in the wooded, flower-filled Emory neighborhood, east of downtown Atlanta.

My first memories are of my father's cruel voice demeaning my mother.

"Never thought I'd end up married to a goddamned Yankee bitch," my father said as he pushed my mother toward the kitchen sink. He was drunk and mean after a day of drinking on the golf course, and though I was only five years old, I knew his rage would fill the house for the rest of the night. Mother had been born in Saint Joseph's Hospital in Atlanta so she was no more a Yankee than General Robert E. Lee. But she was the *daughter* of Yankees, so that was good enough for my father. He was infuriated the maid had slightly scorched that night's fried chicken. He showed his displeasure by hurling the platter of drumsticks and breasts against the dining room wall.

He looked at me and added, "Can you believe the Catholics don't know the difference between a saint and a goddamned angel?"

My mother started to answer and he slapped her hard across her left cheek, causing her to stumble backward against the front of the sink next to me. We both cried.

After he abused us I prayed to be given the strength to someday exact payback. My anger was born. Ultimately he would get the mother of all paybacks.

I was eight when my mother bolted from our new house (and what she had forecast to me as her "dream house" during the time it was built) with her three children early on a humid July morning. My father had not stirred when she stole us away; he had enjoyed a manic Saturday night and was sleeping it off. Her maternal instincts warned her we were all in danger. She feared his violence had no limit.

We sought short-term sanctuary in the home of a friend of the family, a doctor. It was late Sunday morning when my father drove up and knocked on the door. Quickly my mother grabbed my brother and sister and motioned me to follow her. We entered a large study and climbed behind dark green damask drapes that rose from floor to ceiling. We heard his quarrelsome voice muttering down the hall to a servant, and my mother gently placed a hand over each of my sibling's mouths, her eyes commanding me to remain silent. We heard his footsteps when he entered the large room. The seconds that passed seemed like an eternity. Then we heard his footsteps fade away. I only saw him twice more after that eventful day.

He moved to Corpus Christi, Texas, and started a new practice and soon had a new wife and children. He sent us no money; in fact, he deserted us. My mother raised us, working for the federal government, shunning overtures from eligible bachelors. She was *Vanity Fair* beautiful, but since she was a princess of the Catholic faith she chose to avoid romance, avoiding the occasion of sin. With the assistance of my grandmother, the children were able to ascend through Catholic schools, receiving good educations from caring teachers. My mother and the nuns at school were patient with me, encouraging me to control my temper and work on my self-control.

Years later I was 20 and a sophomore in college. My anger had moderated somewhat during my teen years. One evening my mother called and told me my father had been involved in a terrible accident. While on his way to attend a dental convention at the Ochsner Clinic his left rear tire blew out west of New Orleans on a busy road during a thunderstorm on a dark Louisiana night. He put on his raincoat, jacked up the rear bumper, and began to remove the lug nuts. Suddenly a tractor-trailer headed west veered across the highway, hydroplaning on pavement with several inches of standing water. The truck clipped him and hurled him into the steel of his tan Chevy convertible as lightning displayed the nearby overflowing bayou. He lost his right leg, his spleen, and a good portion of his small intestines. Each rib was broken. He was in critical condition, my mother explained, but the doctors expected him to live. I hung up the phone and felt nothing.

Years later my father had been dead for several months when I was told by a cousin from Bradenton he had died. The Corpus Christi newspaper said Dr. Franklin Cox had died of an apparent heart attack. But my cousin added there was some mystery to it, that a rumor existed he had died mysteriously in a hotel room. Once again I felt nothing.

Vietnam rekindled my anger, turning it from smoldering embers into a conflagration. Anger boiled over when I saw Marines sloshing through rice paddies in old leather disintegrating boots while the Air Force MPs at Danang

Air Base strode down the runway in new nylon jungle boots. Anger consumed me when the radio net crashed during my calls for life-or-death artillery fire missions, my words of request going into hyperspace, unheard as if I had been mute, the transmissions negated by old, failed communication gear. Anger morphed to sorrow when I saw American boys waiting to be placed into body bags and when I heard the always-startling news that one of my friends had been hurt badly or killed.

First Lieutenant Jim Pulaski was the company commander of Headquarters and Service Company, Second Battalion, Ninth Marines, upon the unit's arrival in Vietnam. His company operated with productive precision; his orders and the application of them by his Marines ran as smoothly as a parade float rolling along on thousands of ball bearings. His troops appreciated his genuine care for them, so they worked hard to please him. He was usually a paragon of equanimity and self-control.

But it was his anger that fascinated me. He did not tolerate negligence, sloppiness, stupidity, or disobedience. When he discovered dereliction by any of his troops that could lead to jeopardy for his unit, he exuded wrath. The transgressor had to endure the captain's thunderous words of rebuke as lightning flashed from his eyes. The lieutenant was a great intimidator when the need arose. The guilty party received the news of his punishment from Pulaski with glee in order to flee the presence of the displeased officer. Then the dark mood would end as quickly as it began.

Had it been real anger, I wondered? Could he just turn it on and off like a light switch? It was certainly another effective weapon in his powerful arsenal of leadership qualities. He used his anger to intimidate, but he used it sparingly. He ruled it; it didn't rule him. I learned a wonderful secret. Anger could get things done. Like Pulaski, I could draw upon my anger at will.

"Adrenaline-rush junky" is a sociopsychological term bandied about loosely today. The term is used ubiquitously and often describes daring would-be action heroes who take risks in public, like fighting bare-knuckled in enclosed cages or hurtling around NASCAR racetracks. But the term encompasses much more than those examples.

The incredible high gained from a massive adrenaline injection into the human bloodstream can lead to an addiction like no other. Studies show that the subconscious desire to repeat and regain that enervating, electric high is just as compelling as the urges that capture the soul of the heroin addict.

I recall a battle that began late in the afternoon as my rifle company neared our final objective for the day, the northern bank of the Song La Tho River. We had entered into a terrible ambush against a concealed, numerically superior enemy who struck with the element of surprise. After the initial machine-gun fire grazed through our ranks and the first incoming mortar shells exploded, there was an eerie stillness for several seconds. Then the Marines did what they do without hesitation. They attacked the enemy positions.

An hour or so later my radio operator and I were in a depression on the north bank of the river. I was adjusting another artillery fire mission into the tree line that obscured part of the Mainforce Vietcong R-20 Doc Lap reinforced battalion frenetically delivering fire at us. We had already called in and directed several artillery fire missions and close-air support sorties over my radio because the forward air controller's radio net went on the blink. I looked around and saw we were the only two still in the open. The rest of the company had formed a hasty 360-degree perimeter in the woods 50 yards behind us. We trotted into the friendly position. Before the night ended four different artillery batteries expended over a thousand shells all around us, denying the enemy his attempt to destroy us.

The instant the engagement began my adrenal glands broke into a gallop, sluicing and engorging volumes of adrenaline into my blood vessels with such impact there became a vacuum of one single thing ... me and the job at hand, with not one speck of fear, not one thread of doubt, just a furious sweet energy driving me to perform each task just as I had been taught, assisting me to make each decision with resolute confidence, my mind and body consumed by a high I'd never before experienced.

The rush kept coming for hours until the time just before dawn, when the enemy withdrew to avoid the certain arrival of bomb and cannon payloads from Marine warplanes. And just like that, the buzz vanished, to be replaced by a wearied nauseous empty feeling. Weak and tired to the nerve roots we trudged across the river after first light to conduct body counts and damage assessments. There were blood trails everywhere headed in the same direction, away from us, crimson droplets now congealed on leaves shorn from trees by our artillery, red droppings fastened to bushes like the morning deposits of phosphorescence glued to the side of a jar with holes punched in the top containing fireflies caught the night before.

We stumbled listlessly through the bush the next few days, conducting mandated sweeps through the nearby villages. Civil action people kept busy for days, taking wounded villagers back to the medical stations. Finally we went back to the base camp to resupply and rest.

I would chase that adrenaline sweetness for decades.

Back home in America I learned to blend my anger with adrenaline. The combination produced a fuel that drove me to compete with an intensity I had never known.

In 1978 I was a stockbroker with Lehman Brothers, one of the oldest and most prestigious investment banks on Wall Street at the time. It was there I opened my hidden Vietnam War memories and chewed through them. The anger returned and I embraced it. I had been an English Literature major in college and had taken no finance or accounting courses. I didn't know a debenture from a dirigible. But I had an imagination, a passion to compete, the ability to be persuasive, and a God-given gift to paint pictures with words. I combined those assets with a hard-driving work ethic fueled with adrenaline and an edgy anger that I called upon at will. And I worked obsessively.

The sweet mix of anger and adrenaline drove me on a daily pursuit of large accounts and big commissions. It became like combat; I would not take "no" for an answer. I became one of the largest producing stockbrokers in Atlanta and the firm.

Each morning I raced to work, building a business, on a mission. Once at my desk the adrenaline surge engulfed me like firefights once had. The anger was there, too. I was after a different type of body count, but it felt the same. I was as driven by these primitive emotions as the Crusaders were by their love for Christ when they swept into the nonbelievers.

We were hot after huge retail business, cold-calling the richest men across America. We were among the first to use that method; the whole country was our oyster and the fishing grounds were filled with whales. Our strategy was a take-no-prisoners approach, the prospects were valueless to us without that first big order, and we used whatever route it took to begin a relationship ... intimidation, psychological chicanery, begging, prevarication, puffery, tough love, and ass-kissing. We didn't hesitate to employ whatever it took to get the order.

The combination of these hard-sell sales tactics together with the depth of knowledge of the stocks we recommended was remarkably successful. Several of us began to produce obscenely large numbers, right up there with some of the most successful stockbrokers in the country.

One morning I was as prepared as possible for success. I had a perfect-storm mixture of emotions — a small amount of anger and a steady surge of adrenaline. My concentration fused with my will to win. And I knew the complete story about the business and fortunes of a small, domestic energy company I *knew* would triple over the next year.

I grabbed a stack of Dun and Bradstreet cards of prospect leads I had introduced myself to several weeks before and called Roy Nelson, founder and chairman of the board of one of the most successful manufacturing companies in America. The company was in the Standard and Poor's Top 500 companies, and the increase in the value of the common stock had made Mr.

Nelson immensely wealthy. He had become a self-made American success story. At 13 he first gained fame by flying a small plane under a bridge crossing the Mississippi River in his hometown, Moline, Illinois. He was fluent in five languages and became an engineer. In the late 1930s he invented a gearing system that improved the efficiency of heavy farming equipment. After World War II ended, the American agricultural industry expanded geometrically to meet the demand of the new booming American economy, insuring his invention was wildly successful. He was one of the richest, most powerful men in the United States.

"Roy, this is Frank Cox again, with Lehman Brothers. How are you today?" I meshed tones of confidence and camaraderie with my words.

"Fine, Frank. Good to hear from you. What's up?"

I read him a script I had crafted about Energy Reserves, Incorporated, a small domestic energy company. Short, succinct, and seductive, my story was only five short paragraphs in length. After explaining precisely why we expected the shares to run from $4 to $12 I went straight for the knockout. My adrenaline was brimming.

"Roy, I want you to buy 100,000 shares today. If we're lucky enough for the stock to fall to $3 per share I want you to buy another 100,000 shares. When the stock hits $8 in a few months you'll be up $900,000 and on margin it'll only cost you $350,000. Do it now."

Then I became mute. Seconds passed. Roy said he would have his in-house business manager call me back.

Perfect.

"Roy, you told me the same thing two weeks ago when I told you to buy Tosco at $8. It's $12 now and you just left a fortune on the table and you know it. Your business manager doesn't know *horseshit* about Energy Reserves and he didn't know *horseshit* about Tosco or you'd have bought it. Buy Energy Reserves *now!*"

I had challenged him as surely as if I had called him a four-flusher in poker. He had to respond. Seconds passed. No one spoke to him that way. I waited, my chest thumping, my stomach chilled from the excitement.

"Frank, I want you to buy me 100,000 shares today. My business manager will be back with you in five minutes with wiring instruction. Goodbye."

Roy Nelson's account alone put $150,000 in my back pocket for each of the next several years.

It was a dreary, grey, June day when his funeral was held. I rented a small plane in Atlanta and made room for Nelson's in-house money manager for the trip up to Illinois. When we descended I could see nothing but a vast green stretch of flat, rich land with rows of burgeoning vegetables underneath the landing gear of the one-engine plane. The fields were wet from a recent late spring rainfall, and the glistening dirt was as black as pitch. The pilot looked to be in his late 60s and kept popping pills and taking long pulls of breath as my copassenger and I raised our eyebrows at each other. Finally we landed.

The Requiem Mass began and the deceased's women friends from around the globe were swathed in black shawls in the chilled Catholic church of stone and marble. They came from Italy and Spain and Venezuela, and under their mantillas they resembled a covey of ravens. When the words rang out, *Lux æterna luceat eis, Domine* (May everlasting light shine upon them, O Lord), the women softly wept, not knowing each other or the deceased's widow.

It is impossible not to chase adrenaline once you'd had a love affair with it, and if you're addicted to it you will find action everywhere.

I remember Saturday mornings in the shower, thinking about the college football spreads. How could anyone not realize Alabama minus seven points at home wasn't a gift? My heart became turbo-charged. It was action and I was excited, finalizing my plays when I cradled the phone to place the wagers with Marvin, the local cologne-soaked bookmaker.

You're addicted to adrenaline if the placing of the bet is more important than the outcome.

I tried to get my act together late in the afternoon of January 1, 1983. Hopefully I would overcome my slurred speech caused by a two-day binge when I reached Marvin to lay another dime on the Georgia Bulldogs, featuring Herschel Walker set deep in the "I" formation. I knew the Dawgs plus three and a half points in the Sugar Bowl against Penn State was manna from heaven. I'd already bet $4,000 on the underdog. My wife and I were with several other couples in New Orleans, spending the afternoon at Galatoire's restaurant on Bourbon Street before the game. I became convinced I needed to add another "dime." Five Gs sounded like a good round number for a dead-solid lock.

I felt clairvoyant and was truly pumped. Alone in the owner's office upstairs I wiped some vomit off my blazer. Five Johnny Walker Black and sodas, a bottle of Cabernet, oysters Rockefeller, and sautéed Poisson Meuniére Amandine with Crabmeat Yvonne had taken its toll. I was shaking after 15 minutes of busy signals, terrified I would miss the opportunity before our car came to take us so the Superdome. I finally got through to Marvin and placed another $1,000 on Georgia plus the three and a half.

With eight minutes remaining in the fourth quarter Georgia scored a touchdown to make the score Penn State 24 — Georgia 20. For some inexplicable reason Vince Dooley, the Georgia coach, went for two points, eschewing the almost automatic point-after kick, which likely would put me in the winner's circle.

"No, no, no!" I screamed as the Dawgs broke the huddle.

Herschel was lined up deep in the backfield.

"Kick it, Dooley!" I howled.

Everybody in the Superdome knew what the next play would be. The stiff Nittany Lion defense submarined and clogged the middle and stopped Walker short on the six-inch line. I remember nothing about the flight home the next morning.

Adrenaline helped fuel my aggressive acquisition of new business and more commissions, increasing my production numbers to higher and higher levels. But that wasn't enough to slake my thirst for adrenaline highs. To do so I would have to embrace incalculable risks. I would throw $20,000 to $30,000 at a time into out-of-the-money option contracts two days before expiration, seeking 15 to 1 returns. It was insane. I lost hundreds upon hundreds of thousands of dollars. For many years, starting in 1980, I was a million-dollar producer earning hundreds of thousands of dollars each year, but at the end of the year I was back to ground zero. I had earned a lot but had spent and lost most of it. Something was terribly amiss. But every time I got down I came back harder. It was a vicious circle.

When I gave my option orders to the traders in New York on the hotline, the feelings of power and electric excitement were almost the same as when I requested artillery fire missions over my radio while staring at the enemy position delivering fire at my unit in Vietnam. And what the hell, I always hoped; maybe the stock options would go up. So what if I lost? There was always a new day.

27

Mao, Ho, and United States Policy

The enemy advances, we retreat. The enemy camps, we harass. The enemy tires, we attack. The enemy retreats, we pursue. — Mao Tse-tung.

Mao Tse-tung, the Chinese Premier, issued this wisdom to his general officers a long time before World War II dragged us into its nightmare. We didn't need to interpret his meaning in that war; his army and ours were fighting imperial Japs in a death struggle. It was a prime Darwinian laboratory test on the world's battlefields, and the good guys became the winners.

America was robust after that colossal war, a proud, testosterone-charged champion. We had the best leadership, the most audacious soldiers, and the bomb. The strategists of the American organizations assigned to predict political and military threats all agreed on a one-threat consideration. The think tanks, the Central Intelligence Agency, the National Security Agency, the political scientists from Georgetown and Harvard, and Pentagon four-star wunderkinder all decided the might of the Soviet Republic was the one clear and present danger. The notion that an enemy without sophisticated high-technological hardware, armed with only ideas and guerilla riflemen, could pose a serious military threat was dismissed.

Hundreds of thousands of American warriors came home from Pacific islands and German forests to their sweethearts to make babies and create the greatest middle class in history. We contemplated the iron curtain threat and decided on our future course — nuclear brinksmanship. We had the big stick.

The Korean War interrupted our peace but was a nuisance news story, usually on page four. It was a conventionally fought contest. But since the Korean War ended we have faced in our conflicts a maddening enemy, fighting with guerilla guile and insurgent intensity. And our results have been lukewarm, at best.

Since World War II, third-world visionaries, Ho Chi Minh, Fidel Castro, and Che Guevara, mingled Mao's tenets with their own original ideas, setting the foundation for national and regional revolutions based on insurgent warfare.

There was still plenty they would take from Mao, however, including his sensitivity training:

THE SIX PRINCIPLES OF THE RED ARMY
Put back all doors when you leave a house.
Rice-stalk mattresses must all be bundled up again and returned.
Be polite. Help people when you can.
Give back everything you borrow, even if it's only a needle.
Pay for all things broken, even if only a chopstick.
Don't help yourself or search for things when people are not in their houses.

If you follow those simple principles you may win the hearts and minds of the people. And without the people's help you cannot win a war of revolution. History has taught citizens to be wary of interlopers and foreigners. It doesn't take many negative incidents to quickly get on the wrong side of the natives.

The American military has never come to terms with the principles necessary to win over the people, not in Asia decades ago, and not in the Muslim world today. For each child our medics save with tender care, we destroy a village because of our aggression. We have a propensity "to destroy the village in order to save it." We get caught in a conundrum, a no man's land between America's duality as savior and conqueror. We want to help the good people, and kill the bad people but we don't know the difference. It gets pretty schizophrenic.

North Vietnamese aircraft never attacked our troops, and our B-52 bombers dumped 2,633,035 tons of bombs on targets, almost the same amount we dropped on Nazi Germany in World War II. Yet our mighty air power ended up not making the difference our leadership counted on.

In Vietnam we were always kept off balance by the enemy's ability to wage a war on his terms with two different styles, guerrilla/insurgency warfare and conventional warfare. As Ho Chi Minh, the North Vietnamese revolutionary and president, put it, "Our strategy is to pit one against ten and our tactics are to pit ten against one."

But most importantly, Ho understood human nature:

"If the Grasshopper does not stop fighting the Elephant, the Elephant will die of exhaustion."

Ho really nailed it when he said, "You will kill ten of our men, and we will kill one of yours, and in the end it will be you who tire of it."

When Ho predicted how his small country would withstand the awesome power of the United States of America and come away with victory, our intelligence community derided the foolishness of such a statement. The numbers didn't add up. Therefore the spooks and strategists in the clandestine intelligence agencies and the decision-makers in the Department of Defense dismissed Ho's warnings as rubbish.

For years the United States waged the Vietnam War with her hands tied behind her back. But more importantly our leadership never got it right about the enemy, always underestimating him, never taking into account all his history, which he had repeated for hundreds upon hundreds of years while fighting and beating armies who marched against him. His intentions and tactics, politically and militarily, were as discernable as the bullet holes we poured into his huts and pagodas.

If I had been an odds maker when I returned to America in 1966, I would have unblinkingly installed the People's Army of Vietnam/Viet Cong consortium as an overwhelming three-to-one favorite to win. But I'd have lost the other proposition: over-or-under eight more years of war. I'd have bet under eight more years. I couldn't have conceived how mad our leadership would become in order to let it linger on for so many years.

Maybe our country needs more history majors. Our insistence and proclivity to apply quick, high-tech responses to bad situation in nonindustrial hotspots fails us. The past as a history lesson provides an illuminating footprint for the future.

Somewhere along the way our intelligence assets forgot the simplicity of Occam's razor, "When you hear hoof beats think horses, not zebras."

We often watched for zebras in Vietnam, as nonexistent as our chances were of winning the minds and hearts of the citizenry. All the rocket wizardry and smart technology we possessed could not defeat a determined enemy without our adopting a policy whose genesis began with the past.

America's leaders could have studied and understood those prophetic words by Ho Chi Minh and ended the war much sooner, stemming the tide of death and moral bankruptcy that swamped our nation for years unnecessarily. All they had to do was look in the history books, then the TV screen every night, and consider the connection.

The same is true today. Even Alexander the Great had his hands full in his campaign to rule Afghanistan and conquer the forerunners of today's Taliban tribal fighters.

Know thine enemy.

Glossary

ARVN: Army of the Republic of Vietnam (South Vietnam Army).

BLT: Battalion Landing Team.

BOQ: Bachelor Officer Quarters.

C-4: Plastic putty-textured explosive carried by Marines.

CO: Commanding officer.

CP: Command Post.

DI: Drill instructor.

Di-di: From the Vietnamese term *di-di-mau* which means "to move quickly."

Dink: Vietnamese enemy

DMZ: Demilitarized Zone.

FDC: Fire Direction Center. Receives target intelligence and requests for fire and computes firing data for the artillery guns.

FO: Forward Observer. An officer assigned to infantry units to observes the enemy and call back fire missions on his radio to the artillery Fire Direction Center.

Gook: A crude term for Vietnamese people, especially the enemy.

Grunt: Marine infantryman.

HE: High explosive.

HQ: Headquarters.

H&S Company: Headquarters and Services Company. Helps support the four rifle companies of a Marine infantry battalion.

H&I: Harassment and interdiction. Artillery fire designed to limit and alter enemy movement.

Jarhead: Marine nickname.

KA-Bar: A fighting knife issued to Marines.

KIA: Killed in action.

LTV: Amphibious troop-carrier tractor.

LZ: Landing zone for helicopters.

Mad minute: A weapons free-fire and test session.

MAF: Marine Amphibious Force.

MSR: Main supply route for vehicles.

NVA: North Vietnamese Army.

PF: South Vietnam national guard, usually untrained and dangerous.

PLC: Platoon Leaders Course. An innovative Marine officer training program in which candidates train during the summers of their college years.

Pogue: A headquarters or office person in the rear.

PX: Post Exchange. A general store.

Riki-tik: ASAP, quickly.

RPG: Rocket-propelled grenade. A shoulder-fired infantry weapon.

Salty: Opinionated.

Scivvie honcho: A ladies man.

Scivvie house: A brothel.

Section 8: Mentally unfit for military service.

SKS: Russian-made 7.62mm semi-automatic carbine.

SOP: Standard operating procedure.

Short: Very close to ending Vietnam tour and returning to America.

Slope: Derogatory term for Asian person.

Squid: Derogatory term for sailor.

TAOR: Tactical area of responsibility. Area where a unit operates.

Top: The first sergeant is the highest-ranked enlisted Marine in a company or battery.

Victor Charlie: A Vietcong fighter.

WIA: Wounded in action.

WP: White phosphorus. An incendiary material that is not extinguished by water and used in artillery shells.

Zipperhead: Derogatory term used to describe Vietnamese.

Index

Numbers in *bold italic* indicate photographs.